Northeast by Northwest

Road Dog Publications was formed in 2010 as an imprint of Lost Classics Book Company and is dedicated to publishing the best in books on motorcycling, motorsports, and adventure travel. Visit us at www.roaddogpub.com.

ISBN 978-1-890623-51-7
Library of Congress Control Number: 2017936599

Road Dog PUBLICATIONS

An Imprint of Lost Classics Book Company
This book also available in eBook format at online booksellers. ISBN 978-1-890623-52-4

Maps by FreeVectorMaps, http://freevectormaps.com

Northeast by Northwest

Two Restorative Journeys

by

Michael Fitterling

Road Dog Publications

Publisher
Lake Wales, Florida

to those living under a gray cloud

About the Author

Mike Fitterling was born in 1957 in northern Indiana and grew up across the state line in Niles, Michigan, graduating from Brandywine High School in 1975. Mike did a two year stint at Anderson College, in Indiana, before dropping out in 1978. In 1989, he returned to school at the University of South Florida, where he graduated in 1992 with a Bachelor in Fine Arts.

Throughout Mike's youth, family trips hinted at the world awaiting him if he just got on the road. Starting at an early age his family made camping trips to over twenty states.

After his first stab at college, Mike tagged along with his brother on a biology and archaeology excursion Anderson College had organized to Central America. Those five weeks of camping in the remotest areas of Mexico and Guatemala added the twist of adventure to his love of traveling.

As time went on, Mike was drawn to the sea, bought a small sailboat, and took off along the southeast US coast and through the Bahamas and Caribbean. He captained an excursion sailboat in the Cayman Islands for three summers and earned his US captain's license in 1993.

Returning to the States from the Caribbean, Mike settled in central Florida, where he worked as a graphic designer. Later, he became interested in woodworking and worked semi-professionally at that craft for a period while working for Lost Classics Book Company.

When he married in 1997, Mike was working as cover designer and illustrator for Lost Classics Book Company, and later became Managing Editor. He acquired the company in 2010. Finding himself owner of a publishing company, his natural inclination was to turn to publishing books on motorcycling, and so in 2011, the Road Dog Publications imprint was started.

In 2013, Mike became Editor of *Vintage Japanese Motorcycle Magazine*, the official publication of the Vintage Japanese Motorcycle Club of North America, where he also currently serves on the Board of Directors.

Motorcycles had been a distant dream for Mike since his childhood, but bike ownership escaped him until he was in his fifties, when he discovered a 1968 Honda tucked away in a dusty corner of a relative's shop. He extracted the motorcycle and applied himself to learning about fixing and riding them, starting a new episode in his life, which provided him a new means of adventuring. He later acquired a Suzuki Savage, then a modern Triumph Bonneville, and has since added a 200cc Honda Scrambler and a Suzuki GS550e to his garage. Everything but the Triumph have been project bikes, the GS being still largely in boxes at the time this book was published.

Mike loves long-distance riding and tries to get at least one long ride in a year. Between 2009 and the end of 2016 he has put close to 150,000 miles behind him riding in the US and Canada.

Table of Contents

Northwest

Prologue

It had been a difficult couple of years. Issues with the children, with constant trips to doctors and therapists as a result, coupled with the uncertainty of income as a small businessman, where each month's income could make wild swings into the negative or the positive but never in a predictable pattern, had been combining to create a growing wall of stress and worry.

A year before, I had planned a getaway, an epic ride to and around Lake Superior. It had been intended to be a kind of a relief valve, but it had to be cancelled at the very last moment, two days before departure, due to unforeseen financial setbacks.

As another year dragged on, I was feeling more and more trapped. Every time I thought things were looking up, something would happen to quell my optimism. The clock ticked the minutes and hours and the calendar counted the days gone by without relief, while the stress continued to build.

I was only fifty-eight, but I felt like an old man. I found myself counting how many more "good years" I had left. Over and over I asked myself how were we going to live in our old age with the meager scraps of retirement funds we had been able to scrape together. When the kids graduate, how could we ever manage to help them with higher education? Without insurance, what would happen if I got sick? I worried about everything.

I had let circumstances lead me into a very dark place. At times, I could not see a way out of the emotional hole I had been digging.

I felt more valuable to my family as a dead man with a decent life insurance policy than I did as a working man. I had lost my joy, and every time another setback crept up on me, happiness seemed further away than ever. With the gathering gloom of my day-to-day life, it was getting too easy to have that fourth and fifth beer every night.

My immediate response when things went wrong was to mutter "I hate my life," which, at first, I said under my breath. As time went on, I restrained myself less and less. Finally, it broke my heart when I heard my son repeat those words himself in response to being sent to his room or being disciplined for one thing or another. Maybe it was just partly teenage angst that made him say that, but I knew I had set a very bad example. I wasn't only swirling down the vortex; I was taking the ones I loved with me.

"I should get some medical help. Maybe some anti-depressants," I told myself, but having no health insurance and in our financial situation, paying for medical care was just not possible. Our income kept us on the edge by making too much to get assistance with health insurance but also not making enough to afford the outrageous costs of health insurance or pay-as-you-go healthcare on our own. If we paid for insurance, that would mean there would not be enough to pay other obligations. We did get a break on the children's insurance, but if we dared to have a better year and make a tiny bit more, it would all be gone in an instant as their insurance would rocket to twenty times the discounted rate. Yet another wall confronted me, with seemingly no practical options.

I quit looking forward to each new day and struggled to make it to the end of them as they came and passed. I created ways to manage myself. I had to do one task at a time, followed by the next, to make any progress. Performing all my tasks and remembering the things that I needed to do was becoming impossible. I juggled one thing after another, while my stamina was running low. It was getting easy to be distracted by unimportant things and delay the things that needed to be done.

My mind was loosing its ability to stay focused. Once, when standing at a fuel pump getting ready to refill my Triumph's tank, I stared blankly at the pump's debit card screen with not a clue what my PIN was. My mind was completely blank. I stabbed randomly at the keypad and somehow hit the right combination of numbers so I could refuel and get home. I felt what an dementia patient must feel, if only for a moment, and it scared me.

It wasn't only money and work concerns dragging me down, however. For better or for worse, I was a product of late 1960s' idealism, and I had expected that the world would have improved and we'd have made progress toward peace and reconciliation across the planet and between people since then, but all I was seeing was increasing division. Instead of equality, I was watching a world unfold not unlike the age of Louis the Fourteenth, with privilege reserved for a very few and the rest of society left to fend for themselves, in spite of the fact that the rest of society made that extreme wealth of the privileged few possible. Capitalism was draped with the American flag and was made equivalent to patriotism. To criticize inequality was to criticize the "American Dream."

Hate seemed pervasive. No one debated issues anymore. Instead, each group spewed derision on the others. If falsehoods could win the argument, then people were ready and willing to manufacture lies. Scientific and logical truth was lost in a cloud of spurious accusations and personal attacks. Anonymous postings on the Internet took the place of real information, with the truth being whatever agreed with the poster's preestablished position.

The world didn't seem to have improved, in fact, it seemed to be spiraling downward and taking everyone with it. It was a huge disappointment to me, and I felt the world was fast becoming a hopeless sea of hatred and poverty. It seemed that greed had won. I hoped what I was seeing wasn't real, that things were better than what I perceived, but couldn't pull myself together enough to look up, instead of down.

Everything piled up. By the time I was going to sleep not caring whether I would wake up or not, it was obvious something had to be done.

I needed something; something to either shake me up or at least give me escape—something to give me a new perspective, removed from the context of social media and television. I knew once school was out and the kids were with me day in and day out that things would only get more frustrating and stressful. The kids wouldn't benefit from being subjected to me being in that state all summer.

I would need to be out of my usual environment to make any progress toward taming the depression that was overwhelming me. I also knew, from previous experience, that I always felt better on the road.

I hoped that a road trip would help, getting me away and in new surroundings. If I chose to do that, I would only have a small window of opportunity. I would have to get my business affairs in order and pay bills ahead enough that expenses would be covered for a month. I would be giving final approval on another issue of the magazine I was editing on the fifteenth of May, and following that, would not have to focus on the next issue for three or four weeks, when new stories would have to be organized and edited for the following issue. I'd also be receiving some money for my editorial work, probably a few days after final approval, which would be directly deposited into my account and be available for use on the road by using my debit card. The kids would be out of school on June fifth.

My window was established. Although planning and arranging funding for the period during which I'd be gone would add to the immediate stress, if I planned everything well, most of its weight would be gone when I rolled out of the drive for wherever it was I would be heading.

My wife, Andrea, had first met me when I had been fresh off the boat, having returned from being a vagabond for more than a year aboard a sailing boat, mostly alone. So she had been aware that traveling was part of who I was and had a sense of understanding of my need for adventure and for periods of time apart. As stress had worn me down, she had been sympathetic, but didn't really know what to say, but she knew I needed a break and gave the nod to my plans, thinking it would do me good.

Although she didn't say it, I am sure Andrea felt some reluctance to accept my plan because it would mean a lot of pressure would be put on her, being left with the sole responsibility of caring for the kids on top of her work and everything else that would have to be done in my absence. I felt guilty putting all that on her shoulders, which would haunt me quietly in the back of my mind while I was on the road, but I knew that worse lie ahead if I were to stay, and so did she. To be there for others, first I'd have to be there for myself, or what was left of me may not be of use to Andrea or anyone else. I think, as she watched me in my downward spiral, she understood that and allowed me the freedom to do what had to be done.

NORTHEAST

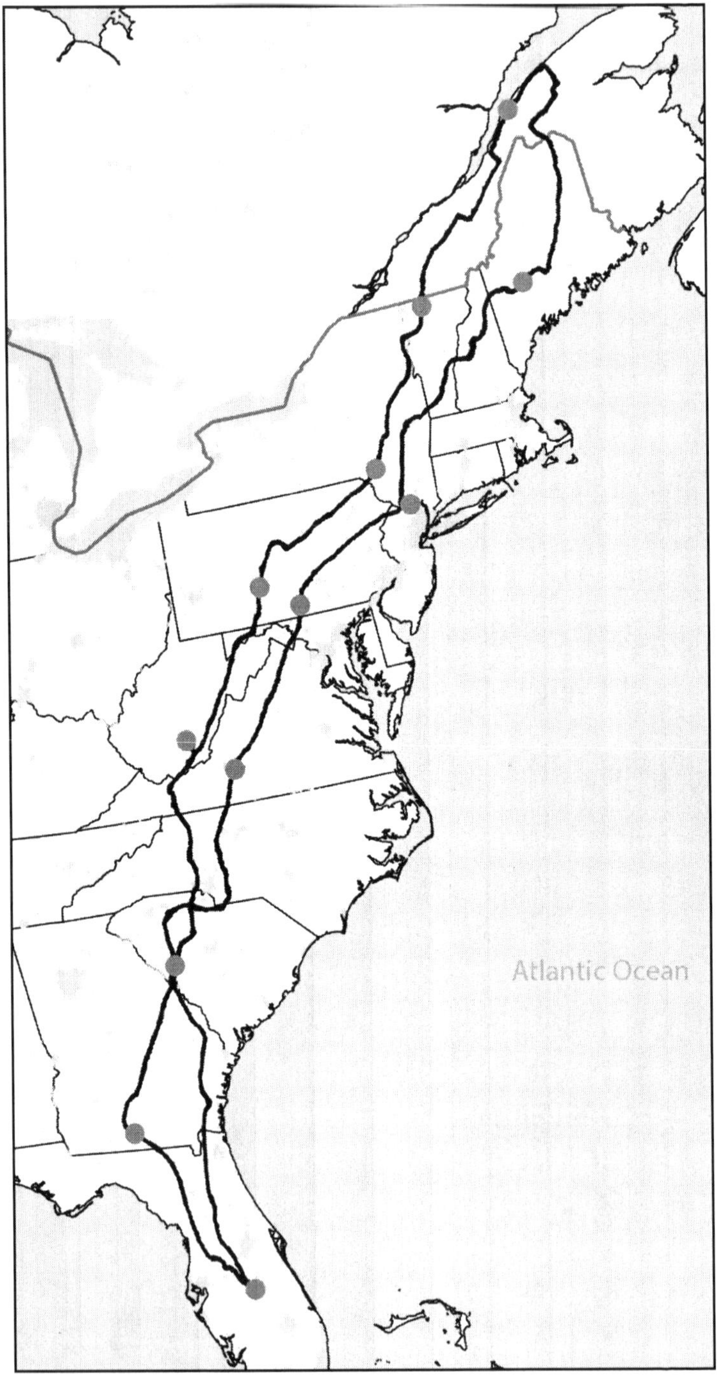
Atlantic Ocean

Chapter One

Planning

I got out maps and started searching. I didn't want to revisit any place I'd already been; this trip would have to be a new adventure into the unknown, something to shake me up and get me out of my rut. I thought the Southwest would be a great place to see, but I'd read so much about it from other riders that it didn't seem so unfamiliar, and if I wanted to write about the trip, which is always in the back of my mind, there had been so many others writing about that region that it would not be unusual or provide any different information than that provided by my antecedents.

I looked on Google Maps for areas I didn't know much about and where I had never been. As a sailor, I had seen the eastern coastal areas of the US from Florida to Virginia, and as a rider I had been all over the southwestern Blue Ridge and Smoky Mountains, and much of western North Carolina, South Carolina, Georgia, and Florida. When I was a young boy my family had taken various family vacations to many different places ranging from Colorado and New Mexico, to the Midwest, throughout Michigan and the Upper Peninsula, to West Virginia, Pennsylvania, and to Florida. One place, however, my folks had never taken us was New England and eastern Canada. Our eastern travels stopped at Gettysburg, and I had never been, even later by any means of transportation, anywhere "Up East."

I studied the map closely. I would pass through familiar areas on my way up, but once north of a line of latitude drawn through Gettysburg, roughly the Mason-Dixon Line, I would be in completely new territory. Having grown up in Michigan, I related to the North in a love/hate kind of way, loving the beautiful summers and rich and tall forests and wilderness, but shuddering at the thought of the long winters and freezing temperatures that seemed to go on forever. Hopefully, I would be there late enough in the season to avoid the worst of the cold weather and be able to enjoy the North Woods in comparative comfort.

Looking for wilderness in the Northeast kept my finger tracing north across the maps and into Canada. The Saint Lawrence River, that long conduit mixing the fresh waters of the Great Lakes with the salty waters of the North Atlantic, intrigued me. Once away from the Great Lakes, it opened up into a giant funnel as it headed out to sea. As a boy, I had lived not far from the extreme opposite end of the Great Lakes and associated waterways, near the southern tip of Lake Michigan, and always had wanted to see where all that water finally ended up.

I looked at the shoreline above Maine and noticed a town named Rimouski, nestled on the coast of the great wide river. That seemed as good a place as any for a destination and a turning point from which to head back home. I knew nothing of the region, but that was the point. I'd discover it on the way. East of the Quebec City area there were no more large cities, and staying south in the countryside until passing that, I could cruise north then ride east along the coastline and see what the area was like. My passport still had a year before it expired, so crossing into and back from Canada would not be a problem. I didn't know French, but that would make it more interesting and different than anywhere else I had gone. Different was just what I needed.

I was a big fan of a list started at the adventure rider forum, advrider.com. In the "Trip Planning" section there was a "Tent Space Sign-Up" thread, where members could post any accommodations they could provide for fellow traveling riders. Members could give their location and contact information, and list things they could provide, like: "fenced back yard, room for 10 tents" or "spare bedroom can sleep two" or "have trailer and can provide emergency bike hauling within 100 miles" and so on. These offers were then combined on a map of the world, with pins stuck wherever a member was who had offered some kind of accommodation. Clicking the pin popped up basic information and a link to the original post of the offer. The list was started in 2006, and by 2015, the map was so crowded with little pins that it was necessary to zoom in to many areas to access the individual offers.

My home in central Florida was on the list. I had hosted fellow wanderers from single overnights to two month stays, and had people drop by when passing through just to say hi. I had also been hosted by members on the list when I had traveled to the Ozarks; in northwestern Georgia near Cloudland Canyon, a beautiful park I had heard about and wanted to investigate, on my way to a VJMC national rally in southern Indiana; and I had dropped in to visit one of the members on the list on my annual pilgrimage to the Barber Vintage Festival, a gathering of over 70,000 vintage bike enthusiasts held each year at the gran prix track and motorsports museum, the largest in the world, owned by George Barber. Every time I had done this it had turned out to be a rewarding experience of meeting truly friendly and generous people. If I made this trip, it would have to be done frugally, so I planned to take advantage of this list. Knowing I was not burning through the family money while on the road would go a long way toward helping me relax and enjoy the ride. Most of the offers, in way of payment, had only asked for stories from the road, which I was sure I would be able to provide.

I also had friends along the route who would put me up on my way. One was my friend and fellow VJMC Board Member, Bryan, who lived in South Carolina, not far from the border that state shared with northeastern Georgia. Stopping at his place would give me a comparatively short first day's ride from Lake Wales. I had often run right past that area on my way north to the mountains on direct non-stop runs. It would be nice to cut those typical long days of six or seven hundred miles down to just over five hundred. A call to Bryan was all it took, and I had a place for the first night, and again for the ride back.

Another friend, Steve, was a fellow ADVRider member whom I had hosted in my backyard the year before. Steve lived in Altoona, Pennsylvania, and had come down to ride in Florida while the winter winds and snow were blowing back home. He had driven his pickup down with one of his BMW GSs in the back. Once in my back yard, we hoisted his bike down, and he set up his tent, which was made to be pitched in the bed of the truck. He also set up a ten-by-ten pop-up, giving him standing room and a place to spend time when he was not sleeping. He had set up next to my shop where I could provide electricity and a fridge just inside the door. Most of the time he could access our Wi-Fi from his pop-up. It made for a nice cozy compact camp. Steve had planned to stay for a couple weeks to ride around the area in the comparatively warm weather, but Mother Nature had other plans, and every time Steve was about to head home he would check conditions back in Altoona only to find bitter cold or snow or both. Every time he checked it was the same story. We urged him to stay. "Why hurry back? You're retired and have all the time you need, and you can stay here as long as you like." Steve ended up staying a couple months. We had fun riding together, and I enjoyed showing him some of the better riding and interesting spots in our area. The kids loved having him visit, and my wife, Andrea, was happy to have him around. He became part of the family and a quasi-uncle to our kids. So, on this ride, I had to see Steve. As I studied the maps, a route began to develop that would take me from Greenwood, South Carolina, where Bryan lived, to Altoona, Pennsylvania, before I would head northeast into New England. Steve assured me I had a place to stay with him.

I scoured the tent space map again. I would be approaching the Canadian border on the eastern side of Lake Champlain, northeast of Burlington, at Richford, Vermont. I would need a spot to stay somewhere in that area. I spotted a pin at Fairfax, about thirty miles northeast of Burlington. I messaged vthuman on the ADVRider site about the possibility of stopping there. Larry is vthuman, but it was Loretta, his wife, who answered my message with, "Excellent. We've got an empty bedroom and a sofa if you're ready to sleep inside...dinner, a beer, and some travel conversation if you are up for that as well. Laundry, shower, charging electronics—all good." I wrote down their address and contact information, and one more stop was secured.

Also in Vermont was Suzanne, Andrea's friend and former schoolmate, who I'd met along with her husband, Ron, on a long weekend spent at the beach together with them and our kids when they were vacationing in Florida. The couple had invited us up to their place near the Canadian border. They had a camper in the backyard, which was offered for our use while there. A quick call confirmed the invitation was still open, even if I was just me, and I had another overnight stop.

On the way back I could pass through Gettysburg, Pennsylvania, and visit my second-cousin, Bonnie, and her husband, Bill, at their historic pre-Civil War farm abutting the historic battlefield where over 51,000 Northern and Southern soldiers had died in the epic struggle to either hold the Union together or divide the United States into two separate countries, one slave-holding and one where the barbaric practice was abolished. I hadn't seen Bonnie and Bill in years. It would be great to catch up with them and see the farm, which dated from even before the Revolutionary War, as far back as 1757. Gettysburg, too, would be a perfect jumping off spot for the next leg of my journey.

Finally, more than any of my childhood friends, I had stayed in touch with an old high school friend, Julie. I've often visited her, usually on my way in or out of the state of Florida. Julie's place was in Valdosta, Georgia, where she lived with her dad, Jack. Valdosta had been a gateway of sorts for me on other rides I've taken, being in the narrow neck of land between Florida and all places north, east, or west. Her place in the countryside outside of the city would be an ideal place to rest up for the final push home on an easy 280 mile final day, while it would give me the opportunity to hang out with her and her dad.

Between Bryan, Steve, Suzanne and Ron, Bonnie and Bill, and Julie, I had six nights covered. ADVRider.com yielded me two more places to stay (which, in the end, turned into three). For the rest of the trip I would wing it, searching for camping spots to spend the nights in between these havens of familiarity and camaraderie. My budget would be enhanced by free lodging those nights, and the other times would be spent camping in small campgrounds that are typically inexpensive. I'd have to look carefully, though, because I remembered from past rides that a "camping" sign didn't mean camping anymore, or at least not my definition of camping. I don't know when or how it changed, but camping had come to mean hookups for RVs, and well, tents usually were not welcome. There still were some places where camping still meant camping, or at least tent campers were allowed, and that was state and national parks. In West Virginia I spotted a state park not far off my planned route, being just a slight jump north. State parks are generally inexpensive; not as much as they used to be, but still I could probably camp for around twenty dollars and have a place to shower and recharge electronics.

There was a gap in lodging for the loop north and east through Quebec and back through Maine, between leaving Fairfax, Vermont, and passing through on the way back at Newport, Vermont. I had mentioned on ADVRider.com that I was planning a ride to the Saint Lawrence and a fellow "inmate," as we called each other, SydQC, messaged me with info on riding the south shore of the huge bay. The communication was very useful, with suggested routes and information on where the best micro-brewed beers were. He was in Rimouski, but it looked like he would be gone when I was there, himself on a two-month ride. He suggested a camping spot at Saint-Andre, but I had hoped to get farther up the peninsula that day, so I checked the camping options near Rimouski. The first place I found was the Camping Centre Naturiste Veille Ferme. It turned out to be a naturist campground, but I thought it might be interesting to try a clothes-less camping experience, and besides, the rates were decent, twenty-eight Canadian dollars without electricity. To save a little money, I could adapt. I called them up, but it was too early at that latitude and they would not be open until May 29, too late for my stay. I hung up, a little disappointed on missing out on a good deal and a new experience. I searched some more and found camping at Parc National du Bic, just southwest of Rimouski and on the bay, but rates were higher at over thirty Canadian a night. On the other hand, it would be open, so I planned to look for du Bic for my overnight stay in Quebec.

On my run back into Maine the day after camping at Rimouski, I had a couple options. I could make a very long run through the central Maine wilderness back into

Vermont to stay at Suzanne and Ron's, a few miles south of the Canadian border at Newport. That would have been a long haul of over five hundred miles and would require me to rush through Maine, which I hoped would be one of the most interesting sections of the ride. My other option was to wing it and hope I would find a place somewhere between Rimouski and Fairfax to pitch my tent, preferably away from running generators and massive RVs. I tentatively chose the latter, figuring in all the North Woods wilderness in Maine there had to be real campgrounds.

I love the mountains and despise most cities and crowds, so as I drew out my route, the tentative route line on the map wound its squiggly way over mountain ranges as I would ride north, then northeast. First, would be the Blue Ridge, a place I loved and had spent many happy days motoring around on curvy two-lanes. I'd be in the Blue Ridge from North Carolina through Virginia and then would enter the Cumberland Mountains of West Virginia. Although I had explored a lot in North Carolina, it was mainly in the extreme western region, so I would try to take mostly roads I hadn't ridden before that lay farther east, before riding into Virginia and West Virginia, two states I had never ridden in before at all.

From central West Virginia, where I'd camp for the second night, I'd be heading toward Altoona to visit Steve and the Alleghenies. Next, I would pass through the Poconos first and then the Catskills. From there it would be on to the Adirondacks of New York, then arriving on the shores of Lake Champlain. The big lake, with its rich history during the French and Indian and Revolutionary Wars, was an intriguing and romantic place in my mind, having read works by Hawthorne and others about the region in that distant, almost mysterious era of the very beginning of the opening up of the North American continent and, sadly, the beginning of the end for Native Americans.

I'd planned to cross Lake Champlain somewhere into Vermont after following the Hudson River, which I'd only known from Hudson River School paintings I had seen and which had inspired me. In Vermont I'd be in the Green Mountains all the way to the Canadian border.

Once in Quebec, I would be close to the terminus of the Northern Appalachians. On the way back, after turning around at Rimouski on the Gaspé Peninsula, I could head south through central Maine and southwest through New Hampshire, passing through the White Mountains. Traveling southwest from there I could roll across the Connecticut River Valley, ride the Green Mountains again, cross the Hudson River, and follow the valley. Turning west after that, I would be in the Catskills again.

Before leaving New York I would detour out of the Catskills and head to the home of another ADVRider, Kevin, in Goshen, who had not known of the tent space list, but had read my first book, *Thoughts on the Road*. He had emailed me as he was finishing reading my book to see if I would suggest some other good motorcycle travel books for him to read after he completed mine. I noticed he was not far off my route, and I ventured to ask if he'd like to meet up while I was on the trip. He said that he would and then generously added that he'd be happy to open his home to me for the night.

After my overnight visit in Goshen, I could head west into Pennsylvania again, with a stop planned at Gettysburg and Bonnie's. It would be an easy ride from there to Front Royal to ride Skyline Drive above the Shenandoah Valley to the southwest all the way to Rockfish Gap, where the two-lane would become the Blue Ridge Parkway, snaking its way, eventually to its end in the heart of the Smoky Mountains. I'd only follow it to just short of Asheville, North Carolina, having ridden it west from there on previous trips numerous times. Going that far would mean that I would have completed the entire length of three great American scenic highways—the Cherohala Skyway, the Blue Ridge Parkway, and Skyline Drive—in their entirety on a motorcycle. Abandoning the Blue Ridge Parkway near Mount Mitchell, the highest point in North America east of the Mississippi River, I'd peel off south through North Carolina, into South Carolina, and to Bryan's place again on Lake Greenwood, finishing my mountain tour of the eastern and northeastern US.

From South Carolina it would be an easy day to Valdosta and Julie's, and then it would be just one last day's ride home. I could do it all in fifteen days, with some wiggle room for extra days, and I would not be late for the start of the kids' summer vacation. I could stay with friends six or seven nights, with ADVRider members for a couple others, and tent camp a few times.

Day by day, the route firmed up as I made emails and calls confirming my stops. I looked for all the twisting lines I could find along the general route and made sure to avoid all major cities. It was looking more and more doable, and if I was careful, I could get by very cheaply. The deposit due to arrive from my distributor looked like it was going to be good for that May. Added to that, after giving my final approval on the next magazine issue for June/July on the fifteenth of May, I would have some more funds deposited into my account just after I hit the road. A huge part of my stress had been caused by the wild roller coaster ride of up months and down months, but those alternating valleys and peaks were promising to even out just in time for the trip. I would still have to be careful with money because future sales, and therefore, income would probably not hold forever, and I had to be ready for possible lean months ahead. But I was going to be on my own and could ride as inexpensively as I wanted, without having to satisfy someone else's need for motel rooms, warm showers, or hot meals in expensive restaurants.

With the goal of the ride to release stress and exorcise some of my demons, I certainly didn't want to be worrying constantly about the welfare of my family while my traveling funds depleted our accounts. If that was to happen the trip would just be a sight seeing tour with no power to heal my state of mind. I had the nightly stays covered. Gas was an inevitable, and all I could do is simply hope for prices to stay low while I was on the road.

I bought a box of granola bars, a jar of dry-roasted peanuts, a box of instant raisin and walnut oatmeal packets, and some "tea bag" coffee. Oatmeal would make a filling breakfast, and while the water was already heated for the oatmeal, it could be used for coffee, too—a simple and quick way to start days at camp. The granola bars could be for my rest breaks, with an occasional gas station coffee to accompany them, and a few fists full of peanuts could be my lunch. For dinners I'd generally keep it cheap by avoiding restaurants, and instead, stop at grocery stores for cheap eats, which I could either cook on my one-burner Dragonfly gas stove or eat cold before hitting the hay on those nights I would be on my own. I would save the cash for dinners with those who had opened their homes to me, in case they wanted to go out.

Unleaded gas had been hovering at under $2.50 a gallon. As I added up the miles I would be covering, I calculated the fuel cost using a pessimistic $2.50 a gallon in case during the couple weeks I'd be gone prices rose. 509 miles to Bryan's; 320 miles to Camp Creek State Park, West Virginia; 346 miles to Altoona, Pennsylvania; 590 miles to Fairfax, Vermont; 422 to Rimouski, Quebec; 830 miles to Suzanne's in Newport, Vermont; 360 to Goshen, New York; 212 miles to Gettysburg, Pennsylvania; 604 miles to Bryan's; 296 to Valdosta, Georgia and Julie's; and 260 miles to home—I kept moving the waypoints on the Google Maps routes until they mirrored my plan—almost 4,200 miles in total. I would use a conservative forty miles per gallon for the Bonneville's fuel consumption rate; in reality I could count on between that and forty-five miles per gallon, but I didn't want to underestimate the fuel cost. I did the math—(4,200 / 40) x $2.50 = cost of fuel; or $262.50. That was reasonable.

With the planning completed, all there was left to do was wait until the time came to take off and to make sure I got the magazine issue done on schedule, so I could be sure funds would be restored while I was on the road. Stress was still weighing me down, but knowing I had a pressure relief valve in the form of the upcoming trip made it more bearable. Of course, time seemed to slow to glacial speed, but I kept my head down and got my work done and waited for the momentous day to arrive.

Chapter Two

The Day before Departure

Final Preparations

The time drew near, and not too soon. The pressure of the magazine deadline floated overhead, while I worried about putting everything together and sending it out to the members of the Publications Committee for their stamps of approval, then the final had to be sent to the designer for upload to the magazine printer's server, and finally, approval by myself on the printer's website by the fifteenth of May.

A delay anywhere along the way would mean a delay to my departure and a narrowing of my window of opportunity.

Luckily, no major delays or barriers to the schedule popped up, and by the evening of the fifteenth, I was checking the "Approved" box on each page online; emailing the printer with final overall approval; sending in the spreadsheet lists of authors, compensation, and contact information to our Membership Director, who took care of the magazine mailing list, and to the Treasurer; emailing my request for extra copies; and sending my final invoice in to the Treasurer for my work on the issue.

I had done it.

While all these final formalities were being ticked off, I started packing the Bonneville, the goal being to have nothing left to do other than to throw on my riding clothes and put on my boots upon getting out of bed. The bike luggage was hauled inside. I packed the tank bag with all the maps I would need, making sure the first day's was folded to the size of the bag to show the first ride segment, then inserted under the clear cover of the bag. Meanwhile, the GPS, phone, camera battery, GoPro and remote, and netbook were plugged in to charge.

My RRR Tool Roll, with virtually any tool I could possibly require inside, secure in it's dry bag, was installed in the very bottom of the left pannier, and the electrical multimeter, extra engine oil, and spare bungees were deposited into the dark recesses of the right pannier. Over the years, the Triumph had proven to be bullet-proof, but being prepared for all the possible mechanical and electrical mishaps that could even remotely occur was a habit I had acquired on all those long rides on my ancient 1968 Honda CB350, which had carried me, more than once, on thousand mile rides and many shorter ones, and which had required my mechanical services from time to time on the road. The tools took up valuable room, but it never hurt to cover all the bases, I told myself.

On top of the tools went clothing, with the stuff for cold weather farthest down, as Florida weather had been in the 90°s F. The pillion bag was expanded on both ends and absorbed any clothing the panniers could not. In spite of warm weather in Florida being almost at the start of summer, I had to plan on any kind of weather this early in the year and going so far north. In a sense, I would be going back in time through the seasons, with spring or even late winter at the northern end of my route. Leaving in summer I would be chasing a retreating spring as my latitude changed, so the bags were jammed full of warm clothes. I made sure, too, that the rain covers for all the bags were in the outer pockets along with kickstand pucks, quick to access when I might need them. The tail bag was unzipped around the base to expand it up another two inches and then filled with the netbook on the bottom, followed by power cords and a dry box with all the chargers and small cords. On the top, where it could be reached easily and quickly, went my camera, a Canon DSLR. In the right side pocket I stuffed extra bulbs and fuses, while in the left went spare glasses, contacts, and other small stuff.

Everything filled full to bursting, I carried it all out to the garage and the waiting Bonnie at the end of the day, along with all the fully-charged electronic gear. While the bags sat scattered on the floor, I set about mounting the already full spare-gallon Rotopax fuel container on the rear rack and the two liter MSR fuel bottles in their holders and on each pillion footrest strut. The MSRs held unleaded fuel for my Dragonfly cooking stove and they, along with the Rotopax, could supply me with almost a gallon and a half of fuel should I find myself in the middle of the wilderness on a very stale low fuel light. They would give me at least an extra sixty miles to find a gas station.

Fuel secured, I attached all the bags to the bike, the panniers to the waiting straps dangling from the footrest struts and across the rear fender, and the pillion bag to receivers on the panniers. The magnetic tankbag was placed on top of the previously filled tank and the emergency strap routed around the handlebars. The GPS was popped onto its mount between the handlebar risers and plugged into the dual USB port next to it. Then the sleeping bag and Thermarest, compressed in a large dry bag, along with the tent and folding camps tool were removed from their pegs on the garage wall. The tent and the stool were strapped above the panniers using the bungees built into the underside of the pillion bag. The dry bag filled with sleeping bag and pad were loaded on top of the pillion bag and secured with two thick RokStraps criss-crossed over the top. Finally, I slipped my knock-around slip-ons under the RokStraps, and the bike was ready to go.

While going in and out of the house during this packing activity, I had managed to finalize all the work on the magazine. I slipped three hundred dollars cash I had withdrawn the day before at the ATM into my jacket pocket and zipped it up. That would have to do for most of my food expenses, so I would have to be miserly with it. My goal was to not use more than that if possible, but I did leave enough extra in the account so I could supplement it with the debit card if it became necessary. Gas would be covered by the debit card, and I made sure that was safely stowed in my wallet along with my credit card that would only be used for emergencies. The wallet was then zipped into the other jacket pocket. In the morning I could slip on the jacket—cash on left side, wallet on the right—knowing all I needed was on me and that it could not fall out of a pocket. Checking to make sure I still had those two items when leaving gas stops was as easy as touching each pocket before I pulled out.

With the loaded bike waiting in the darkened garage, I crawled into bed, knowing it would be hard to sleep but doing my best anyway, and finally settled into a fitful sleep.

Chapter Three

Day One

Traversing the Southeast

By two in the morning on the sixteenth, I woke up, donned my riding clothes, and by three o'clock, had unlocked the garage doors, rolled the now-heavy bike out and onto the driveway, locked up the garage, swung my leg over the mountain of gear, and rolled down the drive and onto the street, heading north in the quiet darkness, with the thrum of the motor and the wind whistling past my helmet making the only sounds.

As I rolled along the city streets and turned north onto State Road 17, my mind was occupied with thoughts of what I might have forgotten and worry about whether this whole trip was a mistake I would end up regretting later. I comforted myself by telling myself that there wasn't anything that might have been forgotten that couldn't be replaced on the road, if necessary. The worry about the trip and the financial risk I was taking was not so easily dismissed, and only time would tell if it was a wise plan. Gas prices could soar and unexpected expenses change the whole landscape of this plan of escape and mental healing and turn it into an expensive experiment with little reward and just more stress and depression.

I tried to shake off my misgivings as I continued toward Dundee, where I'd jump a couple of miles over to US 27, a major conduit from the North that begins in Fort Wayne, Indiana, wiggling south through the country and the middle of the Florida peninsula all the way to Miami, spilling itself into downtown. The usually busy divided four-lane of 27 was quiet at 3:30 AM. That had been part of my plan.

Leaving at the early hour meant that I could run north on that highway during its quietest time and be off it and to the state line by daylight. I rode virtually alone through the stretch I usually dread between the Florida Turnpike and Ocala. From Lake Wales, with Interstate 75 to the west running north to the Georgia line, Interstate 4 crossing the state from southwest to northeast coast to coast, and 95 running along the east coast all the way to Jacksonville, and very little in between them, it is virtually impossible to head north avoiding Interstates, especially northeast, without taking this route at least as far as Mineola.

Just past Mineola, I had often taken a little county road through the area known as Sugarloaf Mountain. That hilly and winding road, by Florida standards, connected to US 19, a beautiful forested route, albeit straight as an arrow, through the Ocala National Forest, that connected with US 301 in the lightly populated north Florida countryside. But this time I opted for 27 because, as quiet a route as 19 promised to be, it also promised to offer an obstacle course of wildlife at that time of night with unpredictable deer, wild hogs the color of tarmac, and even black bear possibly sharing the highway. An encounter with any one of those would put an abrupt halt to my northward progress and most likely end the useful life of the Bonneville and land me in a hospital, something especially to be avoided with me having no health insurance.

My chosen path for this trip, while not a pristine country route and usually a traffic and stoplight nightmare, in the wee hours was devoid of traffic and was easy riding. It got get me to the city of Ocala, where I turned into the quiet Florida countryside, barging through wisps of fog drifting across the highway as I rode north in the early morning darkness. The air was filled with the earthy smell of moist hay, reminding me of the smell released when opening a roll of cork.

At about Hawthorne the chill caught up with me and I stopped. It's strange how much cooler even a temperature in the 60s can feel when you're passing through the air at a mile a minute for extended periods. I realized I had violated one of my traveling rules: to put on more layers than I thought necessary when riding at night. It's easy to stop and pull off a layer, but much harder to park up, dig through the luggage for more clothes, put them on, then suit up again. I layered up before rolling back out.

I raced a ghostly train, barely visible in the pitch darkness while I looked for hot coffee to warm myself. I found my coffee at Starke, whose prison is the dubious home of Florida executions. There I left the US highway I had been following and veered to the north-northwest by a small state road, connecting to another northerly state road about twelve miles away, which then continued north into the little bump Florida makes northward above Jacksonville and east of the Okefenokee Swamp. I skirted the huge Okefenokee National Wildlife Refuge, a huge 438,000 acres of wetlands lying between Florida and Georgia. As predicted, not long after dawn I rolled across the state line and into Georgia. Running north, just west of the Florida state line the road joined US 301 once again in Folkston at the northwestern corner of the Florida bump, defined by the undulating Saint Marys River, which empties itself into the Atlantic Ocean between Florida's Fernandina Beach, a former anchorage of my sailboat *Aries* during my salt water days, and Georgia's Cumberland Island, where ruins of a plantation decay into the earth and wild horses roam the beaches.

I followed familiar roads through east Georgia, which had so many times been my path for getting to the mountains. The wet vegetation smells of Florida were complemented by the omnipresent odor of balsam from the countless pine tree forests of the area and the fresh cut trunks of southern yellow pines passing me on log haulers. The road headed north then made a northeast jog at Jesup and then northwest turn at Ludowici, where the aroma of the pine and wetness was again replaced by the unmistakable odor of the South Georgia paper mills. At Statesboro, 301 continued northeast while I veered northwest, then north, toward Augusta. The empty two-lane road became divided four lane as it approached the city.

There was no avoiding this fairly large city of roughly 200,000 sprawling on the west bank of the Savannah River and the gateway to central South Carolina, without going far out of the way, so I sought a route skirting Augusta to the west. I turned west onto Interstate 520 then north on Interstate 20, the freeways encircling Augusta, before jumping off northward on a small state route, escaping the city. I rode into South Carolina well north of Augusta, crossing the Savannah River and heading onward toward Clarks Hill on the southeastern corner of Lake Strom Thurmond, formed by damming the Savannah River at the Strom Thurmond Dam, named after the centenarian senator, who had spent over half his life in the senate and most of the rest of his life as judge, state senator, and governor.

A large portion of that time Strom Thurmond had striven to retain segregation in the United States, resisting change mandated by the Civil Rights Acts of 1957 and 1964 and the

Voting Rights Act of 1965, euphemistically calling it a fight for states' rights. His namesake now was only segregating one Southern state from another as it lapped the shores of Georgia on the west and South Carolina on the east, the senator's home state.

Along the eastern shore, the road followed the lake up through Modoc, where I stopped at a park on the lake to rest, have a snack, and do a little sketching, which I had promised myself I would do throughout the trip and which I failed miserably to do, except for that single instance.

Strom Thurmond Lake

At McCormick, the route I had been on continued northwest, but I turned inland toward Lake Greenwood, where my friend, Bryan, was waiting for me, having offered a hot meal and a place to stay the night. Bryan's address was actually in a little town called Waterloo. I crossed Lake Greenwood on a low long bridge, then on the far side of the lake, I turned north where the highway split off from a companion state route with which it had shared the roadway toward Waterloo. I went north, while its former partner ran northeast to meet Interstate 26, the major thoroughfare splitting South Carolina diagonally down the middle, from Charleston on its southeastern end to Greenville and Spartanburg at the North Carolina border.

Finally in Waterloo, I typed in Bryan's address only to see the GPS pinpoint a position just where I had crossed Lake Greenwood twenty miles before. While Waterloo is a very small town, hardly a conglomeration of a handful of houses and a fire station, its geographical boundaries must have been considerable. Flipping up the kickstand, I wheeled around and headed back toward the lake, following the directions the GPS gave me as I made quick glances down at its screen. I turned off the highway almost at the foot of the bridge back across the lake and rode down winding residential streets until Bryan's house number appeared on a mailbox. Arriving after twelve hours and 521 miles on the road, several of which were from Lake Greenwood to Waterloo and back, day one's riding had ended.

On my many trips up this way to visit my brother, who had lived at Inman, South Carolina, almost on the North Carolina line, by then I would have had at least another one hundred miles to go. It was nice for once to end the riding earlier and have time to relax, reflect, and share times with friends. I had left Lake Wales, at an altitude of 85 feet, and had arrived at Bryan's at an altitude of 600; I guessed I was making enough progress for the day.

When I arrived it was 2:30 PM. After saying hello and talking bikes and VJMC business with Bryan for while, I was showed my quarters for the night and then went back out to the bike, now parked in Bryan's garage, and unloaded only what was necessary, to avoid a prolonged reloading in the early morning. Bryan's place was on an offshoot of Lake Greenwood, which was really a reservoir of the Saluda River held back by a dam at its southern end. Below the house was a dock where his pontoon boat was berthed. Bryan figured we had time for a boat ride and he, his wife Rosemary, and I walked down and climbed aboard for a lovely ride on the serene waters, skimming along the wilder shorelines of the convoluted lake in hopes of seeing deer and other wildlife on our way to dinner at Harris Landing before heading back and calling it a night.

I realized I had not dwelt for long on problems of home, finances, and the world on the ride today. Riding had taken all my attention and didn't leave room for that, while the constantly passing landscapes and smells offered continually changing sensations to force out negativity. I called home and talked to Andrea, which bolted me back to that forgotten realm when she told me of the struggles she had that day with the kids. I once again doubted that I had made the right decision to go on this ride and hoped my absence wasn't wreaking havoc back home. I drifted into sleep unsettled and distracted by those thoughts, with the darkness I had been feeling creeping back in, but hoping for the best for the future of the rest of the trip.

Chapter Four

Day Two

Reaching the Mountains

My phone alarm woke me early. I slipped into the adjacent bathroom while everyone else was sleeping and took my last shower for a couple of days. Back in the room, after throwing on my riding clothes I had laid out the night before, I unplugged the phone charger from the wall and stowed it in its place in the dry box. I double-checked everything I had brought in, making sure all went back out on the bike with me. Then I crept through the quiet house out to the garage and the bike. Securing everything back in its place, I opened the garage door and rolled the Bonnie out into the cool and quiet morning air. Closing the garage door, I climbed on board, and hit the starter button to wake the bike. I rolled out the driveway and renegotiated the twists and turns of the neighborhood roads until I found myself once again at the highway.

I turned left, bound northeast toward Interstate 26, about thirty-five miles away at Clinton. So far, the route I had taken was well-known, the result of so many trips I had made to see my brother at Inman. I usually would jump on the Interstate for a short run to Exit 15, turn west, and within a few miles I would be knocking on his door. But on this trip, this is where I left my familiar track and started finding myself a new way north. Instead of turning onto the Interstate, I crossed over it and continued east on through Sumter National Forest in the newborn daylight of my second day on the road and on unfamiliar roads.

Still in the forest, I turned onto another route north toward North Carolina. By then, the day had grown and the sun was peeping above the horizon, casting sidelong glances through the trees.

As I rode I was thinking of a story I had written about a hunting trip I had made to my brother's. We had climbed into the trees behind Tim's place and sat through midday and into the night without seeing any deer. We knew there were deer in the area, as Tim had already taken two bucks that year. We decided our lack of luck was due to timing. That evening, Tim had said all the successful deer hunts he had were in the morning; and that the deer there must be "morning deer." After leaving empty-handed on that trip, as I was passing though the countryside in the early morning I had spotted a deer crossing in front of me. I thought, "He must be right." As this episode was passing through my head, I looked to my left and at the wood line across a field a deer was standing, staring into the early morning sun and right at me. Morning deer, indeed.

Between patches of trees, I passed sunny hillsides under blankets of kudzu, with the scent of some flower I could almost, but not quite identify occasionally overpowering the scent of pine in the air.

I passed through a small town ironically, or perhaps prophetically, named Union in this first secessionist state. A few miles past Union, I turned off onto Gaffney Highway, for just a short distance before turning east toward Saratt. There the road turned northeasterly, and I made my way to Hickory Grove, where it veered southeastward, becoming Hickory Grove Road. I turned right and stayed on it until another left put me on another state route heading into York, while North Carolina steadily grew closer.

At York I switched highways again and headed straight north into North Carolina, now only a few miles away, and toward Gastonia. This route would keep me well west of the big city of Charlotte and would not pass through a large city all the rest of the way through the state.

As I approached the North Carolina border, expecting to see the hazy blue profile of the Blue Ridge Mountains out ahead of me, the pecan trees that had been my companions all the way from the Florida-Georgia state line were slowly disappearing. As I passed into North Carolina, around ten, the gentle rising and falling roller coaster road slowly, almost imperceptibly, grew more intense. As I finished each descent, the ascents almost always peaked at yet a few feet higher altitude.

At Lincolnton, another ironically named small Southern town, I took a small connector road to NC 16. This highway would cut straight north across western North Carolina, crossing the Blue Ridge Parkway just north of Wilkesboro, a town I had passed through years before while on the Second Kickstart Classic Ride that had run from the Wheels through Time Museum in Maggie Valley to Denton, North Carolina and the AMCA Swap Meet.

Passing into the now growing mountains, purple flowers appeared, smelling like gardenias, garnishing the mountain roadsides. White jasmine was also blooming, filling the air with a distinctly different odor.

Soon after Piney Creek, I was passing into Virginia. Mount Rogers, at almost 6,000 feet the highest point in

Virginia, rose up on my left in the west in Mount Rogers National Recreation Area. In Virginia the mountains took on a different appearance, many being largely denuded of their trees, revealing how long man has been settled there turning mountains into fields. A lot of hillsides had been cropped recently for their pine and replanted with blankets of tiny pine seedlings in rows, making them look like hills covered with pineapples.

I passed Troutdale where the long Appalachian trail ran just to the left of the road for a short time, then re-entered the countryside. I next passed Sugar Grove and once again I came across the Trail, crossing my route as it ran along a 3,000 foot ridge to the northeast. That would be the first of about a dozen times I would come across the Trail on the ride ahead, but this would be the last encounter for thousands of miles until, on my return, I would be passing Mount Katahdin, the goal of all Appalachian Trail through-hikers, deep in the great North Woods of Maine.

I crossed Interstate 81 as the road became a crazy route of twists, climbs, descents, curves, and hairpins. When I had looked at my maps at the planning stage, the route had looked innocent enough and to be a fairly straightforward direct route dissecting the very narrow western tail of the state and getting me into West Virginia quickly. What I had not known at the time was that this section of road was also known as the Back of the Dragon. I always knew when I would be getting into a good stretch of road when the smell of eighteen-wheeler brake liner was in the air. Even when the trucks were long gone they left their tell-tale odor, letting me know grades and curves were coming my way. I rode 16 with brake smell in my nose all the way to Tazewell, where I jumped onto US 19 headed for Bluefield and the West Virginia line.

Nearing Bluefield, the busy highway I had been on for a short while had run together with US 460 and entered West Virginia. The traffic had increased, but soon US 19 broke off and ran north, roughly paralleling Interstate 77, which continued north through Charleston and eventually would exit the state and enter western Ohio at Marrietta. I would only continue north for ten or so miles to a road leading west off the highway to Camp Creek State Park, the first tent camping stop on my way north, just before the route passed under I-77 only to tag along with it toward Charleston on the opposite side.

Camp Creek State Park, West Virginia

That early in the season, I had my pick of camping spots, and I settled into one undisturbed by neighbors.

I parked up in the wrong spot. I flopped the bike back onto its center stand and found it sinking in the deep gravel and threatening to fall onto its left side. I tried to push it forward off the stand and only made matters worse, digging deeper into the gravel. I climbed back on gingerly, trying not to disturb the delicate equilibrium of the bike's current balance. I fired up the bike, nicked it into gear and eased out the clutch—nothing but a spinning back tire. I shut it down and climbed back off. Determined to solve this problem alone, I once again grabbed the handlebars, planted my feet, and pushed forward and lifted with all my might. The center stand flipped up, and I could feel the bike uncooperatively rolling forward in the deep gravel. I yanked back on the bars and got the bike going in reverse and kept pulling until the wheels were on solid ground. It was the first night, and I almost had to go get help over such a simple operation. I felt good and congratulated myself on having overcome it myself. I reset the center stand and checked the stability of the bike's new resting place before going to pitch the tent.

The tent was simple, a two crossed-poles affair, and it went up in seconds. I staked it down, just in case of wind in the night, then walked over to the bike to unload what I would need for the evening. It wasn't much; this was just a place to lay my head for the night before rising early and heading out in the morning. I undid the Rokstraps holding down my large dry bag containing my sleeping bag and Thermarest pad, opened it up, blew a few breaths into the "self-inflating" mattress, and threw it into the tent, followed by my sleeping bag. I rolled up my riding jacket and tossed it at the head of the bag. It would be my pillow for the night. The only thing left to do was feed myself. I broke out the hoagie and the big can of Fosters beer I had bought earlier and chowed down. Sandwich gone, I decided it was not really camping if I didn't have a campfire, so I gathered up dried twigs and branches from around the campsite, making sure to put ever bigger pieces on the top of the pyramid. I removed one of the one liter MSR bottles I kept attached to the pillion foot rest struts on both sides of the bike, poured a little gas out of it at the base of the wood pile, took the miniscule lighter I had, and flipped the roller. Whoosh! The fire leaped up at me, but I managed to retrieve my hand with only lightly singed hairs on the back of it. I settled down onto my little three legged camp stool and enjoyed the rest of my beer as darkness fell and the sound of night insects began to fill the air. I fed the fire until my beer was gone, then considering it wise to hit the hay before the mosquitoes decided to show,

I climbed into the tent, zipped up the door, stripped down to nothing, and climbed into the bag. I set the alarm on my phone for an early rise. I made a call back home and found out that whatever crisis had developed the day before with the kids had dissipated.

I adjusted the jacket, closed my eyes, and sought rest with a relieved mind. Sleep was upon me before I knew it.

Chapter Five

Day Three

Crossing the Mason-Dixon Line

I only hit the snooze a couple times, then rolled out of the bag and began the third day of the journey. I wolfed down a granola bar while breaking camp. A quick run to the bathroom to brush my teeth and I was ready to roll. I checked the Rokstraps and made sure they were cinched down tight over my drybag, Slipping my cheap camp shoes under the taught straps, with a quick once-over all the rigging, I climbed back aboard, rocked the bike forward, and kicked up the center stand. Rolling backward to the camp road, I rotated the key to start, waited for the buzzing of the fuel pump to stop, and hit the starter button. A click into first, and I was off for another day on the road.

I was starting to enjoy these shorter days riding, yesterday at 340 and today at 361 miles. Those days would be some of the shortest I would be riding on this trip, and I took advantage of the shortness by setting a laid back pace. I rode back south and reconnected with US 460, where I headed east-northeast.

Soon the traffic coming out of or heading into Bluefield thinned and 460 peeled off alone back into Virginia, while I kept going straight on the now narrowed and quiet country road running northeastward, roughly parallel with the Appalachian Mountain ridges.

As I rode north through the wooded mountains, the odor of pines was replaced by the earthy smell of deciduous forest and loam. Passing through small villages I could detect the distinctive odor of oak, hinting at unseen sawmills hidden somewhere among the other structures.

I had been skirting a huge forest on both sides of a narrow expanse that cut its way into the heart of the Monongahela National Forest. Just beyond the tiny town of Edray, I plunged into its heart, bending slightly left and slicing north across the woods to it western edge. I ran along just inside its margin, following it north and slightly east until emerging at Beverly and a bay of privately held land that jutted into the edge of the forest. My exit was short-lived, and at Montrose I dove back into the center of the Monongahela. Just past there, the highway turned northeastward and exited the forest some thirty miles on at the Maryland and West Virginia line. Soon, I had crossed the famously scenic US 50 that runs west through West Virginia and east through Maryland past Winchester and on toward Washington DC and spilling into Ocean City. I'd wanted to ride portions of that highway through West Virginia with all its curves, but this time all I could do was make a mental note to return one day as I sprinted north into Maryland.

Soon, giant windmills appeared stretched in an unbroken line into Maryland. I could see them lined along the mountaintops behind the rolling farmland. A lazy wind was blowing, and only a few of them were turning.

I slowed on a sweeper perched almost even with the blades of one of the huge beasts and pulled onto the wide shoulder. Shutting down the bike and removing my helmet, I could hear the whir of the gigantic blades cutting though the air few hundred feet past the guardrail and drop-off on the opposite side of the highway. It is hard to appreciate the size of those modern power generating mills just viewing them on the mountaintops doing their job from a valley below. Once, on a trip to the Ozarks, I passed a truck hauling just a single one of the three blades, and it was enormous, stretching from the tractor to a small trailer under the tip of the blade, some 150 feet behind it. There at the side of the highway in Maryland was the first time I'd seen one of these up close while working away, and it was an impressive sight, especially when I could see a line of like-sized mills stretching out of sight across the mountains.

Windmills beside the Highway in West Virginia

As I had been traveling north, the colors of the forest trees had been changing slowly from their full dark green summer coats to lighter shades of yellow-green. Some trees still showed their spring flowers as I approached Pennsylvania.

Maryland reminded me of Michigan, with rolling hills, wide valleys, and many iconic traditional farms. Forest smells were replaced with those of the farm—horses, manure, and turned soil. White pine started appearing. German place-names were popping up everywhere as I neared Pennsylvania.

My route continued rolling northeast across the western panhandle of Maryland. A couple miles before the Pennsylvania line, it intercepted Interstate 68, also labeled US 40/219, that ran east into Hagerstown just past the thin isthmus connecting the panhandle with the bulk of eastern Maryland. My plan was to skip past the Interstate and immediately turn right on what was labeled Alt US 40. I assumed it was the old route because it was named *Alt* 40 and traced the same path as US 40 just a few hundred yards to the north, following it west to where the peninsula of West Virginia almost pokes across Maryland into Pennsylvania at Cumberland. I would only follow 40 as far east as where US 219 left the Interstate, and head into Pennsylvania there. As I approached I-68, though, the intersection I was looking for and the Interstate on-ramp were almost on top of each other. It didn't help that US 40 also followed I-68. I took the wrong turn and ended up on I-68 instead. The turn off for US 219 was only five miles farther along, so instead of finding the next exit, getting off, and then trying to get back to my turn, I kept running east on the Interstate. That would turn out to be the only time spent on an Interstate highway on the entire trip. In a few minutes, I caught the exit and left I-68, and in a couple more miles I was crossing the Mason-Dixon line into the North and entering Pennsylvania.

I continued on that highway as far as Berlin, but it would continue north too far west of Altoona, so I took a connector northeast toward the city. My low fuel light was glowing, and I started looking for a place to refill. As I rode through hamlet after hamlet, each time expecting a gas station to appear, I started to realize, that in spite of this being a populated area, the Southern phenomena of a gas station at every intersection big enough to call itself a town was not going to apply in Pennsylvania. By Reels Corner, where I turned right, I was worrying a bit. With still no stations in sight, I turned north towards Altoona. Finally, at New Paris, I could relax when a station came into sight. I pulled up to the pump, inserted my card, and filled the tank. Bullet dodged, I pulled back onto the highway and continued to Weyant, where I hopped a mile or so east on a side road to Business US 220 which ran together with I-99, continuing north into Altoona, where Steve was waiting for me.

Altoona lay in a valley between two ridges of the Alleghenies, sharing it with the Interstate and running roughly north-northeast. Windmills spun overhead on the eastern ridge as I poked around south Altoona looking for Steve's place.

Steve's home was nestled in a little quiet neighborhood west of the highway, and I found it fairly easily. I had a light traveling day of only 361 miles and had arrived early enough in the day to relax and catch up with Steve before heading back out, this time in Steve's truck, to have a look around and lunch downtown at the curiously named Texas Hot Dog, an Altoona fixture since the 1910s. We wolfed down a couple of dogs before Steve drove me around some more, pointing out points of interest. Eventually, back at Steve's, we settled in for the evening, with Steve grilling pork chops on his porch for dinner as the afternoon faded into twilight. The food was welcome as were the beers after having consumed no more than a granola bar and a few handfuls of peanuts during my ride up. While the chops were great, they were made even more delicious, no doubt, by my relative fast during the day.

Soon all the activity of the day caught up with me, and I hit the rack. My usual call home didn't reveal any bad news at home and laid some of my fears to rest before finally closing my eyes and fading into sleep.

Chapter Six

Day Four

The Ridges Surrounding Altoona

The next morning I found Steve in the kitchen cooking eggs and bacon for breakfast, complete with toast and Florida Natural orange juice, no less, straight from the factory in Lake Wales and the best to be had anywhere.

After breakfast, I grabbed a quick shower, figuring this was probably going to be my last for quite a while. Bikes were rolled out and prepped for a day of riding. While the city was waking, we headed out toward the surrounding mountains.

We rode Kittanning Point Road west out of the city, the road's name changing to Veteran's Memorial Highway as we rode into the moutains. It changed again to Glenwhite Road as we flew by Horseshoe Curve, a switchback built in 1854 to help nineteenth century railroad engines tackle the extreme grade over the ridge that fenced in Altoona on the west. At Gallitzin Road we turned south, stopping at Tunnel Hill for a rest and to wait for a train to emerge from the tunnel and pass under the road, a popular spot for train aficionados to observe the objects of their interest.

The Allegheny Portage Railway

Just past Tunnel Hill, we entered Allegheny Portage Railroad Park. Before the dawn of railways, the Erie Canal had been completed in 1825 and was moving tons of cargo between the Hudson River and the Great Lakes and making lots of money and providing many jobs ever since. Pennsylvania wanted in on the action and built a canal system, which was completed in 1834. But the mountains in Pennsylvania were too high and the grades too extreme for the same kind of canal as New York had built. The Allegheny Portage Railroad Park was the site of an ingenious contraption to move barges that had come up the Susquehanna River and canals on the east side of the mountains across a gap of thirty-six miles to canals on the west side at Johnstown, which eventually connected to Pittsburgh and the Ohio River. With this critical piece of engineering, cargo could move from Baltimore Harbor to the

Ohio and Mississippi Rivers, and eventually to the Gulf of Mexico.

The Machinery for Pulling the Barges over the Mountain

The genius of this connecting link was a system of rail cars that could be run into the water. The special barges could be divided into three sections and each one floated onto a rail car. The rail cars, with the barges onboard, could then be pulled up a series of inclined railways and then lowered the same way down the other side. There the rail cars would again be run into the water and the barge sections floated off and reconnected to each other to continue their journey by water. To haul the cars up the steep inclines with the limited machinery they had at the time was done by attaching downward bound rail cars on one track and upward bound cars on another. The enormous weight of the cars and their barges (20,000 pounds) were offset by each other, making it possible to move them with a mere thirty-five horsepower steam engine with a large hemp rope, and later, by steel cable. While enormously useful, the system only operated until 1854 when steam locomotives had come to rule US transportation.

After our brief rest, we continued west for a short distance, before we turned south heading toward Portage. From there we turned back to the east for the run to Blue Knob, where Blue Knob Run would take us into Blue Knob State Park and, we hoped, to the second highest point in Pennsylvania. Once inside the park, however, we came across a closed gate barring our way to the very top—close but no cigar. At the southern edge of the park we turned east again heading back to Altoona, passing through Queen on our way back into town. The ride was pleasant, through hills, mountains, and forests, and it demonstrated how quickly you could leave the quiet countryside and be in Altoona.

Back at Steve's we put away our bikes. Steve's went into the small separate bike-only shed and mine into the car garage at the front of the house. With it only still mid-afternoon, we decided a walk was in order, so Steve and I wandered over to his neighbor's place, where I was introduced to Tim and his barn-busting collection of motorcycles, none of which he rode anymore because of his health. Tim offered me a glass of wine and we sipped while he showed me around, pointing out the new Indians, a Scout and a Chief; BMW K1600 GT; a BSA, and more.

After chatting for a while, we said goodbye and wandered down to see another riding friend of Steve's just a block or so away, Mac and his wife, Linda. Mac was the "Indian Larry" of Altoona, but instead of Indians, he worked with Harley-Davidsons. He showed us a couple of project bikes he had been working on out in an outbuilding in his backyard with custom frames, motor/transmission arrangements, and other doodads, before walking back to the house, where we had beers while chatting about riding, about my trip so far, and other places I had gone.

It was getting near sunset by the time we left Mac's, when we walked back in the cooling air to Steve's house. Once there, we discussed dinner. Steve had the idea of riding over to a place called Caesar Battisti, or "CB" as it was known by the locals. It was an Italian club, but anyone could eat there. We were only restricted to not drinking, as only members could do that. I had just had a beer and Steve didn't drink, so that was not a problem. We ordered a large pizza. When it appeared, I was surprised at its size, stretching across the small table, but by the time we departed, not a scrap was left. We rode home stuffed but happy, with sixty-five miles on the clock just riding in the area that day.

Back at the house, I rolled my Bonnie into the garage while Steve put his GS away in the shed. It had been a long but fun day, and it was not long before we were saying good night and settling down for the evening. I took my netbook out of its neoprene sleeve and took advantage of Steve's Wi-Fi, posting on Facebook, for the first and the last time on the trip, a couple photos of what we had seen that day. Everything that needed charging was plugged in for the night, and I called home, happy to find no issues had arisen yet and all was still going alright there. Fortune was on my side...so far. I slept soundly, grateful that I had nothing at home to worry about to take some of the luster out of my, so far, glorious ride.

Chapter Seven

Day Five

Into the Pennsylvania Wilderness to the Foot of the Catskills

We got up early the next morning. I was heading on toward the northeast, but we were going to make time to have breakfast together at Nicoletta's. I went out to the bike and reloaded all the gear in the chilly morning air and under an overcast sky. Steve got out his GS again, and soon we were heading out to breakfast.

We arrived at Nicoletta's while the regular breakfast crowd was there eating and telling stories and lies to each other. It was no tourist stop. The people in there were locals, and it turned out Steve knew a few of them sitting near our table from high school. Across the table Steve and his pals bantered while questions were flung at me about where I had come from and where I was heading. It was a jovial group, full of jokes and quips, and it made for a cheerful start to the day. We filled up on bacon, eggs, and toast between comments flung from table to table. Steve picked up my tab and would not listen to my arguments about why I should pay for my own. After our fill of food and talk, we all wandered outside. I shook everyone's hands and said my goodbyes and thank yous to Steve. I climbed onboard my laden Bonnie, made one final wave, nicked it into first, and rolled away.

I headed out of town, exiting the city on its northeast end and shadowing the Interstate as I rode a parallel highway. I passed through a few towns, each diminishing in size as I left Altoona until Bald Eagle, where I turned left and headed north across the western ridge toward Phillipsburg. By then the chill had reached me under my jacket and through my normal riding clothes, so after pumping gas, I changed into my cold weather gear, adding a two-layer wool and cotton shirt under my jacket with its thermal liner in.

At Phillipsburg, I switched roads to one which arced more northeasterly toward Moshannon. Another turn put me on PA 144 and running straight through the heart of Sproul State Forest. I had a glorious ride through the wilderness on 144, also called Elk Scenic Drive, climbing and descending and curving my way onward. As I rolled along this route, every so often I spotted stacks of small boulders along the roadway, and I wondered what they signified. Were they entrances into the woods to hunting spots or old trail markers? Between Moshannon and Renovo, the sun started to appear, fitfully at first, but gaining momentum, with lengthening periods of sun as I rode north. The trees were shorter in the forest, making me wonder if there had been a fire years ago and what I was seeing was new growth.

Before arriving at Renovo and my turn east, I spied a small park-like area and pulled off for a rest and a granola bar. There were trails leading off from the picnic area, and I decided to take a short hike. As I walked down the hillside and into the brush, the sun had come out and the wool shirt I had donned earlier, combined with my walking, warmed me up considerably. I walked to one end of a trail where I could get a good look out over the rolling hills below and then walked back up to the junction with another trail heading off to the southeast. I followed the new trail for a short distance from which I could see the parking area above, with my bike perched waiting for me. Soon I was back up the hill and climbing onboard the Bonnie ready to roll back onto the highway refreshed.

A Hike in Sproul State Forest

It was not long before I reached Renovo and my next turn, to the east on State Road 120. I had intended to take a shortcut to PA 44 via a tiny road called Hyner's Run that promised to be scenic and that would cut across the mountains from the North Branch of the Susquehanna River Valley to the hills above Pine Creek, eliminating a large U-shaped dip that was otherwise necessary to get to the same point on my next highway. But when I passed the turnoff, I spied a sign saying the road was closed. I continued on, now running southeast, following the West Branch of the Susquehanna River, walled in on both sides by 1,000 foot mountains, toward its inevitable connection with the main course of the mighty Susquehanna River at Northumberland. Before the branch's joining with its namesake parent, I was back on US 220, the route I had taken out of Altoona that morning, heading east to PA 44, the highway Hyner's Run would have put me on much farther north. The detour had me backtracking north-northwest until Tomb, where I cut east toward Salladasburg.

The route bypassed the largish city of Williamsport, on the West Branch of the Susquehanna, and ran east to Loyalsockville, where I turned north after crossing Loyalsock Creek. The road ran north for a very short way before bending once again east, following the creek and roughly mirroring the Loyalsock Trail, which wound its way through state forests to the south following an old Native American path. To the north was more forest, and the road whipped left and right with 1500-1600 foot peaks towering overhead. The route made an abrupt turn north, passing Kettle Creek Gorge on the way to Hillsgrove, where the road twisted right again and continued on its east-northeastward track again past World's End State Park at Forksville and on toward Russell Hill. The highway ran southeast briefly, then wove up over and around the Pennsylvania hills, heading roughly east-northeast toward the northeastern corner of the state.

I passed through pleasant countryside and forest, enjoying the sunny day and without a thought or trepidation about trouble at home, the wisdom of taking this trip, or worry about money. Riding is such an all-encompassing activity, especially in new surroundings, filling all the senses and requiring concentration on the job at hand that it leaves little room for thoughts of anything else. The road lifted my mind's dark clouds high, so if I still saw them at all they appeared to be fluffy white cumulus, far overhead and non-threatening.

The highway had dropped Loyalsock Creek and soon picked up the North Branch of Mehoopany Creek and crossed the Susquehanna where the creek joined its mother river. Before Tunkhannock I jumped onto US 6 for a short distance, turning onto PA 92 where it veered off the highway, continuing on its independent way winding to the northeast through the countryside, leaving 6 to roll on into the urban sprawl of Scranton.

Tunkhannock Creek Viaduct

Beyond Nicholson, I passed underneath the massive Tunkhannock Creek Viaduct, which spanned the wide floor of the Tunkhannock Creek Valley. From where its shadow fell below it onto the creek to the railroad bed high above, the bridge stood 240 feet and stretched its arms for over 2,300 feet from Station Hill to the north across the creek and its floodplain to the hills on the south. Looking like a Roman aqueduct, with numerous arches along its concrete expanse, the bridge held the title as the largest concrete bridge in the United States for fifty years after it was built in 1915. Connecting to the viaduct on both ends, the Norfolk Southern Railway wound its way, loosely mirroring US 11, also know as the Lackawanna Trail, from Binghamton, New York, to the north, to Scranton, Pennsylvania, to the south.

Just beyond the viaduct, a glance in my mirrors revealed the impressive sight much more clearly than it had appeared coming toward it from the west. I found a small side road on my right that ran over the creek and across the flat farmland of the valley to the south and pulled off the highway. Coming to a stop on the far side of the much more modest modern low concrete bridge across the creek, I shut the Bonnie down and was left with only the sounds of the water moving quickly in the stream below. The camera came out of the tailbag, and I put it to use trying to capture the massive structure stretching across the broad and green fields and hanging above the flowing brown water of the creek below. It was a good time for a snack and a short rest in that tranquil place, but soon I was off again, pointing east toward southeastern New York.

At Gelatt I abandoned 92, which wandered north into central New York, and turned east, wiggling my way over to another state highway on tiny local roads. A turn to the north soon had me at Ararat where I turned right, shooting for the northeast corner of Pennsylvania and the Catskill Mountains beyond.

Crossing over the West Branch of the Delaware River into New York, a first for me, I stopped for more gas at Hancock on NY 17, which now became my route, inching ever closer to the Catskills and turning north and south trying to keep up with the turns of the East Branch of the Delaware. Frost heaves appeared, shaking the bike violently and continuing like endless rows of topes, trying to shake me off the bike. Highway 30 peeled left and northeast, and relieved I followed its smooth asphalt, continuing the dance with the Eastern Branch, trying to keep an eye out for the road that would lead me to my second paid camping spot at Peaceful Valley Campground. When I spotted the little bridge I turned right, crossing the river, and rode into the campground, nestled inside a oxbow and along the eastern shore of the Delaware's East Branch.

I crunched over the gravel to the combination camp store and check-in, turned off the ignition, kicked down the stand, threw my leg over, and walked in to register. I was told inside was that it was going to be a cold night, down to 40 degrees Fahrenheit. I was glad I had brought a good quality mummy bag for the trip. I asked for a tent camping spot, got the location, and went back outside. I rolled slowly down the gravel road, turned left before the river along the many small cabins facing the water, and looked for my spot on my left. I didn't have a specific site, because it was so early in the season that no one else was tent camping, but there was a large grassy area where I could the pitch tent to my left. It was a huge, more or less, flat area, looking like a grass runway. The wind was blowing hard from the northwest so I picked a spot on the downwind side of a line of trees jutting out into the green space from the road and not too far from the restrooms.

I stopped the bike in the now diminishing late afternoon light, detached the tent from the bike, and erected it. I went back to the bike for my sleeping bag, which had been stored in a large dry-bag on top of my pillion bag along with my Thermarest sleeping pad, only to discover it was missing along with my knock-around slip-on shoes that I had tucked under the straps. Both RokStraps were still securely attached to the bike with the buckles still connected to each other, but the bag was gone. My heart sank. I didn't relish the idea of lying down inside the tent fully clothed in my riding gear, lying on the ground, and freezing through the long night. I left the tent where it was and rode back to the office, hoping that somehow I had knocked the bag off the bike without knowing it when I had dismounted and kicked my leg over the rear of the bike.

Inside there was no good news. I was dejected, but that was when the owners did something that started the trend, that was to continue restoring my faith in my fellow human beings. It was early and few people were in the park. The owners, knowing how cold it was going to be that night, offered me one of their small cabins at the same price as the tent space. There was no heat, but I'd have electricity and solid walls to keep the cold wind off me. I'd still have to sleep in my clothes, but at least it would be on a mattress and inside and out of the wind.

I went back to the tent, took it down, folded it, and put it away and then rode just the fifty or so yards to the cabin I had been given. I took my dry-box with all the cords and chargers for my electronics in it, and went inside and plugged everything in.

It was all but dark by then, and the temperature was falling fast. I had gotten this far using the debit card only for gas, and of my cash I had still not used up the first twenty dollar bill. With a cold night ahead and my disappointment at having lost very important items I would need for the rest of the trip, and so would have to replace somewhere, I took a bit of pity on myself and decided to treat myself to a hot dinner to try to cheer myself up if I could.

I climbed back on board the Bonnie and crunched my way back up the drive, asking at the office where I could get a bite to eat. Armed with that knowledge, I headed back out and across the river, heading back the way I had come in. Not seeing what I was looking for, I stopped at a small convenience store to ask again about a dining place, then headed out again with new information. I got confused where 30 junctioned with 17 and rolled through the stop sign in plain view of a police car that was sitting at the crossroads. As I realized my mistake, I looked behind me—no flashing blue lights. I had been lucky. I made a mental note to pay more attention and turned around to go back to the junction. I turned left and rode west back on the frost heaved highway. I watched in the dark for the bag on the side of the road, but saw nothing on the darkening evening roadside. The bag was a smooth vinyl, and my best guess was that all the slamming over the heaves had dislodged the bag, and I hadn't noticed it as it went sailing off into oblivion, down some ditch or into the river. I gave up the search when I spotted Beaver Del Hotel and Campground, which I had passed on my way to Peaceful Valley. I didn't stop to camp there because it catered to RVs only, but I had failed to notice the restaurant.

I ground to a halt on the gravel parking lot among a row of cars. Lights were glowing inside the building. I walked into the contrast of a cheerily warm and cordial interior, with small tables scattered around and a large wooden bar. I chose a small round table at the window near the bar, where I could keep my eye on the bike, a habit I usually try to satisfy when eating out. I climbed out of my thick riding jacket and hung it on the back of the adjacent chair.

A waitress approached and read my mind, offering a list of beers they had available. There were several locally brewed ones, and I chose Floodwatch IPA from Catskill Brewery. I also order a bleau cheese burger and fries, then sat back to relish the beer, and very good beer it was, and enjoy being warm for what I thought would be the last time that evening.

When I left the bill was $17, about the same amount as I had spent on the entire ride so far on all my expenses except gas. I was a little disappointed in myself, but shook it off and told myself I would be more careful from then on as I walked back to the bike in the bitter cold.

I found my way back to camp and rolled back to the cabin. Upon entering, I found that another kindness had been offered me without my asking. Folded neatly on the bed were a couple of warm-looking and welcome blankets. My spirits bumped up as I got ready to go to sleep.

I had ridden 358 miles that day, and was 1,645 miles from home.

I made my evening call home—no problems there—and told Andrea about my bad and my good luck of the day, then said good night, hoping her good luck would hold as well.

Chapter Eight

Day Six

The Catskills, Adirondacks, and Lake Champlain

I awoke in the dim rosy dawn with the sun yet to show its face over the surrounding mountains. I climbed out of the warm blankets into a chilly room and started unplugging all the electronics and packing them up for the road. I folded up the kindly offered blankets and stacked them where they had been left on the bed. I added my wool shirt under my jacket, expecting a cool ride through the Catskills and Adirondacks. I wandered out into the frosty air, surprised at the overnight drop in temperature, and ambled over to the bathrooms to brush my teeth. The Canadian geese were calling and landing in the nearby river as I returned to the cabin. All the stuff I had brought in for the night got replaced on the bike and tightened down, with special care given to make sure everything was tight, after my unfortunate experience with my dry bag the day before.

I had a quick granola bar breakfast and then mounted the Bonnie and crunched back down the gravel road to the office. I climbed off and approached the door. No one was in the office yet, and there was no sign of anyone working around the campground in the early morning air, so I scribbled a hurried note thanking them for the generosity they had shown me the night before and stuck it in the closed door before remounting and riding away for another day on the road.

Roadside Lake in the Adirondacks

Back at the highway, I turned right and rolled east. In a few minutes, I was following the twisting shore of Pepacton Reservoir on my left. I soon crossed the Pepacton and continued with the lake on my right and PA 28 joining the highway from the north. I veered north-northeast toward the Adirondacks when the two routes parted ways, continuing to follow the East Branch of the Delaware, where I soon spotted more "morning deer." At Roxbury, I stopped and broke my promise to myself and splurged on a breakfast of eggs and corned beef hash at Cassie's Café. Leaving Cassie's, I put the Catskills behind me and the Adirondacks straight ahead and headed into the land of the fabled Mohicans and the early days of the American experience. I had considered heading east to the Hudson River Valley, a place immortalized by the stunning works of the Hudson River School painters, then north to Lakes George and Champlain. As I looked at the maps noting many towns lining that route and a major Interstate, however, my disdain for traffic and cities won over my desire to follow the Hudson. The mountains prevailed, as they usually do when planning my routes.

The trees had grown to truly huge heights by the Catskills compared to what I had gotten used to in the South. While at the Georgia-Florida line they had leaped well above the scrubby Florida trees, but now I was in the North Woods and all the vegetation took on enormous proportions. I imagined the forested earth seen from far above as covered with a carpet of trees and how that pile would change as the latitude increased. In Florida, the short scrubby ones were like a short commercial carpet, flat with no texture, and in Georgia, especially as the mountains began to appear, it was a Berber, with textured rolls of thick carpet, but by the Catskills, it had turned to full, thick, shag carpet, where the forest floor fell far below the soft tops of the green weave.

Continuing along the Eastern Branch of the Delaware, I saw signs of days gone by, of barge traffic being towed along the quiet waters, evidenced by grassy pathways on the side of the stream where oxen once trod pulling the heavy canal boats laden with goods for the frontier.

Pass the turnoff to Northville, I stopped to take a photo of one of many snowmobile crossing signs I was going to see, thinking, "You know you're in the North when..." Riding past fast flowing rivers and up and down increasing grades, the landscape was incredible and dotted with little lakes and ponds. I stopped at one that looked like the background for an ad for L.L. Bean, with the light green leaves of birch trees, with their canoe-building white bark, rustling in the breeze surrounding the pond and beaver lodges poking up from its depths here and there.

You Know You're in the North When...

Colonial names appeared on signs, like Lord Howe, Roger's Rock, and Essex. At the southern corner of Siamese Ponds Wilderness I aimed further east and was heading slowly toward the mighty Hudson River Valley north of the non-stop string of towns farther south. I eventually caught up with the famed river and crossed it at Riparius, then continuing on past Brant Lake. At Hague the north end of Lake George spread out before me and followed me north to Ticonderoga, stronghold of the French during the French and Indian Wars. With the lake on my right, I rolled northward toward Lake Champlain, the natural barrier between New York, with its wild Adirondacks, and Vermont, with its rolling Green Mountains.

At Crown Point, I had arrived at the extreme southern end of Lake Champlain. I stopped for gas at a small combination gas station and convenience store called Hap's, and after filling up, I went inside to ask the locals how I could get up above the lakes and, hopefully, have some stunning views of the land and lakes below. I was in luck, although the two clerks debated whether a bike could make it up because it was dirt and pretty rough. "ATVs go up there on the weekends; yeah, you can probably make it on a motorcycle if you're careful. You'll find a small cemetery called Lang. From there you'd probably be better off walking the rest of the way up, which is just a little farther."

At Hap's corner, the highway turned right toward the water, which it had meandered away from earlier. I was told if I kept on straight west on Creek Road to White Church Road and turned north I would eventually see a small dirt road named both Lang Road and Big Hollow Road heading east into the woods. That little dirt road would lead me to the vista I wanted. I had installed dual sport tires on the Bonnie so I figured this was the perfect opportunity to give them a test and see how they would do. I turned onto White Church Road and started watching for both names. About fives miles out I spotted a sign for Lang Road and turned right.

It was a two-track wooded trail paved with small rocks thrust up from the rocky core of the land just beneath the surface. After the first couple houses the track grew more rustic with a grassy center ridge and increasing grade. I stood on the pegs, ducking larger branches while small branches occasionally swiped across my face shield. I found the small cemetery and parked the bike, making sure the Bonnie was steady and secure on the sloping ground. I slipped a kickstand coaster under the stand to make sure it would not sink into the soil then started up the steepening trail. There the track was no longer a road, but simply a cleared path climbing over exposed boulder surfaces with trees encroaching left and right. As I crested the ridge I was rewarded with what I had hoped for, a wide open view from boulders topping cliffs that fell into the forest below and a view northeast to the main body of Lake Champlain and its southern end to the southeast and Vermont's Green mountains receding on the far side of the lake into diminishing ridges of lighter and lighter blue.

Parked Up at Lange Cemetery

The sunshine was warm, but there was a hint of chill in the air as I clambered over the rocks and boulders taking photographs and savoring the moment. Over the lake was my future and looking south toward Lake George was my past. I was living in the moment and had completely forgotten my worries and anxiousness, which I had left behind. I spent an hour or so climbing over rocks and ledges on the cliff edge before heading back down the trail.

Arriving back at Lang Cemetery, the bike was still there waiting for me, my silver helmet still dangling from the left handgrip and my gloves shoved down behind the windscreen and above the headlight bucket. I geared up and climbed back on the Bonnie, for once remembering to remove the coaster from under the kickstand and stick it back in my bag. I had my GoPro perched on the top of my helmet and decided to fire it up for the ride back down the mountain. Although the footage would not capture the steepness of the downhill ride, it was more challenging than going up, but by then my confidence was up, and I stood on the pegs and rolled down the mountain, glad that I had taken the time to get up to the mountaintop and that I had the nerve to test my dual sport skills. In Florida riding off pavement usually means deep sand, which is very taxing and difficult. But I found riding in New York, with hard packed and rocky ground, to be a much more pleasant and less stressful experience. I told myself not to shy away from doing it again when the opportunity presented itself.

Lake Champlain and the Green Mountains in the Distance

I retraced my path back to the corner at Hap's, completing the detour loop of eighteen miles, then rejoined my original route north toward Bullwaga Bay, where I had the choice to turn right and cross the lake into Vermont by bridge on NY 185 or continue north along Lake Champlain's western shore. I noted a ferry crossing the lake at Essex and decided to take that across as a more interesting alternative to a bridge. If it cost a bit, so be it; I was here to see and enjoy this area, and a ferry fee was a small price to pay.

At Westport, the road veered west, back into the Adirondacks. I veered right onto NY 22, which wandered inland a while crossing Bouquet River twice before following it north. West of Essex, the road turned east and back to the lake, leaving the Bouquet to find its own way into Lake Chaplain a few miles north near Willsboro. At the shore, the highway made an abrupt left and continued along the lake shore without me, while I rolled east onto the Essex-Charlotte Ferry. As luck would have it there was no charge, and I was able to continue on my own frugal way.

The ferry was a small one hundred ton vessel, with room for about ten cars and a few motorcycles, although that day I was the only bike on board. As we crossed the glassy waters of the immense lake, our wake was the only thing disturbing its surface. People got out of their cars and leaned on the rail gazing across the water. I turned on the GoPro and panned around the ferry while chatting with a couple fellow passengers who had noticed my Florida plate and wanted to know where I was heading. "Six days out and headed to Fairfax, then on to Rimouski," I told them while watching the lines of the Green Mountains approaching on the far side of the lake.

Departing the ferry, in a bid to avoid the large city of Burlington perched on the western shore of Lake Chaplain directly north of our landing place, I headed east on Ferry Road crossing the busy US 7, the most direct route into the heart of the city, and east toward Hinesburg. There the plan was to turn north, skirting the city on the east side. At Essex Junction I would continue north into Fairfax, where Larry and Loretta were awaiting me. I hoped to find a camping supply store where I could replace my sleeping bag along this route, which was the closest I'd been to a metropolitan center in the last couple of days, but I never saw a likely place. The missing bag was my only worry, with the falling temperatures and the next day or two that I anticipated camping out. In spite of my distance from the city, it was about five o'clock and the road was crowded. I got confused and thought I was lost, but somehow I got past the traffic and ended up in Fairfax.

Scenic River in Vermont

I passed a dual sport bike going the other way as I entered the little town. The temperature had rapidly dropped as the day wore on toward evening, and I thought how odd it was for someone else to be out on a bike in such cold. There was a gas station and convenience store called The Steeple Market on the side of the road just after I crossed the Lamoille River, so I pulled off there to check my final directions to the house. As I was pouring over the map, which had precious little detail of the area, the same dual sport rolled into the parking lot, the rider raised his shield, and asked, "Are you Mike?" It was Larry, who'd grown bored hanging out at his house and had decided to see if he could spot me riding in on the highway, figuring, as I had, that few riders would be out in that cold so if he saw one, the chances would be that it was me. Having confirmed I was, indeed, Mike, with a shout of "follow me!" we were off. I followed him to the next road that turned right, which was aptly named River Road, and followed the river. The road was gravel, but graded well and an easy ride to Larry and Loretta's place, nestled among the trees, clothed in their early spring foliage.

I was invited inside, where Loretta and warm food were waiting. We dug in, and between mouthfuls, I filled them in on the highlights of the trip so far. Larry and Loretta were both motorcycle instructors and loved to moto-travel, and Loretta would soon be on an adventure herself within a week or so of me heading on. We talked as the sun set and the twilight faded to darkness outside,while the temperature plummeted.

I told Larry about losing my bag back in New York and asked him if there was anywhere in the area I could pick another up. He said there was nothing closer than going all the way back into Burlington, but he thought he might have an extra sleeping bag and even a dry bag I could carry it in. I could just mail back the dry bag when I got home, but he told me not to bother returning the sleeping bag. Once again, a stranger, who I'd not known further than a couple emails back and forth before I had left, was demonstrating generosity and kindness that had seemed to me just a couple weeks earlier a quickly disappearing quality of my fellow human beings. Face to face, and perhaps especially with the bond that riding provides fellow motorcyclists, humans do interact with selflessness and charity, and it warmed my heart to have that confirmed, once again, in my hosts.

After a bit more conversation with Larry and Loretta, who is also a teacher, sharing our views on life, people, politics, and education, Larry showed me upstairs to my waiting bed. He pointed out where I could recharge all my electronics and where I could grab a shower in the morning. He examined the possible sleeping bag candidates and offered me a zero degree one, which was especially welcome, knowing the temperatures were expected to drop further as I rode north. We said our good nights, and I called Andrea for the scoop on how things were going in Florida, receiving good news that she was having no major problems with the kids and that no major appliances had broken, which always seemed to happen when I was on the road. I drifted off to sleep with an untroubled mind under the luxury of sheets and quilts.

Chapter Nine

Day Seven

Into Canada

I woke up early and grabbed a shower. By the time I made it downstairs, pancakes were on the table, and of course, maple syrup to top them—a fitting meal before my venture back into the cold and into Canada. Loretta was off to school early, and after saying her goodbyes, Larry and I were left alone chatting and discussing the day ahead. Larry mentioned that he had grown up in central Maine and very near the route I would be taking on my way back south, outside the tiny town of Sangerville. He said his family still had a farmstead there that they kept for whenever family members wanted to get away. He said I was welcome to use the place, telling me how to find it, where the key was, how to turn on the electricity and hot water. He also mentioned his neighbor, Sally, whose boys he had grown up with as a kid. He said to make sure I stopped and said hi to Sally. He said she might even feed me.

Topping Up the Scottoiler before Leaving Larry and Lorretta's

I rolled the heavily laden Bonneville out into the driveway, and added to its burden the few things I had brought in with me the night before. On top of it all I strapped down the sleeping bag, secure in the dry bag Larry had loaned me. I checked my Scottoiler and realized I had not considered it when I was leaving Florida. The reservoir was empty. Larry loaned me some chain lube, and I lubricated it the old fashioned way, with a squirt and a roll, a squirt and a roll. I was not too concerned because the Bonnie had an X-ring chain that required little care, but I felt better knowing it got a shot of lube occasionally. I shook hands with Larry and thanked him for Loretta's and his hospitality, and once again, offered to ship the sleeping bag back to him upon my return home, which he still told me was unnecessary. I swung my leg high over the bike and climbed onboard, said one more goodbye, thumbed the starter, and crunched back out of the driveway and down River Road toward Fairfax.

It was cold and there was not a prospect of much warming through the rest of the day. I headed west, back toward Lake Champlain, then north until I found my route that veered off to the northeast, east, and then again north toward Canada. A little north of Sheldon, I stopped and topped off my fuel tank and took a short break, then continued as the route made its final turn north toward the Canadian border just past the little town of Richford. There, just before the border, the road I had followed veered once again off to the east, so I turned north on another state road for the short jump to the border.

A New Country and a New Language

I entered Canada at the post between Richford, Vermont and Abercorn, Quebec. Passage was easy, and I never had to step off my bike. A simple check of my passport through the officer's window and a short "Two days" answer to his query of how long would I be in Canada, and I was done. There was no traffic behind me, so after the minor formalities, I chatted with the officers a bit, but the news was not good when they mentioned the weather. "Supposed to get down to 0° (32° F) tonight. The forecast is for snow overnight." At least they didn't mention rain, too, I thought. Riding in the cold is one thing, but riding in the cold and getting wet at the same time is a very different thing, especially when cutting through the air and rain at 60 miles per hour on a bike. I considered my options, realized I had none, knowing turning back was not acceptable. It was what it was; I would just have to layer up and roll with it. All I could think of to reply was, "That will make for interesting photos." I said goodbye, nicked it into first, and headed into Canada.

Finally in Quebec

It was chilly and overcast as I began my first day in a new country, but as I rode north the sky was slowly clearing. North of Granby, the road ran east for a short distance then hooked north again. Somewhere in the area I made a wrong turn and ended up on gravel road. After a while I ran across QC 241, a paved highway, turned north, and rejoined my original route at Roxton Falls. In less than six miles I spotted my turn and headed toward the east then northeast as I passed the major highway of Canada 55.

So far, the day's ride had been through large but gently rolling hills where place-names such as Asbestos, both a county and a village, revealed the kind of industry in the area. I stopped at Victoriaville to fuel and warm up in one of the dozens of Tim Horton's I had spotted on the Canadian roadways. Tim Horton's soon became my favorite stops. They were everywhere and had excellent coffee at good prices that not only warmed my insides, but gave my hands welcome relief as I wrapped my fingers around the steaming cup. At one, I was able to tap into the free Wi-Fi and shoot an email out to Andrea. Phone calls from Canada would have been extremely expensive on my cell plan, so other than email, I would be out of contact with home for the next couple days. The road I was on aimed for Quebec City on the far side of the narrow stretch of the Saint Lawrence Seaway. I followed it as far as Plessisville, with the aim to miss the traffic near the large city, turning southeast on another provincial route to cut over to a more rural road to the northeast that split the area between the Saint Lawrence and the western Maine border.

Heading southeast, I was cutting perpendicular to the ridge of the northern Appalachians that eventually fall to the sea at the end of the Gaspé Peninsula, only to pop up one more time in the form of the island of Newfoundland, before disappearing completely under the ocean waves. Between Lac William and Lac à la Truite, I turned left, continuing northeast through the heart of the mountains. Another mining name appeared as I passed the turnoff to Thetford Mines. On my new route, grades grew steeper. Those seven percent grades, considered extreme in the Blue Ridge Mountains, fell to insignificance as I rolled up and down eighteen percent grades in the Canadian Appalachians.

I climbed higher and higher in latitude with the thermometer stuck at 45° Fahrenheit. There were no Tim

Horton's by then, so I had to tough it out and wait for a break from the weather until I got into more populated areas. Up and over and down again, the road kept climbing northeastward, obliquely approaching the northwestern border with Maine. At Frampton, not long after crossing Canada 73, the main route directly from the Maine border to Quebec City, the road T-ed. I jogged left, northwest, just long enough to connect to the next road, where I resumed my previous heading to the northeast.

Once in Quebec the Grades Started to Increase

My path abruptly halted at a T-junction with QC 204, running southeast only to stop before kissing the Maine border and northwest to the wide Fleuve St-Laurent, as the Saint Lawrence was called in Quebec. I turned left and made my way toward the bay and civilization, with a stop at Ste-Perpétue for more fuel and a warm up. At those stops, my lack of French made communication cumbersome, but not impossible. A simple point toward the bike parked up beside a fuel pump had pretty obvious meaning without the need for words, and coffee at these small stops was no different than coffee in American gas stops—just fill up a cup yourself and walk up to the counter to pay.

Twenty-one miles later I was at the immense river that had become a bay. I turned right, running northeast on the coastal flats which sometimes were on the left and sometimes on the right as the road wandered away and then closer to the coast. The cold, wide, blue bay was on my left and the last vestiges of the Appalachians in the form of rounded knobs were scattered here and there on my right in long strings, sometimes close at hand, and sometimes off across a wide expanse of rich flatlands and sometimes surprising me by appearing between me and the sea. Even then, some refused to give up and poked their heads up out of the sea offshore or formed little hilly jutting peninsulas. Small farms whizzed by, the fields too early for planting. I passed through small quaint towns planted beside the Saint Lawrence many years ago, which I imagined would not be out of place in the other France on another continent.

I had finally gone back in time far enough for the start of spring; the trees' new leaves barely open. I had not only caught spring in its infancy, I was on the very edge of winter. The temperature had failed to budge any higher than 44° F and the cold wind was taking icy stabs at me, which were finding their way into the cracks of my riding gear. I had on every layer I had available, and still my core was freezing, and my hands were brittle and refused to cooperate. Tim Horton's stops became necessities, with half-hours of a finger-wrapped coffee cup required to restore enough feeling to them to be able to return them to the clutch and throttle and head back out.

One thing the cold did was block out thoughts of anything else. I rode along without worry about how things were going in Florida, and enjoyed the selfish pleasure of being in the moment and not thinking about anything beyond the next curve. Part of the sensation felt wrong, as if I should feel guilty for not worrying about my family and duties left behind, and another part felt good, as if my cares were shed for the moment, with the freedom to live for just for what I was doing, if only for a short while. I never stopped caring about my family, but the worry was gone.

My goal had been Rimouski for the day, but by the time I had cut through the icy air for twelve hours, I found myself at Rivière-du-Loup, miles from my intended camp spot at Parc National du Bic. Other than my exorbitant cheeseburger and beer dinner back in New York, I had been careful not to spend too much money, dining on peanuts and granola bars and occasional coffees. So, I ditched the idea of tent camping and looked for what I hoped would be a cheap motel with warm shower, clean sheets, and a place to eat nearby. It was twilight when I found a suitable place after tooling slowly around Rivière-du-Loup, watching and stopping to ask at hotels with no vacancies.

I pulled into Motel Cartier, with a restaurant named St-Hubert connected to its eastern end. I pulled in, climbed off the bike, free at last from the relentless frigid wind, and walked inside. Lacking French, I still somehow got my message across that I wanted a room and was handed a key. I walked back outside and moved the bike as close as possible to the room and started unloading. The rooms were laid out in typical motel fashion, in one long string with one side toward the bay and the other toward the street. But, instead of the rooms opening directly to the outside, there was a long corridor running its length, perforated with occasional entry doors, that insulated the room doors from direct contact with the weather outside. I unloaded the gear from the bike outside the closest door into the corridor and near my room and labored inside with all my baggage, then opened the door to the room and piled the stuff inside.

I didn't waste much time in the room and immediately headed down the corridor to St-Hubert. It looked a bit pricey for me, but I threw caution to the wind and walked inside. All around me were well-dressed couples and families enjoying their meals, while I sat alone at a booth for four, looking like a homeless wanderer in my well-worn riding clothes and with seven-day's growth of beard, which I had decided to leave unattended during this trip.

The waitress approached and addressed me in French. I apologized for my complete ignorance of her tongue and asked if they had a menu in English. I had assumed anyone working at a resort town like Rivière du Loup would have a good working knowledge of English, but if she understood me, she didn't show it. I sensed a little disdain as she walked off in search of a foreign menu. Nevertheless, she was back soon, and understood my Neanderthal finger pointing enough to take my order. The chicken pot pie, one of the least expensive items on the menu, looked like just the thing for warming up after a day of bitter cold, with a photo of its golden baked crust enticing me, and with sides of both salad and coleslaw. I also splurged on a beer to celebrate my reaching the Saint Lawrence. The pot pie lived up to its menu billing, and I left for my room full and warm, albeit a little less wealthy.

Back in the room, I filled all the outlets with chargers, re-energizing the netbook, camera, phone, and GoPro and its remote so all would be ready for the road the following day. I coveted the luxury of warmth, which I thought would be the last for me for a while. I slipped my clothes off, glad to not have to sleep in all my gear in a tent somewhere in the freezing night, and slid beneath the clean white sheets and fell instantly asleep.

Chapter Ten

Day Eight

To Rimouski and South to Maine

I woke early and turned on the television to try to see if I could find a forecast for the day. I flipped through the choices searching for a weather channel. Once I found one, I sat and waited for it to cycle to the day's forecast. It looked better than the day before, with the promise of a high of 16° Celsius (61° F) with sunny skies, at least for Montreal, 250 miles southwest. I could count on a bit less at my higher latitude but was happy the trend was up for the day and the upcoming week. The next image I saw was radar of the night before, showing a swath of snow blanketing an area diagonally from the northwest at Quebec City to the southeast all the way the Bay of Fundy, on the New Brunswick coast.

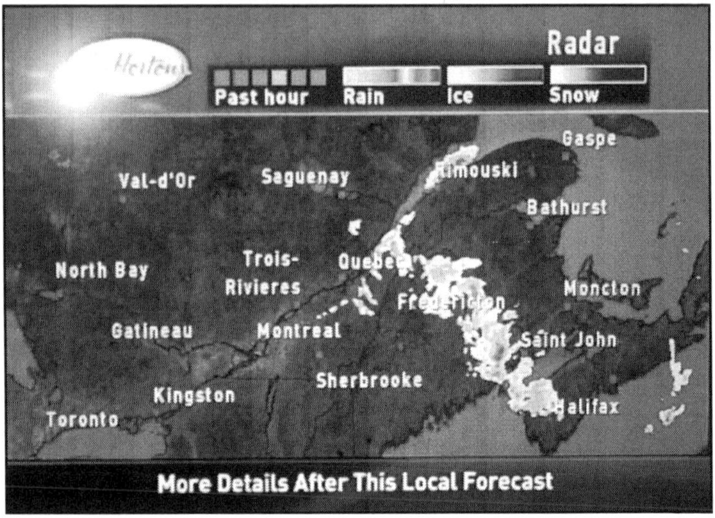

Snow across Quebec and Maine

I flicked off the television and headed to the bathroom to brush my teeth and take a hot shower. Cleaned thoroughly, I put on my dirty clothes from the day before, not having brought any extra warm clothes to go under my riding gear and only having one set of riding pants to my name. I unplugged all the electronics and stuffed them in their places, then closed up the baggage, opened the corridor door to the biting cold, and lugged it all out and reinstalled it on the bike under the early morning lightening sky. While working on the loading, I briefly chatted with an American couple who were motorcycle riders and surprised them when they asked where I had come from.

Breakfast would be fare from my pannier while on the road. I hopped on board, clutched, fired the Bonnie up, clicked into first, and was off.

My arbitrary goal had been Rimouski, farther up the coast. Having come as far as I had and being only seventy miles away, I decided to complete the run up the shoreline before turning south toward Maine. I continued northeast past Cacouna and L'Isle Verte before paralleling Canada 20, but closer to the coast, until 20 ended abruptly just before Rivière-Trois-Pistoles.

Rolling beside My Goal, the Bay of Saint Lawrence

My former route continued without me, and I followed the Saint Lawrence south coast toward Rimouski. I rode northeast toward my goal with hills occasionally on one side or the other, and sometimes on both. After passing Porc-Pic, I came to a halt behind a line of vehicles. We did not sit still long and soon we were herded off the main highway onto a smaller side road that paralleled the main highway a hundred yards of so to the north. On the detour, I could see the reason for the traffic and diversion. There was a small car, which obviously had impacted a box truck head on. The roadway was clear and straight, with nothing to impair view. I guessed one of the drivers had dozed off on their early morning drive and never woke up again. I reminded myself to be vigilant and not let a similar scenario play out on my ride.

I stopped for fuel at Saint-Fabien. The attendants inside just gave me curious looks when I spoke English, but eventually my intentions to fuel up were made clear, and I topped the bike up. There was a display of fresh muffins at one counter. I picked out a chocolate chip one to go with a hot cup of coffee, struggling with the attendants less that time because I used cash instead of a debit card, as I had for fuel, and walked outside to relax in the sunshine and absorb some of its heat at the east side of the building. A car driver had fueled up and came over to talk to me. He perceived my lack of French so talked to me in good English, telling me he had grown up in that area and had come home for a funeral but now lived in Montreal. He also rode motorcycles and asked all the usual questions: where had I come from, where was I going, and how long had I been on the road. So much for the smug disdain of French Canadians; he was friendly, and we talked for quite a while. I started to wonder if my expectations had colored my perception of the hotel attendant and waitress the night before and of the attendants inside the gas station. Many people there truly did not speak English, and what I took for disdain was probably just a lack of understanding.

Finally, I passed Parc National du Bic, which had been my originally planned stopping point for the night before, and entered the last of the coastal flatlands approaching Rimouski, which would end completely a bit farther up the road, once and for all at Matane.

QC 132 eventually circumnavigates the entire Gaspé Peninsula and returns to itself at Sainte-Flavie, a few miles northeast of Rimouski. What a beautiful ride that must be, I thought. The route passes the last cross-Saint Lawrence ferry at Matane and continues in magnificent solitude, with only tiny villages rarely interrupting, all the way around the peninsula. The coastal road passes the highest mountains in the range, which fill the entire peninsula and sweep down all the way to the coast from Matane, on the north, to Matapedia, on the south. Less than a day's ride from Rivière du Loup on the same route would have put me in the shadow of Mont Jacques Cartier, the highest point on the peninsula, at over 4,000 feet. These are the northeastern tip of the Appalachians, known as the Chic Chocs, running northeast until they drowned themselves in the Gulf of Saint Lawrence at Gaspé. There the only barrier to the wild North Atlantic is the island of Newfoundland, where the last remnants of the Appalachians make their final appearance, only to disappear finally and for good into the North Atlantic Ocean beyond. I was tempted to ride on but knew that was too big a stretch and decided that would have to wait for another trip.

I parked downtown looking for another Tim Horton's, but failed. I walked to a visitors' bureau in the park, but found the doors locked; it was probably too early in the season. I looked back over the Saint Lawrence River for the last time, turned away from the coast, found my highway, and rolled into the heart of the Gaspé and toward Maine.

The route headed inland, passing the Camping Centre Naturiste I had looked into for booking a campsite. I was a little sorry I had not been able to get in, but on the other hand, with the temperatures that night there'd have been no clothes coming off to enjoy a new experience of being au naturel in nature. The highway T-ed with another provincial highway, and I made an abrupt left and ran southwest into the heart of the interior mountains.

The temperature had not risen much yet and had probably not reached forty, and I was freezing. Passing Rèserve Faunique Duchénier on my right, I noticed wet spots appearing on the arm of my riding jacket. I cringed, thinking cold was not so bad, but cold and wet together was not a welcomed development. Combining the two portended a miserable day ahead. As I peered ahead into the falling moisture, I noticed it did not fall straight down but, instead, floated down with a sort of weave from side to side. It had been a long time since I had seen it, but I recognized it as snow!

With my teeth chattering, I continued southwest on the country road, which went on endlessly up, over, and down innumerable hills. Almost before it had started, the snow disappeared as I rode toward the northernmost tip of Maine. I passed the northern end of Lac Témiscouta, where

I stopped for more fuel and a quick bite at a McDonalds and my route intercepted the major highway, Canada 85. That highway runs southeast to Edmundson, joining Canada 2 which parallels the eastern Maine border on the Canadian side, eventually turning east then southeast into Nova Scotia. At Tèmiscouta, my route jogged southeast then back to southwest again. The border with Maine was approaching quickly, but right before kissing it at Rivière-Bleue, I turned left toward Lac Baker and the border crossing at Fort Kent, crossing a thin arm of New Brunswick that extends across the northeastern tip of Maine in a handshake with its southwestern neighbor.

Crossing the border on the Canadian side was not much more than a wave and a bonjour. On the other side at Fort Kent was another matter. There were just two vehicles crossing, myself and a van full of a family and their dog. All of us were detained and both vehicles thoroughly searched. After an hour and a half, I had passed muster and was given the go-ahead to enter my home country. I walked back out to the Bonnie and closed up and reattached all the luggage that the guard had pulled off and rifled through. I guessed at the little lonely crossing, far from any cities and off the main route to Caribou, the officers had plenty of time on their hands, and they didn't mind using some of it to practice their search techniques.

In Maine, I was then on ME 11, which headed south through the interior of the state. Between that highway and the western Maine border there were only private roads, requiring special permits and fees, that ran past the small mountains on my right, into the huge Allagash Wilderness, back into more mountains on the far side of the Allagash River valley, and past a series of long lakes in the North Maine Woods wilderness.

Passing Moose Mountain, I started to see snow still on the ground in white banks under the shade of the roadside trees and other places the sun hadn't found yet. I watched my mileage carefully, because it was a very long way between the widely scattered little villages along the way. I was glad to have my spare gallon Rotopax on my tail rack, tucked under the rear bag, and my two MSR litre bottles perched beside my panniers. The mountains grew as I moved south, from the over 1,000 feet heights in the north to 2,000 and 3,000 foot peaks farther south.

Back in the US and Maine's Rolling Woodlands

South of Knowles Corner, where ME 212 branched off to the southeast, I caught my first and only view of a huge porcupine as it ambled across the road, dragging its load of long sharp quills with it.

Passing Mount Chase, my view to the west opened up. By Patten, I could see the granddaddy of the Maine mountains, Mount Katahdin. I pulled over and climbed off my bike where a pasture provided a treeless view of the mountain that has been the ultimate goal of so many hikers of the Appalachian Trail. Strung for 2,200 miles, the Trail winds its way along the mountain ridges from its southern end in North Georgia at Springer Mountain all the way to this mountain. I could imagine a hiker's thrill upon standing at its summit after months of hiking. I walked up and down the road and stood on both sides taking a variety of photos to help me remember that moment.

At Sherman Mills, I came upon the tail end of Interstate 95, almost at its terminus at the New Brunswick border at Houlton, Maine, after a long haul from Florida of 1,919 miles. Before the Interstate, the road made an abrupt right and ran back out into the wilderness and toward Stacyville. The route continued southwest at Stacyville, and only a few miles out, I caught up with a car stopped in the road for no apparent reason. I slowed as I approached, and as I did I looked to my right, where I discovered the reason for the car's halt. Among the small trees beyond the edge of the road was a huge moose ambling about in the scrub. I rolled to a stop behind the car as it started to move, and then it was my turn to sit and stare at this enormous creature of the North Woods. I doubt my head would have been higher than its underbelly as I sat on the bike, which confirmed the story I had heard earlier that usually when a car hits one, it runs under its belly, knocking it off its feet, and the bulk of the moose lands on the car roof. That explained the caved-in car roofs I had seen.

In Maine these Signs Appeared for Good Reason.

When the moose wandered into the jumble of brush and small trees and disappeared from sight, I kicked it into first and continued south. I would intersect the Penobscot River in just a few miles and follow it south-southeast. As I approached the river, I spotted another moose in the roadside tangle. That convinced me that I did not want to be caught out in that area riding at night.

The river and road made their way back to Interstate 95, where the highway, once again, abruptly turned away and to the northwest along another river, across Dolby Pond, and toward Millinocket, the gateway to Baxter State Park, within which Mount Katahdin stood above all. The highway continued its southwestern heading past the southern face of Mount Katahdin, rounding the mountain in a wide sweeping circle and finally leaving it in my mirrors as the road veered south into Brownville.

Mount Katahdin, the Goal of Hikers of the Appalachian Trail

As I rode south I was starting to catch up with spring again. Trees wearing spring's white flowers were appearing the further south I got while the shadows' remaining snow banks were disappearing into the grass, leaving the only snow visible on the top slopes of the distant mountains in Baxter

State Park, home to the terminus of the Appalachian Trail, which I had crossed many miles before in western Virginia. The northern end of the Trail was high above on the top of Mount Katahdin, which was surrounded by the lesser peaks of Soubunge, Burnt, Beetle, Horse, Traveler, and Jo-Mary Mountains in a great rugged circular ring.

At Milo I turned west. I was approaching my turn to Sangerville beyond Dover-Foxcroft and just before Guilford. I slowed, keeping a watch for my left turn, which would take me south a few miles from the east-west highway I had been on. Sangerville was a tiny place, not even appearing on my map, so I could not count on any signs pointing toward it.

Luckily, the little side road was marked. I spotted the corner and turned left. From that point I could follow the map Larry had printed out for me a couple days ago with its handwritten notes scribbled on top. At the bottom, Larry had also typed out the directions for when I got really close and at the last turn. I followed the road south through the rolling Maine countryside looking for a hard left where Sangerville Grange Road was supposed to intercept my path. I came across an odd intersection where an east-west road cut across my path, and another road crossed that heading north from its intersection with the road I was on just ahead of me and forming a unique small triangle in between the three paths.

I spotted a farmer near the road on my right across the road from the triangle and pulled over to ask if he knew where Sally lived. As I turned off the Bonnie, the man walked over and introduced himself as Wilson. It turned out Wilson was Sally's neighbor and he pointed to a house across the triangle and said that's where I'd find Sally and her boys. He went on to tell me he used to have a Honda CL350 Scrambler and I told him about my old 1968 CB350, the street brother to the dual sport CL. We chatted a while over the three-strand barbed wire fence about bikes, the weather, and Larry's and Sally's families. So much for the taciturn and stranger-wary backwoods Maine natives.

After a while, I thanked him, reaffirmed which house was Sally's, then climbed back on the bike, transited the triangle, took the east-west road east, then turned into the first driveway on my left. As I pulled in, a small older woman walked toward me from the house with a tall, broad-shouldered bearded man, the epitome of the Northern backwoodsman. Before I could turn off the bike and ask if she was Sally, I heard them both say, "You must be Mike on a bike!" And Sally said, "Come on in. Dinner's ready and we have a place for you to stay the night." They both wore broad smiles, and as I climbed off the bike my hand met the clasps of George, one of her sons, and then Sally. They told me Larry had called them and said they might have a visitor, and they had been looking for me to pull up all day. All thoughts disappeared of heading to Larry's family's homestead up the diagonal road minutes away as I was swept into the house, where I was welcomed by the comforting smells of home cooked food.

I was invited to sit down at the long table while Sally went to the stove and I talked to George. There were stories of growing up with Larry, of motorcycles, and farming. Soon a large bowl of baked beans and a pile of sage sausage, fresh from a neighboring Mennonite farmer, were placed in front of me. Homemade bread was laid out with butter. Sally said that it was traditional Saturday night dinner fare for central Maine, and I dug in with gusto, having eaten little all day as I rode through the cold but sunny North Woods hills. Hot black coffee rounded out the meal, culminating in ice cream with rhubarb sauce drizzled over it. Rhubarb; that was a real Northern food. I recall my father growing it in the backyard in Michigan and my grandmother making pies from its green and red stalks. Somehow, I had never tried it. It must have been a kid thing, but now I was keen to give it a try and was surprised at its strawberry-like sweetness. What had I missed out on all those years?

While I ate, the rest of the family filtered in from their various daily tasks. Warren, George's brother, who still lived with Sally, soon joined us. Chris, Sally's grandson, came in next with Kelsy, his girlfriend. Chris and Kelsy worked the farm and were transitioning from dairy to beef cattle and talked about the differences in the two types of farming. Sally was a teacher, and we chatted about how schools worked in Maine and compared our educational philosophies. I asked Sally about the wonderful white-flowered trees and was told they were apple trees. I thought there had been something familiar about them, and when Sally told me, I instantly saw all the flowering apple trees from my youth growing up in southern Michigan, where they constituted one of the primary harvests in the crisp, cold autumns.

After I had more than my fill of the wonderful farm fare, Warren invited me to the basement to show me his collection of old Japanese motorcycles. That was right up my alley, and I followed him down where a Kawasaki KZ1000 sat, along with a CL175, Honda XL, and a Honda 500 Four. All were in decent shape, with only a frosting of dust from sitting for years. Most had work started on them, but sat unfinished—a typical bike collector's scenario. Warren had a love of all things mechanical, and so the tour moved into the garage to see the cars. He loved Caddies and Buick Rivieras, not to mention tractors. If it had a motor, Warren knew something about it. I heard stories of traveling in the old cars that were sitting dusty in the garage and all the mechanical attributes of one engine compared to another.

We headed back in as all were settling down for the evening. Sally would not take no for an answer, and I was led down a hall to a bedroom, all ready for an overnight guest, and given directions to the bathroom and asked if I needed anything else. What else could I possibly need?

Again, the amazing hospitality and good nature of people, and especially people born to the soil, showed a light on my previously dark appraisal of my fellow human beings.

Warmth and kindness radiated from these people and so many I had met on the road. My dim view of humanity was lightening with every mile.

Surprisingly, I was able to get a cell signal and called Andrea to check on things at home. They were still going alright, and I guessed my absence was not as destructive as my dark thoughts had made me believe. One change to my plan was necessitated when Andrea told me her friend, Suzanne, and her husband, Ron, were not at their home in Newport, Vermont. They had gone south with their trailer to North Conway, New Hampshire, to camp for a while in anticipation of attending the huge motorcycle rally at Laconia in a couple weeks. I was still welcome to head to their house in Vermont, but also was welcome to go south, instead, and join them for a night in the camper. I decided not to backtrack north, knowing they were actually more directly on my route south, so I planned to join them for a night around the campfire.

I undressed and fell into bed, pulling the quilt up under my chin with a smile on my sleepy face.

Chapter Eleven

Day Nine

Sally and the Boys in the Mirrors and the White Mountains Ahead

I was up early, by about six, and I was not the only one. Life starts early on the farm, and by the time I had showered and entered the dining area, Sally was already at the stove and asking me what I would like and whether some eggs, bacon, and toast would suit me.

I made quick work of the country breakfast, washing it all down with cup after cup of hot coffee. I could have stayed there for weeks and had a blast hanging out with Warren and George, exploring the area and taking in the warmth of their friendship, but the road was calling. I thanked them for their overwhelming hospitality and carried my kit out to the bike to load up, while invitations to return with the entire family were sincerely offered. I hugged Sally and shook Warren's big hand, climbed on the bike, throwing my leg high over the piles of gear lashed on my pillion, and fired up the Bonnie. With one last wave, I kicked it into gear, rolled backward in the drive as I turned around to face the road, then rolled slowly out into the chilly early morning air. I turned back up the road toward ME 16. I hadn't even made it as far as Larry's place, which had been graciously offered days before. But Larry had told me Sally and the boys were friendly and he would not be surprised that I had gotten no farther than their friendly farmstead.

On 16 in Maine

Back at the east-west highway, I turned left and rolled west toward Bingham, where the road took an abrupt sweep to the south, and joined US 201, following the Kennebec River. On the far side of town, 16 left its course along the river and jumped across it to the Kennebec's west bank, where it continued to mirror its partner as it shot south.

At Anson, I stopped for more fuel. From there, 201 crossed the Carrabassett River and went on alone, while I turned to the northwest following the north shore of the river for a few miles before it veered away and crossed its tributary of Gilman Stream at North New Portland. There the highway started climbing out of the river valley and into the foothills of the mountains to the north.

At Kingfield, I headed north, deeper into the mountains and aimed at Carrabassett Valley and the south side of Bigelow Preserve, bounded on the north by Flagstaff Lake. The road arced passed the over 4,000 foot high Sugarloaf and Saddleback Mountains in a large counter-clockwise semi-circle. At Bigelow the route veered northwest, crossed the Appalachian Trail, which would be my on-and-off companion for many miles on my ride south. The route continued west to Stratton, then it dove southwest, following the track of the South Branch of the Dead River, leaving it at Dallas for a short jump down to Rangeley, and completing the arc at Rangeley Lake.

I followed the north shore of the lake as the road twisted and wriggled its way toward New Hampshire. Crossing Bear Brook, I soon crossed the line separating Maine from its neighbor to the west. The highway turned south past the border, hugging Bear Brook on it east bank as the river turned and twisted its way through New Hampshire, flanked by the White Mountains.

Bear Brook changed names to Androscoggin River where the highway crossed the Pontook Reservoir and the road ran south on the west bank. On my left, in the middle of the river, curious small pyramidal rock islands appeared standing above the water. They were separated from each other at regular intervals of about one hundred yards. As I sped south, the islands were my constant companions, dividing the river into two distinct sides. I made a mental note to ask Suzanne and Ron about them when I arrived that evening at their campsite, but forgot all about when I got there. It was not until over a half a year later that I discovered what those islands were. Logging had been a huge industry in New England ever since colonists settled the area. Those little islands were "boom piers." Logs were chained between them forming a floating fence, keeping rival logging companies Brown Paper Company and International Paper Company's precious products from mixing as they floated down the river to mills. It's not known when the piers were built, but they continued in use until 1963. At Berlin, home of the mills, I pulled over for another tankful and a short rest before moving on.

At Gorham, the river made a sharp left back into Maine, about ten miles to the east, while my route turned right and headed south along the Peabody River, flanked by 3,000 foot mountains climbing up from each side of the road. The highway made its way between those sleeping giants, while approaching increasingly tall mountains, Mount Madison at 5,367 feet close on the right hand and Middle Carter Mountain at over 4,600 feet a bit farther to the east. Squeezing between those last couple of peaks, I was soon at the road to the base of Mount Washington, the highest peak in New Hampshire at 6,288 feet, and the start of its famous Auto Road to the top.

Back in Lake Wales, I had made the acquaintance of one of the loan officers at my bank, due to our mutual habit of riding motorcycles on long trips. Once in a while, when I was in the bank on business, I would stop and chat with John and maybe give him the newest issue of *Vintage Japanese Motorcycle Magazine*, knowing he had an interest in joining. One of those times, John told me about a trip he had made into New England. On that ride, he had mentioned riding Mount Washington, telling me not to miss it if I ever got the chance. He said it was hair raising, but it was a ride he's never forgotten. And now, the same mountain was towering overhead, the same mountain viewed for the first time by Europeans by Giovanni da Verrazzano from the far away Atlantic Ocean, at least seventy-five miles distant, in 1524. I turned off 16 and headed for the entry gate, stopping behind a line of cars. It had been very windy that day, and from talking to John, I knew if it got too windy they closed the road. As I pulled up to the officer at the toll booth, I mentioned the wind and that I had thought they might not be open. He told me that they were just under the wind speed threshold that day. Throwing financial considerations to the wind—when was I ever going to have that opportunity again?—I handed the man seventeen dollars and rolled ahead and toward the foot of the mountain, clicking on my helmet-mounted GoPro using the remote dangling around my neck.

The View from Mount Washington, with the Bonnie below

I had ridden to the top of Mount Mitchell in North Carolina, just off the Blue Ridge Parkway, to an altitude of 6,684, the highest point anywhere east of the Mississippi. But the road to that summit had been only a bit higher than the Blue Ridge Parkway, and being so far south, the peak was well wooded at that more southerly latitude. Even the Blue Ridge Parkway's highest point is at 6,047 feet, noted by a huge sign at a pullover, in front of which many photos have been taken of bikes and riders. Mount Mitchell is almost 36° N, and while Mount Washington is not as high, at its latitude of just over 44° N, its timberline is at only 4,000 feet, above which you enter the completely tree-less sub-arctic zone at 4,300 feet. What a difference eight degrees of latitude made. At Mount Washington, you also don't have the luxury of riding a few hundred paved feet up from a main roadway; you, instead, travel narrow two-lane, with a mile of gravel halfway up, from 1,527 feet to the summit, a climb of 4,618 feet with grades up to 22 degrees. Not only is it a long way up, the mountain is famous for its high winds. At the summit the highest wind speed ever recorded on earth that was not part of a tropical cyclone was noted at 231 miles per hour by the observatory at the peak in 1934.

After clearing the gate, I began the seven and a half mile climb. The maximum speed limit on the trek into the sky is twenty-five miles per hour, but with all the vehicle traffic, I was climbing at fifteen to twenty at the maximum, and usually at around fifteen or lower, often coming to a complete stop on a steep grade while wide vehicles passed going the other way. There were no devil-take-care speeders on that road, but moving at that speed has to be one of the hardest ways to ride a motorcycle, and it certainly added to the stress of the ride. On an empty road at twenty or so, things would have been much easier to manage. The road wound up and up, with few turnoffs in which to take a break, I was happy when one or two of the lead vehicles did just that and opened up some space in front of me, until I ran up on the next turtle. I just plodded ever higher, twisting left and then right then left again and tried to not run into the bumper of the vehicle in front of me or wriggle off the road and into oblivion past the unguarded road edges.

Earlier, the day had warmed and had made it up to 50° F. By the time I arrived at the entry gate, I had dropped a layer of clothing and switched from my cold weather gloves to my perforated leather ones, which made it much more comfortable to manage left-hand duties while riding. Now that I was steadily climbing, the temperature was rapidly falling. I started shivering, and my teeth were chattering, while I tried my best to not have a death grip on the handlebars. When the gravel section appeared, my four-wheeled companions slowed even more, forcing me to ride almost exclusively in the friction zone in order to keep my revs up. Past the gravel, the road improved, but that 22 degree grade was thrown in at the very last section approaching the summit. Relieved pulling into the gravel parking area, I found several other bikes parked up and wriggled in between a couple of them pointing up hill in the loose gravel, where I clicked into first and turned off the Bonnie.

I managed to climb off without catching my foot on the mountain of gear behind me or on one of the bikes packed in beside me. I slipped a kickstand coaster under my stand and headed to the stairs that led up to the summit proper. Climbing the short series of steps I found myself at the top in the chilling wind, which felt like a big hand shoving me one way and the other, depending on which way I walked. I took a quick peek into the gift shop; nothing much of interest in there, just the typical key chains and logoed coffee cups. I wandered back out into the wild wind and tramped across the top to the former guest house. Unbelievably, people had come up here since the 1850s. The road was completed in 1861, so it must have been an incredible journey before that just for the sake of spending the night in such a rare, wild, and beautiful place.

I walked past the cog railway train station and cafeteria building, passing snow banks still sleeping in the early spring sunshine, up to the very tip spot that all the tourists were posing at. Stepping to the edge, I spun slowly, taking a series of panoramic shots of the mountains surrounding me on all sides. There I ran into my traveling companion again, the Appalachian Trail, as it passed right over the summit.

Satisfied with the accomplishment of planting the Bonneville's two wheels on this summit and the fantastic views around it, I returned to the bike, pulled out my cold weather gloves, remounted and did the whole ride in reverse. I was engine braking all the way down as I passed through invisible olfactory clouds of burning brakes emanating from the cars in front of me. There was less of a crowd going down, and in twenty-five minutes I was back at the highway and in the relatively warm temperature of the valley. With my "This Bike Climbed Mount Washington" sticker in my tank bag, I continued on my way toward North Conway and, within minutes, was crossing the Appalachian Trail once again where it crossed the road just south of the Auto Road entrance. The Ellis River joined the highway on its run south as I passed a number of ski slopes and crossed the Appalachian Trail again, destined for yesterday's mountains in Maine.

At the bottom of the valley I had been descending, the road ran into to North Conway on the east side of the Saco River. As I approached, the traffic increased until it was dense in the small vacation town. It seemed so strange after riding 525 miles from Rimouski, two days before, where I last was in anything resembling traffic.

Entering town, I had no clue where to find Suzanne and Ron. I passed a pub with a few bikes parked up outside. I turned around, thinking it was as good a place as any to sit in the cool, have a beer, and try to contact my wife's high school friend. I rolled to a stop in front of Delaney's Hole in the Wall Pub, flipped down the kick stand, extricated myself from my motorcycle, and walked inside. I found my way to the bar, ordered a Harp, and looked for Suzanne's number in my phone's contact list. Suzanne and Ron were camping close by, but I would need directions to get to their camper. I made the call, and by the time I was on my second pint, they walked in. We had only met once before, when the whole family had joined them for a beach weekend, so we got reacquainted and I updated Suzanne on Andrea and the kids. I finished my pint, and we left. I climbed back aboard the Bonnie and followed them down the road just a few miles, where we turned off into a shady campground near the Saco River, parking up at their tow-behind get away pad.

Beer and steaks were the order of the day, in that order. Soon the steaks were sizzling on the grill as the sun disappeared behind the mountains. We sat down to some great food and conversation as the sky darkened. A camp fire was lit. More beer and conversation followed. They had brought their dog with them, so our conversation and beer consumption was only interrupted now and then by a little time taken out to scratch his ear and pat his head. Soon all was dark and we were all getting sleepy. I was shown my spot on the main cabin's couch and where the bathroom was in case of need in the night, and we all said our good nights. I made my evening call to Andrea and then fell fast asleep.

Once again, the kindness of friends had provided a safe and warm spot for the night. It had been only the second time I had met Suzanne and Ron, but I was welcomed like one of the family.

Chapter Twelve

Day Ten

The White and the Green Mountains, Schenectady, and the Catskills Revisited

I rose early, knowing I had three states to cover that day. Suzanne and Ron were up and offered hot black coffee, just what I needed to get myself motivated. We sat around the gray ash of last night's fire and talked about alternate routes I could take that day, the Kancamagus Highway winning out over my originally intended course down south and west across the state on NH 25. Soon, three coffees were consumed. It was time for me to leave. I thanked my hosts, made sure everything was on the bike and that the map I would need to start the day was on the top under the tank bag's clear vinyl, and fired up the Bonneville. A hug for Suzanne and a hearty handshake for Ron and I was off in the early morning light.

Just a few miles south, the Kancamagus Highway intersected my route from the west. I turned right onto this famous scenic route. It would take me a little out of my way by heading northwest, instead of southwest, but by all accounts the extra miles were worth it, in spite of my expected ride of almost 599 miles. I rode west through the White Mountains National Forest, following the Swift River upstream, wedged in a narrow valley bordered by 3,000 foot peaks. About halfway across to Lincoln, I passed the headwaters of the Swift and soon found myself mimicking the route of the Hancock Branch, now following downstream. I briefly left Hancock, crossed the East Branch of the Pemigewasset River, and continued west downstream in the new river valley.

On the Kankamagus below Green's Cliff

At Lincoln, my cruise of the Kancamagus ended shortly after passing under the major thoroughfare of Interstate 93, which ran to join Interstate 91 in Vermont for the short run to the Canadian border at Derby Line, just northeast a few miles from Suzanne and Ron's place in Newport, Vermont. Heading south, 93 ran all the way into Boston. I skipped the Interstate, and, instead, opted for a US highway, roughly paralleling 93.

I had been told while in the Northeast to make sure I tired a lobster roll, a traditional fare. I had mentioned them to Sally, back in Maine, and she said they would be pretty easy to find, but didn't know what all the fuss was about because all they consisted of were some lobster chunks in a sauce thrown on a bun. However, I am a big fan of lobster, although I have to admit to a preference for the clawless southern kind, also called crayfish. Still, lobster is lobster and I had been seeing signs for lobster rolls for a while.

I stopped in a small town, where I found a likely diner, but was told lobster rolls were not on their menu. However, they pointed me back a few miles up the road I had just come in on, to a small truck diner that was reputed to have the best lobster rolls around. I remembered passing that place, but had a desire for a place I could sit down inside and take a little break from the saddle and be out of the sun, so I had passed it by. Having seen it had probably prompted my now overwhelming desire to consume a lobster roll, so I turned around and backtracked to the little stand by the side of the highway.

After a few miles, I was rolling across the gravel and parking in front of the truck. I walked up to the window and handed the proprietor a whopping ten dollars. That hurt, but what the hell, I got coleslaw with it, too, and how often am I going to be able to taste this Northeastern delicacy once I was back in Florida?

I sat in the shade of an umbrella at a picnic table and waited. When I saw my order was up, I trotted back up to the window, and while gathering my lunch, was asked about the Triumph, about where I was going and had been, and where I was from. The food truck owner told me he wintered just a few miles away from my place in Florida—small world. I should have gotten his contact information in case I had the urge for another lobster roll after I got home. Maybe he could be talked into whipping a couple up off season, and perhaps he'd be willing to use the nontraditional crayfish instead.

The roll was delicious and so was the slaw. I was good for another few hours in the saddle, so I mounted up, got back on the road, and headed back the way I had come, passing the little town and diner as I caught up with my previous course.

Small town traffic slowed my pace for the thirty-five mile run south to Meredith, where I made a stop for fuel. West of town I stopped again to souvenir hunt at the Meredith Trading Post. I wandered around the shop, looking for something that would be representative of the Northeast. I spotted blankets and thought one featuring bears or moose would make a nice gift for Andrea. There was nothing small to fit the bill, but I did spot a Northwoods plaid wool blanket that I thought would look right in place on a lumberjack's bunk. I walked up to the counter, and as I checked out, the owner and I chatted. He asked if that was my Triumph out front, where I had been, and where was I going. He, too, rode and had a BMW, and the talk revolved around the pros and cons of different models and good places to ride. He helped me wrap the blanket in plastic so it would stay dry on the bike, then I walked outside to load it on top of my borrowed sleeping bag. Leaving Meredith and the trading post, I was soon back in the countryside and headed west, following the Smith River.

Soon, I found myself in Danbury, where the road shot northwest then west toward the Vermont border. I crossed once again into Vermont in Lebanon, crossing the Connecticut River at White River Junction and heading northeast with the White River on my right and Interstate 89 on my left. My city riding did not last long, and within a few miles, I turned south, shot over the Interstate, turned west again, leaving I-89 behind, then followed the Ottauquechee River into the heart of Vermont and the Green Mountains.

At West Bridgewater, with the northern section of the Green Mountains National park and Killington Peak dead ahead and 3,235 feet above me, I turned south along the Black River. The route wove its way at the bottom of mountain valleys with 2,000 and 3,000 foot peaks towering overhead, diminishing in height as I rolled south. By Ludlow, the summits had decreased by 1,000 feet, but soon began to grow again as I passed the southern section of the Green Mountains National Forest, close by on my right.

Back in Vermont

As I approached Stratton Mountain, standing above me at almost 4,000 feet, I stopped at Rawsonville for another fill up. From there the route veered southeast, then back to the southwest around the base of that giant. One more jog to get back on track and going south, I was soon at the junction with VT 9 at Wilmington. I turned right, passing Glastenbury Mountain on my right. I passed through Woodford and crossed the Appalachian Trail yet again as I was making a beeline for the New York line, just beyond Bennington, and leaving the Green Mountains for good.

Heading into New York I continued west-southwest toward Albany, the one big city I could not find a good way to avoid completely. There was one last ride through the country before approaching Troy as the mountains became hills and I approached the Hudson Valley. I was now on the east side of the Appalachians, where white men have lived for close to five centuries. The population was much more dense and towns closer together and more congested. The roads also got more confusing, being established long before modern technology could straighten them. Houses were planted right against the road, built when that was plenty of right-of-way for single-horse carriages to pass by. Now everything seemed jammed packed, and it increased as I crossed the Hudson River and searched for my route around Albany.

My intended plan was to continue past Albany on the north, then to take a jump to NY 155 west of the city via a connector labeled County Road 151. The plan was that I would shoot me between the two large cities of Albany and Schenectady and pop back onto my route on the far side, hopefully in the country. It looked pretty clear on my inset map of the city but the scale was not right for maximum detail. In reality, 151 didn't intersect my route, but stopped short.

Of course, I did not know that at the time, so I plunged into the city traffic, eyes peeled for that little county road. It should have been just past the airport, which would be on my left. I flew northwestward, and never saw anything saying 151. The problem with maps is that they usually refer to highways by their numbers, but especially in metropolitan areas, the road signs use the road's name instead, like Valley Road or Main Street or Albany Shaker Road. Miles passed, and I realized I had missed my supposed bypass route. The highway I was on had become a major artery, with four lanes, plus a middle turning lane. I tried to keep up with traffic, and with no clue where to turn, I continued on into the heart of Schenectady. When it intersected Interstate 890, I continued straight, and when that road intersected the Interstate again, I turned off and rode southwest toward Rotterdam and away from Schenectady.

The Dutch settlers of this area left obvious signs of their heritage. As I looked on my little inset map, I saw roads with names like Guilderland, Ten Eyck, and Heidelberg Avenues and towns with names like Rotterdam, Voorheesville, and Guilderland.

I turned left and, ironically, found myself back on NY 7, which had jogged south a few miles on Interstate 87 only to leave it again. I kept poking my way south and east on the suburban streets. Eventually, my path intersected a road shown on my map, and I turned east. After passing Guilderland Center, US 20, which I had passed earlier, appeared ahead of me. I turned right again, because my map showed it intercepting NY 155, my intended route out of the city. Turning right I was finally at a location I could definitely spot on my map. At Voorheesville, I turned east again toward Slingerlands, where I turned right again. The road passed through Delmar and then Elsmere, where I turned south and finally connected with NY 32, leading south to the Catskills. At least, that's the best I could reconstruct the thirty miles of detours in city traffic to reconnect to a road I knew would lead me away from Albany and toward the mountains.

My plan had been to breeze by Albany and ride through the heart of the Catskills from northeast to southwest via a series of small state roads and exit on even smaller county roads west of Denman Mountain. After leaving the mountains, I had planned to run east to Goshen, where a fellow ADVRider was waiting for me to spend the night. Catskill Park was a big blob of green on my map, stretching from the straight line of border between it and Pennsylvania on the west, to the Hudson River Valley on the east, and spanning most of the width of the southeastern triangle the state made, with its southern apex being the great city of New York. The detour to Schenectady had cost me a lot of time, however, and it was already late afternoon as I approached the northern limits of the block of green and I turned west toward its northern end.

I was hopeful that light would hold long enough for me to get to the other end before complete darkness. As I turned off into the woods and toward Catskill Park, however, it was becoming obvious I was not going to make it back out in time on the route I had chosen. On the same road I saw deer, another sign I should get out before the night creatures started wandering out onto the dark roads. I sped on until the road merged with one which ran east. I was still on my original planned course, but light was fading fast. Seeing NY 214, I turned right and headed into the very center of the Catskills. I passed through Lanesville, and then at Phoenicia, I made a decision. To follow my original plan I would have needed to turn west and make a westward jog to intersect my county road then continue south through the mountains. Instead, I turned east and headed toward the eastern edge of the Catskills at Kingston, just before hitting the Hudson once more.

Light steadily faded as I continued riding, racing the sunset that was hidden in the trees somewhere behind me. I skirted Ashokan Reservoir in the dusk, and after a short delay due to an accident, I emerged. I took a right and ran southwestward toward NY 17, a big highway and major thoroughfare running toward New York City. All the time it was getting later and darker. It had been farther than I had anticipated and was fully dark and getting late as I approached NY 17. In the darkness I turned south-southeast and settled in for the ride among all the other vehicles zooming toward the cities along the Hudson and the Atlantic Seaboard. That was the biggest highway I had ridden on the entire trip, with the exception of the short stretch of Interstate when I had made the wrong turn way back at the Maryland and Pennsylvania border, and the most traffic I had seen, other than the traffic during my tour of Schenectady. Passing Interstate 84, I was soon in Goshen and looking for Kevin's place, or as I had originally known him, opinion914.

By the time I was in Goshen, it was well into the evening. I got off of the highway and entered the address for my layover and then followed the green arrow dutifully At about 11 o'clock, I stopped at a house with the number I was looking for. I parked up and walked to the front door. I felt bad arriving so late, but Kevin had said he might be out until evening and not home until late, so I knocked. There were lights on inside, and I could hear television and other noises emanating from somewhere behind the locked door. I waited, but no one appeared. I knocked again and waited. After a few minutes and another knock, someone finally came to the door. It was only opened a crack. I told him I was looking for Kevin and gave him the house number, and a voice wound its way through the crack and to my ear, "You have the right number but, no, no one here named Kevin." "What?" I thought, "This is the correct house number." I spoke to the door, "I'm sorry. I am traveling and was supposed to stay at a house on this road with this number tonight. Do you know anyone named Kevin who lives nearby?" "No; never heard of him, but maybe you should be looking for *Lower* Reservoir Road." "You mean there's two?" "Yes, he must be on the other, up that way." I apologized for knocking on the door so late and thanked him for the heads up about the other road. The crack closed, leaving me alone in the dark. I walked back to the bike, rolled backward out of the driveway, and went in search of the other Reservoir Road.

Eventually, I spotted a green sign in the beam of my headlight and LED spots. It said Lower Reservoir Road. "Must be it," I thought, and soon I was knocking on another door. This time I had it right, although it was almost eleven-thirty. Kevin came out, greeted me, and helped me carry my gear inside, where I met his beautiful wife, who was up working on a paper she had to electronically turn in by midnight. Kevin was a young architect, and Amy was pursuing the same line of study.

I stowed my gear, washed up, and went back into the living room. I apologized for my lateness and told them the story of my getting lost and ending up in Schenectady and arriving at their house number only to discover there were two Reservoir Roads and I had been on the wrong one. They both graciously replied that it was not a problem and not to worry about keeping them up and that Amy would be up late into the night working on her paper, anyway. We all chatted a short time, then Kevin guessed I must have been hungry. He said he knew a place nearby where we could still grab a bite. Amy stayed behind to continue working, while Kevin and I climbed in his car and drove through the dark streets to a brightly lit diner, talking about the trip, architecture, motorcycles, and books on the way.

The conversation continued inside over hamburgers and fries. Kevin was both a motorcycle racer and a book lover, so we had plenty to talk about. I described to Kevin the route I had taken through the Catskills to his place, and we talked about Melissa Holbrook-Pierson's *The Perfect Vehicle*, which I had suggested he pick up when he had asked me about other motorcycle travel-related books. He said he had tried to get a copy but found it was out of print. The author happened to live in the Catskills, so he had arranged to go to her house to pick up a copy. It turned out that I had passed by her house on my route through the Catskills as I had made my way to Goshen that afternoon.

When the check came, before I could grab it, Kevin snatched it and refused to let me pay for anything, saying it was adequate payment just getting to hear stories about the trip. We left the diner with the doors being locked behind us and the lights going out as we drove out of the parking lot and back to the house.

Back at Kevin's garage, Kevin showed me his bike and the vintage Japanese Honda 400 Automatic that his wife rode. I always think it is pretty cool when people ride those old bikes like they were intended to be, instead of just parking them and cleaning them between bike shows. Amy was light as a feather, and I couldn't think of a better bike to fit her.

Back inside, we realized it was past midnight. Kevin and Amy wandered back to their bedroom, while I stretched out on the couch. I messaged Andrea good night, not wanting to wake her with a phone call but wanting to fulfill my daily required check-in so she would know I made it to the next stop. I hung up, set the alarm on the phone, then flicked off the lights, and soon fell into a restful sleep.

Chapter Thirteen

Day Eleven

The Road to Gettysburg

I got up before light and grabbed a quick shower. Kevin was up and offered, considering the trouble I had the night before trying to find his place, that he would ride with me and get me outside the worst of the city traffic and on my intended route for the day. We had a cup of coffee then went outside so Kevin could get Amy's Honda 400 out and I could load my baggage back onto the Bonnie and check things over. I borrowed some spray chain lube from Kevin and gave my drive chain a good coating. We both fired up the bikes, his with that distinctive vintage Japanese overhead cam sound so familiar to me and the Bonnie with its deep-throated grumble exiting the Arrow pipe, and rolled out of the driveway with Kevin in front. I was soon to find out what following a racer was like, as we swept along city streets and curvy country roads, with me lagging behind at my usual sedate pace.

We negotiated several neighborhood side streets and soon were past NY 17, the route I had come in on, and were flying under Interstate 84. A couple of turns later we were through Mount Hope and on to Otisville, where we stopped at a corner convenience store. After fueling up the Bonneville, we went inside and picked up a couple breakfast sandwiches and coffee. Again, my money was no good as Kevin stepped up and paid for everything before I knew it. We sat outside on the curb enjoying the morning, talking, and taking our nourishment. Before I had finished, Kevin disappeared inside and soon was back out with a gift of chocolate covered berries to give me some energy as my day went by. I chucked them in the tail bag, where I could get to them easily, and thanked Kevin for his hospitality and generosity and for helping me get out of town and back on track. He was heading on to a meeting, so we would be parting there. With one more handshake, I climbed on board my bike, waved goodbye, and headed out.

From there, I just had to turn left for the short distance to US 209, the highway I had been on yesterday afternoon coming south from the Catskills. I was ten miles to the south of where I had turned off 209 last night and well on my way away from the city congestion. At my turn onto 209, I had only another ten miles or so to leave New York and re-enter Pennsylvania and the Delaware River Valley.

At Port Jervis, I crossed the Delaware near its junction with the Neversink River. There I paralleled Interstate 84 westward for a while but soon my route veered southwest and traced the contour of the Delaware River through the Delaware Water Gap National Recreational Area where the highway also went by the name Federal Road as it wound its way through the park-like and wooded recreational area with New Jersey on the far side of the stream.

The Delaware River at the Delaware Water Gap NRA

I had completely caught up with late spring, and all the leaves of the trees and bushes were bright green, and no bare branches still dared to show themselves. Between me and the river, among the riverside trees, brush, and poison ivy, was a walking path skirting the edge of the Delaware with pull-offs ever so often to enable access to this quiet natural setting. The coffee from this morning had caught up with me, so I pulled over in one of the lay-bys to take a break. After taking care of my pressing business behind some shrubs, I tip-toed carefully through the ivy, being careful not to touch any with bare skin, and down to the river walk. I brought my camera with me and took this chance to snap a few photos of the quiet river that had been a principle pathway to so many pioneers in days gone by exploring the vast wilderness that in those times stretched from there to the Mississippi River and beyond. I tried to picture the barges and the earlier native birch bark canoes plying their way upstream. Rambling back up the bank to the bike, I grabbed a handful of the chocolate-coated fruit, pulled on my helmet, and set off once again.

The road left the verdant recreational area behind just past Bushkill, and soon I was hurtling on toward another city. Luckily, my route continued straight through, so there was no need to strain myself looking for turnoffs. All I had to do was watch for signs confirming I was still on the same road and I would soon be on the far side of Stroudsburg, Pennsylvania. Within ten miles I was out the other side and rolling through the quiet countryside once again.

I was running west-southwest on the southern edge of yet another group of Appalachian mountains, the Poconos, which stretch from the Delaware River on the east and run between the major metropolitan areas of Wilkes-Barre and Scranton to the northwest and Allentown on the southeast. I was riding along in gently rolling foothills, with the mass of the gentle mountains to my north. Even the highest point in the Poconos, Camelback Mountain, is a modest 2,133 feet, and most are at much lower elevation, with flat topped ridges making up part of the Allegheny Plateau. The most dramatic areas were where the plateau dropped off into the river valleys along the Delaware and Lehigh Rivers. I would not see high mountains again until I revisited the Blue Ridge Mountains on my way south the next day. Heading west, the mountains were dissolving into rolling hills and wide farmed valleys with picturesque farms planted on their margins or along waterways.

My goal for the day was Gettysburg, but first I would have to negotiate another big city, Harrisburg, that lay in my path west and south. About twenty miles north of the west end of the Allentown metropolitan area, I crossed Interstate 476, which shot straight for the heart of the huge city of Philadelphia. There I switched to a smaller state route, ensuring I would be able to roll through farmland and hills all the way to Harrisburg without encountering any other large cities. That made it easy to navigate because all I had to do was follow the road signs and make sure to stay on that route, and it would take me all the way to the wide Susquehanna River that divided Harrisburg on the east from Enola on the west bank. On my approach to Harrisburg, I rode through Swatara State Park, where the Appalachian Trail made another couple appearances, crossing my route first on the northwestern curve around the park, then just before a hard right where the road ran turned back to the west and toward the river.

Reaching the Susquehanna River, I turned left on US 22 and followed the river south until the entrance ramp to Interstate 81, which I was obliged to take for a short way, as it was the only practical way across the river. I picked up speed and joined the maelstrom of other vehicles for the wild ride across the Susquehanna, then almost as soon as I had gotten on, I was spat out into the countryside toward the little burg of Wertzville, with a conspicuous 1,200 foot ridge following me on the north. Beyond Wertzville, the Appalachian Trail crossed my route again as the road turned northwestward and began to close with the ridge, until I found myself climbing to a notch on its rim. On the very top, I turned south off 944 and rolled back down the ridge to the southwest. The new highway veered south and shot me over Conodoguinet Creek and back under the Interstate.

I had made good time and the navigation was easy from then on, other than the last few miles trying to follow the GPS instructions to my cousin's farm. The highway ran straight into Gettysburg; all I had to do was stick to it and I would soon be in the historic town, less than thirty miles ahead. Five or so more miles from there, I would end the day's ride at Fairfield, at Bonnie and Bill's farm on the southwestern edge of the great battlefield.

I rolled through progressively lower land, away from the ridges of the Appalachians running west toward Pittsburgh and eastern Ohio, until they petered out in the flat cornfields of the Midwest, which lie from central Ohio all the way west to the Mississippi River.

About halfway to Gettysburg, I crossed Yellow Breeches Creek in the valley between the string of ridges behind me and a straggling string of hills that arced northeastward across my path beyond Mount Holly Springs, a symbolic last stand for the Alleghenies. I shot across through Holly Gap at almost the bitter end of this branch's eastward arc—the last hurrah for this southern ridge. The gap was cut by the rushing waters of tiny Mountain Creek. On my left, on the far side of the creek, were heights of 1,000 feet, and on the right close at hand were 1,200 foot peaks. I shot out the southern side into a wide valley and continued following the creek as it wound its way to lower elevations. I skirted a final 1,000 foot hill on the left then emerged into the low and rolling hills of central Pennsylvania farmland, crossing the Appalachian Trail again.

My route didn't just run toward Gettysburg, it ran straight into the heart of the old city's downtown. I putted through the streets crowded with tourists, even so early in the season, negotiated the roundabout in the very center of the town, and ran south out of downtown on Baltimore Street. Passing historic homes and businesses catering to a bustling tourist trade, the street veered left onto Steinwehr Avenue and continued out of town and across the heart of the scene of the bloodiest battle on American soil.

Everywhere I looked stood monument after monument, some honoring fallen Union soldiers and generals and others lamenting over the loss of Confederate soldiers and their generals. The field was paved with low grasses, and pathways criss-crossed to sites of strategic victories or crushing defeats. In spite of the bright sky, the warm air, and the beauty of the rolling field of green grass, there was a palpable sadness in the air.

I rode slowly through the early summer fields that had become the graves of so many, but as I left I had to switch my thought from contemplation to navigation. I stopped to enter Bonnie and Bill's address. The GPS was in charge from there until I found the farm. It was only midday, so I could take my time locating the place. The GPS ordered me to turn right on Bullfrog Road, and I dutifully complied. Within a couple miles the GPS once again barked its orders, "Turn left on Gordon Road." Again, I complied. Gordon Road ran past farmland and cantilevered barns, that I later found out were called bank barns, typical of the area. The field and farms were on my right and woods to my left. Ahead I could see a line of trees across the road. As I approached, I could see it was turning into gravel as it entered the woods and made a curve to the right. As I crossed onto the gravel there was a sign to my right saying, "Creek Crossing Ahead" and another one in red below it saying, "Warning Cross at Your Own Risk." "Well," I thought, "this is why I put dual sport tires on the bike; I'll just see what it's like and then decide what to do." Then I rounded the curve into the treeline.

I stopped. Middle Creek lay across the road. It was perhaps only twenty or thirty feet across but was flowing briskly from right to left across baseball-sized rocks. Luckily, the water was clear, and it did not look like any of it was very deep. I pulled in the clutch, clunked it into first, and eased out the clutch while keeping my revs up and started moving ahead. Soon water was up to the footpegs, but still too low to get into the air intake under my seat. The rocks were covered with algae and were slippery. As the bike sank another couple inches I put my feet down and felt them slide over the slippery rocks. A slight dip caught me off-balance, I pulled in the clutch and came to a halt in mid-stream with my feet planted on the rocky bottom. Water poured in over the top of them. So much for wearing waterproof boots. I got the bike steadied, revved it again, slipped the clutch, and climbed out of the small hole and up onto dry ground on the other side of the creek. It was actually exhilarating doing a little more than mild gravel road travel. It was only my second time to ever cross flowing water on a bike, but the first time the water flowing over the road was only a shallow trickle and not a full-fledged stream. I might have gotten wet feet, but I felt proud of getting across.

Middle Creek

A year later I would cross it again, with a different result, but that's another story...

Gordon Road followed the creek for a hundred yards, then made a left through a field and through the middle of a farm. The road looked more like a private farm drive and I saw private drive signs, but I kept going. Passing the farm house without anyone chasing or chastising me, I came upon paved Middle Creek Road and followed the GPS's instructions to turn right. I saw Pumping Station Road and turned left. I had to be close. The road made a hard right and continued following the creek but now was several hundred yards from it. Within a minute, I saw people I recognized standing and waving in front of an old farmhouse. I had arrived.

It was only mid-afternoon, and I was invited onto the porch for some homemade lemonade. Between sips and talking I wriggled out of my soaked boots and let the sun dry my feet and laid my socks out in hopes of getting them a little bit drier.

Bonnie was my dad's cousin, so was my second-cousin. She and Bill had bought the place and had been fixing it up ever since. Being an owner of such an old historic home had gotten them involved with local historic preservation efforts, as I know is almost inevitable from my own experience when Andrea and I had bought our hundred-year-old house (old for a central Florida house).

After quenching my thirst, I was offered the barn for storage of the bike for the night, where it would be out of the night dew. The barn was one of the bank barn types, with a cantilevered section protruding from what was the second level on the downhill side, and which would be the ground floor on the uphill street side. I rode up the street a hundred yards and turned down the dirt driveway that led past the south side of the barn, down the hill, and to the backside facing the pasture, with the creek far on the other side. I pulled under the cantilevered upper floor, looked for a relatively cow patty-less spot, and put down the kickstand. Climbing off I squished around on the barn floor and unloaded the bike of what I would need for the night, trying not to let it land on the cow patty plastered barn floor, and headed back to the house on foot.

Back at the house, I got the story of the farm, how it had come to be the way it was and when it was built. The oldest structure was across the street from the house and had been a blacksmith shop. It was built in 1757 with local stone, and Bonnie and Bill had converted it into Bonnie's office. Bonnie had been a professor before and was doing consulting work and visiting lectures. The blacksmith shop was all hers for a quiet and rustic place to relax and think. It had taken an enormous amount of work to get it back into liveable shape, with major work to the stone wall on the back, uphill side. Everything that could be saved from the original structure had been, while some had to be replaced by new. While looking just like a blacksmith shop on the outside, the inside was beautifully done and had its own bathroom facility and cooking area, while the one main room spanned the entire rest of the structure with high open ceiling overhead.

Bonnie and Bill's Historic Farm

The house was really two houses, one small stone two-story structure close to the main house, which was also two story but much larger and made of red brick. They thought the smaller house, which was a simple one room per floor structure, probably had been the summer kitchen. Back before our modern conveniences, like air conditioning, farms would often have summer kitchen apart from the main house, to keep the heat produced by cooking from making the living quarters unbearable in the warmer months. These summer kitchens were usually one story, so theirs was a little bit unusual, but the thought was that it probably served as the farm house while the newer big house was being constructed. The summer kitchen, they thought, was probably built in the 1760s and the big house soon after. The bank barn had been built many years ago, and local artisans who had kept the old traditions alive had been working re-pointing its stone walls before I had arrived.

With the afternoon waning, Bill proposed we go into Gettysburg and get some dinner. I had been in contact with the Vintage Japanese Motorcycle Club's event coordinator and fellow board member, Peter, who had been wanting to do a new event in the Gettysburg area; I asked my hosts if they would mind showing me some places on the way into town that might work for a four day event, with group dinners, rides, and a bike show. They were glad to oblige and suggested the Eisenhower Center, not far from the farm, where plenty of rooms would be available, catered dinners could be enjoyed, and a convention center building was available where we could do a really top-notch bike show inside and not have to be dependent on good weather. There were also a couple other good hotels with facilities. I put back on my slightly drier socks and slipped my feet into my still drenched boots. At least I had been able to pour the standing water out of them. Then we all climbed in the car for the ride into town.

We headed back to Emmitsburg Road by way of Middle Creek Road, this time with no water crossings involved. Turning left on Emmitsburg Road, we headed back toward downtown Gettysburg. After crossing Marsh Creek, we soon saw the Eisenhower Hotel and Convention Center complex. We turned right into the huge complex where a sizeable hotel was located along with a large convention center building, perfect for a bike show, with plenty of parking adjacent for all the trucks and trailers that would be hauling bikes to the show. I took a few photos as we drove slowly past the main buildings and through the grounds to send to Peter when I got back home.

Back at the roundabout in the center of town, we turned east onto US 30 and drove out toward the intersection with US 15, about which were clustered hotels and eating places. There was a Wyndam, Sleep Inn and Suites, and a Hampton Inn, and surrounding them was a mix of inexpensive fast food restaurants, mid-range chains, and more expensive eateries. Just beyond the exit to US 15 was also the Battlefield Harley-Davidson with an intriguing large steel outbuilding. I wondered what they would think about hosting an all-Japanese motorcycle show in their establishment. I jotted down all the pertinent details to pass along to Peter as we drove by each of the places.

The venues near the crossroad with US 15 were nice, but there didn't seem to be any place that was all-inclusive, where our event attendees could stay, eat, and have the show all in one location. I gave Peter a call and gave my recommendation for the Eisenhower Center, which had the added bonus of being on the quiet side of the battlefield, but close to the next exit to US 15 and an outlet mall, in case some of the guests who came with members would want other things to do. And those who wanted to camp instead of staying in a hotel would have that option eight miles away at the Granite Hill Campground, which hosts a biker weekend and Bluegrass Festival every year. I said I would send along all the details by email when I returned.

My club obligations out of the way, we headed downtown for dinner at the Blue and Gray Bar and Grill, right on the roundabout. It was a little bit early in the year for the tourist crowds, so we were able to get a seat right away. Menus came with Civil War-themed meals. The burger plates were named after Union and Confederate Generals. I don't recall which general I ordered, but I as I recall it was a Confederate. I had a stupendous burger with cheddar, onion rings, and, of all things, apples. Of course, I was once again told to keep my money in my pocket by Bill. To wash it all down I chose a micro-brewed beer, which got Bill talking. Bill was somewhat of a brewer himself and back at the farm had stores of homemade beers and wines. Some of the best beer I have ever drank was homemade, so I looked forward to test tasting some of Bill's brew.

After cleaning our plates, we headed back to the farm with all intentions of sampling the beer. But talk took over, and before we knew it we were all heading to bed, having forgotten all about the beer—a failure I regret to this day. I climbed the stairs to my room on the second floor and settled in for the night in my period-correct farm bed.

I made another call back home, and everything was still running smoothly. I guess I had really been rather egotistical to think my family couldn't function without me there all the time. They got along without me just fine. I wasn't the essential stabilizing factor I thought I was. As I started realizing that, the pressure I always felt to take care of everything eased.

I set the alarm for early and fell asleep, looking forward to getting on the road again the next day.

Chapter Fourteen

Day Twelve

Back to My Beloved Blue Ridge

In the morning, an omelet was waiting for me, courtesy of Bill. We sat around the kitchen island revisiting our talk from the last evening and both of us regretting our forgetfulness of the beer. It was too late to sample them with a whole day ahead of me on the bike, so we let it go.

After breakfast, I gathered all my gear and walked out to the barn to reload the bike. Already, men were perched on scaffolds pointing the stonework. As I walked by, I got the "That your Triumph?" query from above and had a little chat about Bonnevilles "back in the day." I rolled the bike out of the barn and fired it up. Bill and Bonnie came out, and we said our goodbyes, with me promising to return one day and offering them an invitation to come see us next time they found themselves in Florida. I thunked it into first gear, rode up the hill past the brick-pointers, turned right onto the road, then headed off. I turned right on Bullfrog Creek Road and headed back toward the Emmitsburg Road. I could smell the earthy and fertile, almost erotic, smell of mushrooms and the loam under the trees along the creek. As I passed Gordon Road, I couldn't resist turning off toward the water crossing from the day before for a photo of the bike by the Middle Creek crossing. Souvenir photo safe in the camera, I headed back onto the main road and back to the highway out of town. Soon I was on US 15 and headed southwest toward Frederick, Maryland.

Passing Frederick and approaching the mountains again, US 340 ran with 15 but divided past the city. I took 340 where it veered off and continued south along the slope of the easternmost ridges, while my new road headed toward the Shenandoah Valley.

The exit to Knoxville, on the nearby Potomac River, flew by and then another crossing of the Appalachian Trail. The Trail, heading south, ran along the river following the old Chesapeake and Ohio Canal Tow Path that served commerce early in the area's history by delivering supplies to outposts along the river and shipping goods from them to the Eastern Seaboard cities.

The road dwindled from the major highway it had been to a two-lane road as I crossed the first ridge of the Blue Ridge Mountains. After transiting the first great wrinkle in the earth, I skirted the next at the place where it kissed the Potomac River, crossing the river before the next ridge met the water. The AT crossed under my route one more time as the valley floor along the river dropped under the bridge crossing the river. Following the old tow path along the river, the AT continued until it, too, crossed the Potomac on an unused railroad bridge just below Harpers Valley Tunnel, out of which trains still emerge to cross on the second track bridge beside the one now accommodating foot traffic.

On the far side of the bridge, I slipped into Virginia then back out and into West Virginia. The Shenandoah River was closing fast when I met up with the AT again. It had doubled back once on the Harpers Ferry side of the Potomac and shared my bridge across the Shenandoah River, after which it departed again, shooting south into the countryside, zigzagging for miles along the West Virginia and Virginia state line. I continued west, crossing the Shenandoah River and riding into famous Harpers Ferry, one of the very earliest ignition points of the American Civil War, leaving the AT to wander until I caught up with it again later along my route.

In the 1850s, Harpers Ferry had been one of only two federal government arsenals in the United States. John Brown, an abolitionist who was willing to use violence to end slavery in the South, with less than two dozen men raided the arsenal on the evening of 16 October in 1859, less than two years before the start of the American Civil War, hoping to foment a slave uprising. He planned to arm the slaves, who he thought were sure to join them, with the spoils of the arsenal before moving through the South in the hopes that more slaves would join the uprising.

Brown and his men managed to capture the arsenal, but because of the secrecy of the raid, the local slaves didn't know what was going on, and the uprising did not gain momentum. By the eighteenth, then Brevet Colonel Robert E. Lee, later the military leader of the entire Confederate army, led a detachment of Marines, along with J. E. B. Stuart, also of Confederate fame, to take the arsenal. By mid-afternoon John Brown and his men were captured, and by December second he was dead by the executioner's hand.

While the raid failed, it did demonstrate the intensity of disagreement between the North and the South and alarmed many Southerners. Tension only mounted after that until shots were fired on Fort Sumter in the spring of 1861.

From Harpers Ferry, I sliced across the tiniest corner of West Virginia, then continued south into Virginia, roughly following the Shenandoah River and entering the legendary valley as parallel ridges rose on the east and west. Eventually, the route ran straight into Front Royal, standing at the northern terminus of scenic Skyline Drive and Shenandoah National Park. It was midday, and I looked for a place I remembered from a family vacation we had taken a few years before. It had been a quiet diner in a quiet little town, but nothing looked familiar to me anymore. I remembered the place was directly on my route, but no sign of the restaurant appeared. I needed fuel, too, before hopping onto Skyline Drive, where it would be miles before I would have the opportunity to gas up again. I pulled into a station and filled up and then went inside to find a snack that would have to substitute for the real meal I had hoped for, before climbing into the mountains above the beautiful Shenandoah Valley.

The Shenandoah River zigzagged its way south-southwest across a wide valley between two long ridges with altitudes of between 2,000 to 4,000 feet, On the east were the easternmost of the Blue Ridge Mountains with more parallel ridges marching toward the west and across West Virginia. I left Front Royal, took a left on Skyline Drive and ascended from the northern terminus of the first ridge. Skyline Drive shoots skyward then follows the ridge, sometimes on the crest and sometimes just below on either side as it snakes its way southwest. The road is smooth and well maintained and offers beautiful views across the spectacular Shenandoah Valley when the route rides on the westward flank of the mountains and expansive views to the east, across the foothills of the Piedmont, which follow the Blue Ridge in a huge triangle, narrow at the top, east of Front Royal and the Maryland border, and widest where it meets North Carolina, there stretching 190 miles to the east.

As quickly as I got on Skyline Drive, I was stopped at a gate and toll-taker's booth, where I shelled out fifteen dollars, the discounted price for motorcycles from the usual $20 for automobiles. The fee is not so much for the road but for entrance to the Shenandoah National Park, which the road happens to pierce from the north end to the south, exiting 150 miles farther on from where I entered.

Within a dozen miles I had caught up with my old friend, the Appalachian Trail where it joined Skyline Drive at Compton Gap. From there the AT would be my constant companion for most of the day. It would mirror Skyline Drive and the Blue Ridge Parkway; sometimes on the east and sometimes on the west; sometimes close at hand and sometimes wandering a few miles away. The Appalachian Trail would cross my path twenty-nine times on Skyline Drive and another nine times on the Blue Ridge Parkway for a total of thirty-eight crossings.

It wasn't long before I found out why the pavement looked so pristine, when I was stopped behind a line of cars waiting for a flag man to wave us on to proceed behind the "Follow Me" vehicle. Road work was underway, and we were in the middle of it. This happened twice, and each time the single lane ride behind "Follow Me" was five or more miles of slow and stacked traffic. "You'd have thought they might have tipped me off at the entry gate," I thought to myself, "or given me a discount." But who was I to complain; I was on top of the mountains riding a motorcycle, not stuck in some office behind a desk, so I sucked it up and let it go.

The road had a speed limit of thirty-five, which seemed pretty slow on the straights, of which there are few, but perfectly reasonable on all the twists and turns. The oleander was blooming in the woods along the road, and it lent a wonderful smell to the mountain air.

No sooner had I gotten rolling again, that I looked to my right and saw a huge, beautiful deer with velvet antlers climbing the steep ascent at the side of the road. As I rode south, I tried to correlate what I had just seen to my mental image of a deer. What I had seen was not only large but bulky and heavy-looking, with a thick chest and large rump and antlers that were much wider and thicker than I had ever seen on deer. It started to dawn on me that what I had seen had not been a deer at all, but an elk. Judging by the size of antlers that bull had so early in the season, it was going to be enormous when fully developed, too. What a rare site; I was so lucky to see one, although I was glad it was climbing the hillside instead of standing in the road.

Elk had completely disappeared from Virginia by 1970, in spite of twentieth-century attempts to reestablish them in their native habitat. In the late 1990s, elk were released in Kentucky, and eventually some of them made it into Virginia again. By 2010 only 150 were in Virginia, although more introduction was begun in hopes of sustaining a herd of 400. When I rode through, the number was closer to 100, so it was a very rare sighting, indeed.

Not long after spotting the elk, the road was running below the crest on the west side with views down into the valley. I noticed a pull-off with great views and stopped. It was time for a break and snack and a better, non-moving view of the valley.

Pleine-Aire Painters on Skyline Drive above the Shenandoah Valley

There were a couple other cars pulled off, and when I walked to the low stone wall separating the parking area from the drop off, below on large point of rock jutting out over the mountainside were two pleine-aire artists working on canvases mounted on portable easels. I took a couple photos from above, then made my way down the hillside to see their work and have a chat. My friend, Julie, who teaches art at Valdosta State University, specializes in pleine-aire oils and often can be found sitting in her kayak working on a painting on-site. I also studied painting at art school in the 1990s. So the painters and I had something to talk about. The work they were doing showed they were experienced painters with good technique, and their finished canvases I am sure would turn up on someone's wall. I didn't want to interrupt too much, so I didn't talk long. I climbed back up the hill, had a bite or two of a granola bar, then climbed back into the saddle and resumed my cruise south.

A Rest Stop on Skyline Drive

I passed a doe and her fawn, but forgot until too late to turn on the GoPro perched on top of my helmet so missed getting them on video. The day was warming and the sky was sunny with scattered white puffy clouds—a summer sky.

As the day progressed and the road heated up, I noticed long squiggly lines across the opposite lane from time to time.

Stopping and turning around to take a look, I could seen the lines were large black snakes, half the width of the lane, out soaking up the afternoon heat from the dark tarmac. I had the GoPro on so got a nice view of them as I passed Soon I spotted yet another snake that looked a bit different than the others. I did a U-turn and approached it until I could clearly see it was not black but was unmistakably a diamondback rattler. It was large and menacing with the diamonds and rattles clearly visible. I backed off a bit before negotiating another U-turn and continuing in my previous direction.

I exited Skyline Drive at its southern end at Rockfish Gap and stopped for more gas. From there I would be on the Blue Ridge Parkway through the rest of Virginia and into North Carolina.

The Appalachian Trail had been following close by Skyline Drive since Front Royal, and now it mirrored the Blue Ridge Parkway. It was getting late in the afternoon as I was approaching Roanoke. Just a few miles before the road wound its way around east of the city, at Blackhorse Gap, the Trail headed southwest passing Roanoke on the opposite side, parting company with me as it wandered west-southwest, toward its end in far-off northern Georgia, and I continued south-southwest. I wouldn't cross or be close to the trail again. It seemed like I was leaving an old companion.

I was past Roanoke as evening was falling fast. With my GoPro battery dead, of course, I saw numerous deer. They were appearing thick and fast. There were no close calls, but I knew I had to start thinking about where to camp for the night. I stopped to check the GPS to see what campgrounds were close by, hoping I wasn't far from one of the sporadic campgrounds right on the Parkway, but the GPS showed none of those. I found the closest camping spot to be Deer Run Campground in Ferrum. I made that the GPS's destination and got back on the road, following its lead.

Within a couple miles, I was directed to turn left on Runnet Bag Road, according to Google Maps, although I never saw a sign stating that or any other name or number. Soon the road had turned to gravel and was descending rapidly down the east slope of the mountain, dropping from the Blue Ridge Parkway's 2,000 feet elevation. The trail twisted and turned its way down the mountain prompting me to give it a new name: Unpaved Tail of the Dragon. I swooped right and left down the relatively unstable surface, using engine braking to keep my speed down or dragging my rear brake on occasion as the situation merited it.

The track wound down for a few miles until, finally, pavement began again and a few scattered houses began to appear. After a couple more miles, I arrived at Franklin Street, where I was directed to turn left. Darkness was falling, and I was hoping I might find the campground before I lost all light. Franklin was almost as twisting as Runnet Bag had been, but it was paved and ran fairly level along recesses between the mountains. I switched back one way and then the other. About to make a right around a sharp corner, I spotted Deer Run Road on the outside of the curve and heading northeast. I slowed, but not in time, and I watched Deer Run fly past my left mirror. A came to a halt on the far side of the curve, made a U-turn, then approached my last road. I turned onto the gravel and soon saw the campground on my right. I turned in with the last of the daylight quickly disappearing, parked up beside the office, and went inside to make arrangements for a tent spot. It was over twenty-seven dollars, but it was no time to argue, and it looked like a nice family spot with few campers this early in the season, so I took out the debit card and laid it on the counter.

Soon, I was back outside and searching for my site number. I spotted a BMW GS at a site, and as luck would have it, mine was right next to it and across from the showers and bathroom. It had been a wild ride down the mountain in late afternoon wooded darkness, but seven miles from the Blue Ridge Parkway I had a nice quiet spot for the night, and hopefully, a neighbor who might share my love of riding and traveling.

I crunched across the gravel and to my spot, cut off the bike, climbed off, and pulled off my helmet to the sound of campers talking and children playing. Night was upon me, but there was enough artificial light in the campground to find my way around. I unloaded the tent and quickly had it pitched and ready for the night. I pulled the borrowed sleeping bag from the borrowed dry bag and tossed it inside. I unfurled the Thermarest, blew a few puffs into it, and tossed it inside, crawling in after it to tuck it under the bag and to lay everything out flat in readiness for climbing in later. I rolled my jacket up and laid it at the head of the bag. It would suffice as my pillow.

Everything stowed and organized inside the tent, I climbed back out, dug through a pannier, and pulled out my MSR Dragonfly stove and set it on the tent site's picnic table. I released one of the one liter MSR storage bottles from one of the pillion peg strut mounts and connected it to the stove and gave it a few pumps. I opened the valve just a little to let a small pool of gas flow from it into the base of the stove, then turned off the flow. I flicked the only igniter I had, a short regular cigarette lighter and touched it to the stove at arm's length, ready to snatch it back as soon as the flame shot up. While the liquid gas burned, I filled my pot with water at the nearby spigot and went back to the table. The flame had almost burnt out when I turned on the flow of fuel once again. Instantly a hot blue flame, accompanied by the stove's usual roaring sound, made a nice clean and hot circle around the burner.

I sat the water on to boil, and while it was heating I offered to share some of my coffee with my neighbor, Bill. I poured the steaming water into my cup over a coffee "tea" bag while Bill walked over cup in hand. He brought over some Starbucks' instant coffee packed in little straw-like packages. He said they were very good and comparable to regular brewed coffee and offered one to me for myself and made himself a cup, leaving a few more straws for morning, too.

Over our coffee we compared notes on our bikes and our travels. Bill was riding a BMW 1200 GS, and was from Massachusetts. He was only a couple days out on an extended ride to the Southwest, with the plan to stay out for a few weeks. It turned out he had been in Gettysburg when I was there and had probably just been a few miles ahead of me on Skyline Drive and the Blue Ridge Parkway that day. He took a look at my bike and kit, and then we wandered next door to his site to examine his GS setup with BMW aluminum panniers—a very nice rig for long-distance riding.

Eventually, Bill went back to take care of things at his campsite. I was getting hungry. With the remaining hot water, I saturated a couple packs worth of instant oatmeal with dates, raisins, and walnuts, a super easy to store and fix nutritious food handy for these kind of rides. I straightened out my spoon, bent to fit inside my stacking cooking kit, and ate my dinner in the quiet of an early summer night in the Blue Ridge Mountains—early enough in the year to not be cold but late enough not to have to fight off mosquitoes. After dinner, I cleaned up my oatmeal dish and spoon and rinsed out my coffee cup then gathered my stuff and walked across the gravel driveway to brush my teeth and take a quick shower.

Back at camp, Bill and I bantered across our campsites while I wrote notes of what had happened that day on the road. That little chore done, it was time for bed. I plugged in the stuff that needed to be charged at my little power post adjacent to my water spigot then headed to the tent. I stripped down, not needing to worry about cold that night, and slipped inside my sleeping bag. One last call home assured me everyone was getting along just fine without me.

I hung up, set the phone alarm, slipped it onto the tiny net gear hammock that hung under the peak of the tent and drifted off to sleep.

Chapter Fifteen

Day Thirteen

Into Familiar Territory

The sun had not made its way above the surrounding mountaintops when I awoke. I got to work breaking camp. I drug everything out of the tent and plopped it onto the picnic table. I squeezed the air out of my sleeping pad and rolled it as tight as I could and stuffed it in its storage bag, rolled up the sleeping bag and compressed it enough to fit it in its dry bag, then walked around the tent's perimeter pulling out stakes and slipped the poles out of their channels and broke them down for storage. I quickly folded the tent, with the poles rolled inside, and wriggled it into its bag. All the big stuff restored on the bike, I went through the ritual of lighting the Dragonfly again. I made a breakfast of oatmeal again, and when the coffee was ready I called Bill over. We had a last short chat and I asked him to stand beside his GS for a photo. The stove and pot were disassembled and stored, and I was off on another day of riding, waving goodbye to my new friend as I rode away from the site and out of the campground.

Getting back onto the Blue Ride Parkway was a much easier task than getting down to Deer Run Campground the night before. I rode back to the main road, turned left and rode a few miles to Woolwine, where one more turn right returned me to the Parkway just a few miles farther southwest from where I had left it the afternoon before for my wild ride down the mountain to the campground.

The sun was out again and I had fully returned to summer. I snaked my way along the Blue Ridge Parkway but was running low on fuel. With my wheel about to cross into North Carolina, I took a quick exit north away from the state line in search of fuel. When I got to the crossroad, there were no stations in sight. If I was not going to have to break into my Rotopax spare, I was going to have to find a station soon. The sign pointing right at the intersection said, "Galax 6.5 Miles." I recognized the name, the "home of traditional mountain music" that my friend, Zoë Cano, loved so much and described in her book, *Bonneville Go or Bust*. I would have loved to head that way and stay a while and absorb some of the mountain culture that so enthralled her when she passed through a couple years ago. Unfortunately, my day had just begun, with an expected day of riding at least 400 miles, so I would only be going far enough to refuel before heading back to the Parkway and on into North Carolina. I stored the location away in my memory banks for future reference sometime later on a different ride.

I saw a man standing near the empty road in front of his house and stopped to ask which direction would be closer for finding gas. He had been watching me ever since I launched from the stop sign onto the road leading to Galax. When I stopped, he immediately started talking bikes, and especially Triumphs, having had a lot of experience himself riding them. After a few minutes of pleasant chatting he pointed me down the road, saying I could find gas just a little farther up. I thanked him, said goodbye, and pulled off the grass verge and back onto the road in the direction of Galax. In a very short time, I had found my fuel and was back on the road heading the way I had come. Approaching my new friend's place just before my turn-off I beeped the anemic horn and waved in his direction then sped off back to the Blue Ridge Parkway.

Within seconds of climbing back onto the Parkway, I was over the border and in North Carolina following the curve of the great Appalachians now trending more southwesterly as the mountain chain headed toward Chattanooga and northern Alabama. I crossed US 21 at a right angle less than fifteen miles from the North Carolina border. In another fifteen miles, as I rolled past Stone Mountain State Park, then Doughton Recreation Area, and Thurmond Chatham Wildlife Management Area, I crossed my northward track, NC 113, that I had traveled over a week earlier and over three thousand miles ago on my way to spring and the edge of winter on our northern neighbor's coastal roads on the Gaspé Peninsula.

I had ridden much of the famous parkways in North Carolina, both the Blue Ridge Parkway and the Cherohala Skyway, and now I had completed the entire length of their sister highway to the north, Skyline Drive, but there was a small section left of the Blue Ridge Parkway I had never traveled from Deep Gap, North Carolina, to where I was now. I was determined to close that gap.

I passed Glendale Springs where the Blue Ridge Parkway was mimicking its neighbor, the South Fork New River to its north. The Parkway ran at heights of 3,000 feet and slowly climbed higher as it approached the tallest peak of them all, Mount Mitchell, standing at 6,684 feet, the highest point in North America east of the Mississippi River.

Approaching Linn Cove Viaduct and Grandfather Mountain

At Deep Gap I crossed above US 421, completing my navigation of the three famous scenic highways, and zoomed past Laxon on the now familiar road. I still had some traveling to do on the Parkway before leaving it, almost at the foot of Mount Mitchell, so I continued following its twists and turns as it made it way through the Blue Ridge Mountains. Grandfather Mountain appeared above my windscreen, towering over the surrounding ridges, after passing the turnoff to Blowing Rock. The road followed the contour of Grandfather Mountain, which stood directly overhead on my right, culminating in Calloway Peak at its craggy summit, thirty-six feet shy of six thousand feet. I stopped at one of the numerous pull-offs for a break and a photograph. Ahead was visible one of the mountain's lesser peaks, Linville Peak at 5,280 feet. Up there, the Mile High Swinging Bridge accessed Linville Peak over a eighty foot deep gorge, running 228 feet dangling across a mile above sea level. I remember that suspension bridge from a childhood family trip, when Dad, my two brothers, and I walked across, while Mom waited for us at the start of the bridge biting her fingernails in terror and praying we would return alive. I wonder now how she even made it up there at all.

In the distance I could see the Linn Cove Viaduct snaking its way around the flanks of Grandfather Mountain below Linville Peak. I clicked on the GoPro to record my passing on this 1,243 foot bridge carrying the Parkway past the mountain. The viaduct was the last section of the Blue Ridge Parkway to be completed, and that was not accomplished until 1987. Camera on, I climbed back on the Bonnie, clicked into first gear, and rolled back onto the highway. Passing milepost 304.6 I was on the bridge, the mountain towering above me on the right and a fall of hundreds of feet to my left. The views across the mountains were stupendous. The ride along the viaduct was a nice finish to my ride on the BRP, which would be ending in just forty more miles.

I passed the picturesque village of Little Switzerland and finally found my route south off the Blue Ridge Parkway to US Highway 70. I had ridden up NC 80 before along with my brother on a weekend of riding and on our way to Mount Mitchell. It was a wild ride going up, but going downhill as I was, the route was more than a little challenging. For ten miles the small rural road hurled me down the mountains around left twists and right twists and throwing in a few hairpins to keep me awake. That route is one of my favorites in the region, although I have to admit to preferring going uphill where gravity is your friend, allowing quick deceleration before flying around the crazy curves. Going downhill you have to constantly check your speed by engine braking on the straights to keep from building up too much speed and being whisked right off the mountain. From 3,400 feet the route dives for ten miles to 1,300 feet where it turns and straightens out at Buck Creek. From there it is an easy two miles along the Buck Creek valley floor to US 70, two or three miles west of Marion.

By the time I reached the busy highway it was time for refueling. I pulled off at the first station and topped up the tank. I was not looking forward to this section of road. I had seventeen miles to go to Black Mountain, where I could turn south, duck under an Interstate, and be back in the countryside in the mountains again. I was on the old main route into Asheville coming from the east from the Greensboro/Winston-Salem metropolitan areas, running parallel to I-40 in the broad valley created by the diminutive Catawba and Swannanoa Rivers, sometimes traveling directly beside them. The highway crossed a hump between the sources of each. The Swannanoa ran west toward Asheville, eventually joining the French Broad River and hence to the Tennessee River, mixing its mountain waters with those of the Ohio River, then the Mississippi River, and finally the Gulf of Mexico after a journey of thousands of miles from the mountains around me. The Catawba ran east, eventually joining other rivers and pouring itself into the Atlantic Ocean at Charleston, South Carolina, many miles away, after joining the Wateree, the Santee, and the Cooper Rivers.

The highway was filled with auto traffic and big trucks and was void of interesting scenery, except for the occasional glimpses of the mountains to the north. Black Mountain appeared soon, however, and I turned south, happy to be leaving the traffic behind but a little sad that the majestic mountains were in my mirrors instead of in front of my windscreen. Still, I had miles yet of riding through scenic countryside populated by mountains, although the farther I went south the smaller and less rugged the mountains would be.

I followed the road as it wiggled its way through the smaller mountains, now at more modest heights of 2,500 to 3,500 feet. Following the Broad River, it joined up with US 64 at Bat Cave. US 64 was the major east to west artery through the Blue Ridge Mountains, shooting west and southwest from Statesville, North Carolina, and skirting the south edge of the Blue Ridge and Smoky Mountains all the way to the very western end of North Carolina, where it joined US 74 for a run out of the state in its extreme southwestern corner. Eventually, it would end at Four Corners, far away in Arizona. But I was not going to follow it to its extreme that day, so I turned left and toward Lake Lure. Ahead lay Chimney Rock, a spectacular mountainside rock formation of a chimney-like rock tower jutting three hundred and fifteen feet up beside the mountain proper with a huge American flag flying in the mountain breeze planted on top of it. From the touristy town in the valley below it is an impressive site, and a trail to the peak of the chimney had been built to accommodate visitors to Chimney Rock State Park. Of course, this is modern America, and an elevator option to the top is also available, except when its not, which seems to be often. On a previous visit I had driven the road into the park, only to find out that entrance was fifteen collars per adult and seven for children. With my entire family with me then, we found the forty-four dollar fee too steep for the chance to stand on a piece of rock. I satisfied myself with the beautiful views of the chimney across the Broad River as I rolled though and out of town.

Just a few miles down the road was Lake Lure, a favorite place that I had ridden to before with my brother and had taken my family to more than once. I followed the contours of the mountainsides lining the rim of the lake, taking extra care in what was now a busy tourist and residential area, with driveways emptying into the road on both sides and often on blind corners. At the southern tip of the lake was a favorite restaurant, Larkin's on the Lake. Often, bikers heading up into the mountains from the big cities of Spartanburg and Greenville make it a stop, being positioned at the dividing point for those heading northeast on US 64 and those heading northwest, the way I had come in. Remembering the prices, I decided a stop was not in order for me and I turned south, my back toward Larkin's and my wheel pointing at South Carolina. I continued on hungry, but richer.

The South Carolina line was approaching fast, just over twenty miles ahead. I was entering the Piedmont, a broad plateau between the Appalachians and the wide coastal lowlands. The mountains quickly diminished in height until I was surrounded by low foothills. At Mill Springs I turned southwest and soon joined US 74 for a short jog west. I passed over Interstate 26 and then left 74, which rolled off west across southern North Carolina without me. I rode south, and just over a mile past Tryon I crossed into South Carolina.

I approached Landrum and very familiar territory. My brother, Tim, had lived just beyond Landrum in Inman, the next town. I had ridden up to his place many times, sometimes to hunt deer in his forested backyard, and sometimes to join him for some mountain riding. In less than fifteen miles I could have been at his door. Unfortunately, Tim had separated, amicably, from his wife a few months before and had moved to Florence in the coastal lowlands of South Carolina. His wife, Pam, had stayed on at their place in Inman. I considered what I should do. I really should stop in and say hello to Pam, but was feeling a bit awkward but convinced it was the right thing to do. In spite of their differences I still loved Pam like a sister, and just because things had changed between them it shouldn't mean they had to change between us. Then I realized it was a work day, and she would not be at the house anyway. That removed any indecision, so I headed away southwest with the aim of intercepting SC 11, also known as the Cherokee Scenic Highway.

Highway 11 was one of my favorite rides, not for twist and turns or technicality, but for the wide, usually empty, highway and beautiful vistas. The route runs along on the South Carolina side of the North Carolina border and sweeps eventually southwest where it joins Interstate 85, the main conduit between Greenville/Spartanburg and Atlanta, Georgia. It skirts the southern edge of the Blue

Ridge Mountains, with a wall of peaks towering above on the north side and rolling hills to the south with only a light sprinkling of scattered mountains poking up among the hills. On this ride I was not going to be enjoying the entire length of the scenic highway, but I followed it to a few miles north of Traveler's Rest.

I turned left and headed south toward Greenville, while the skies darkened ahead. I had resolved to just stay on this major highway and ride directly through Greenville and out the other side. To completely avoid this wide metropolitan area surrounded by busy suburbs would take me very far out of my way, so into the city I dove. By Travelers Rest, rain was imminent, so I stopped to don my jacket's interior rain layer and my Frogg Togg pants.

My feet, shod in "waterproof" touring boots, were going to get wet. The boots had never been waterproof, even right out of the box, in spite of the manufacturer's claims. The previous pair from a different manufacturer were exactly the same when it came to their claim of being waterproof. On top of that, both pairs had holes worn all the way through the right sole resulting from pressing down on my centerstand arm when parking the bike each night. I decided I was done with inexpensive waterproof boots and next time I would spend double the $125, if I had to, in order to have truly dry feet and to get boots that would hold up to the common task of parking the bike.

As I approached the city and the traffic thickened, the sky let loose and the rain fell in buckets. I was tempted to pity myself, but could not justify that. After all, I had ridden from Florida to the Saint Lawrence and back, some 4,500 miles so far, and that was the first precipitation I had to endure, other than a light sprinkling of wet snow above Maine for a few minutes. I had been very lucky until now and really was lucky again, now that it was raining while I was in a warm climate.

I zoomed through Greenville, keeping my eyes on the signs saying I was still on US 25, and shot out the south side aiming for Waterloo and my friend Bryan's home again. The rain had stopped by then, and I was back under partly cloudy skies with increasing temperatures.

I, obviously, was not paying enough attention and found myself on the wrong road about 17 miles out from downtown Greenville. I needed to be on the east side of the Saluda River, but now was crossing over to the west. At the next highway, I turned left toward Honea Path. There I turned left making my way back toward 25. Immediately after my turn, I stopped for fuel and rechecked my map carefully, in place of the distracted scans I was trying to do while on the road trying to manage the bike, watching for cars and road signs. I rolled out, now confident of where I was going. I was getting close; the Saluda flowed into Lake Greenwood, and Bryan lived on a little fork of the lake on the east side.

Just beyond the corner station where I had stopped was a small state road, and my map showed it running southeast and closing with the Saluda River at Ware Shoals, where I would cross the river again. I turned east and continued on another small state highway. Having looked at the GPS and comparing it to my much too large scale map, I saw that, just after crossing Reedy River, a tributary of Lake Greenwood's northeastern branch, Neely Ferry Road headed south toward the lake, following the river. When I spotted the road sign, I turned right after a quick stop to recheck my map and GPS at the corner. The rain returned as I pulled out and fell in torrents as if to give me a final vindictive "Take that!" in return for all the rainless days I had up until then. Almost reaching the lake where two branches split off, northeast and northwest, Neely Ferry turned off to the east and I continued south on Todd Quarter Road, crossed the eastern branch, and was soon at US 221. The rain had eased off and then quickly cleared.

I turned right and moved south, riding through the tiny downtown area of Waterloo, where I had accidentally found myself on the way up while trying to find Bryan's. In five more miles the route intersected SC 72, which going southwest crossed the lake and rolled through Greenwood and to the northeast headed toward a crossing of Interstate 26. I was meeting my track I had taken on my way north a couple weeks ago.

After the confusion the last time on the way to Bryan's, on the way out I had paid attention and now had a clear idea of where to turn to find his place again. I turned right onto 72, then immediately left it again and wound my way through a residential area arriving at Bryan's place on a bay of Lake Greenwood.

I arrived as Bryan was in his workshop working on yet another vintage motorcycle. Bryan welcomed me with his usual warm hospitality, and after talking bikes for a while in the shop, he ushered me inside. Bryan cooked up a big meal, and if I had known what a good chef he was at the time, I might have made up an excuse not to eat out on the lake on my last visit. I ate until I was stuffed then was handed a cold beer to enjoy in the sun room. It had been a long day, over 400 miles, with the rain thrown in for good measure, so it was not long until I could feel the exhaustion creeping in and my eyes drooping.

I called home and hoped for good news—still all clear. I asked her if it was going well enough for me to take another day. It was a long haul all the way home from Bryan's, and I wanted to stop by and visit my friend, Julie, in Valdosta, Georgia. Stopping there for the night would give me an easy last day's ride of less than three hundred miles. I was given her blessing and actually encouraged to not push it and to take my time.

I had another reason to stop by Julie's and that was to see her dad, Jack, who lived with her. The last couple times I had stopped, Jack had not been doing well. Jack was in his mid-80s and I wanted to see him again before anything worse happened. It had been a good call, unfortunately, because later that year Jack took a turn for the worse. Then toward the end of that summer, I took a ride up again to check in on him and Julie, but in the fall, we lost Jack, one of the greatest generation, a soldier of the German occupation after the war. Jack came back to the States and studied psychology, becoming a psychologist and practiced in the 1960s and 1970s, specializing in the new trend of art therapy. He was a kind person, true friend, and rare intellectual. I had not known him very well growing up, and was glad over the years of riding through and visiting Julie to have really gotten to know him.

It had really relieved my anxiety to hear Andrea encouraging me to take the extra day to see Julie, so after plugging in the electronics and setting the alarm on my phone, I fell asleep instantly.

Chapter Sixteen

Day Fourteen

The Empty Georgia Countryside

Before the sun had risen I was gathering up all my gear, and by the time it was up I was loading it all back on the Bonnie and strapping it all down. It was going to be a short ride of less than three hundred miles that day.

Leaving Bryan's, I retraced the winding residential streets back to the main highway and turned right, crossing Lake Greenwood. I quickly passed around the town of Greenwood as the highway made a southern bypass. Passing into the countryside to the southwest of town, I was soon riding along through Long Cane Scenic Area and heading for the state line. At the Savannah River the route turned south-southeast, roughly following the river to my crossing at Strom Thurmond Dam at Clarks Hill.

At Strom Thurmond Dam

I rode along the top of the dam with Strom Thurmond Lake, a widening of the Savannah River, on my right created by the dam. Below, on the left, the river continued toward the Atlantic Ocean in its natural bed.

I hadn't topped up my fuel before stopping the night before and was getting low, so I stopped in Appling for the first fill up and rest stop of the day. From there it was a run through the mostly empty east Georgia farmland toward Vidalia, where the air smelled like sweet onions for miles around. The lack of traffic gave me a chance to think as I rolled south and the day grew warmer.

Since leaving Quebec, slowly the trees had been gathering their clothes. In Quebec the trees had been naked, but then soon put forth buds, then blossoms in Maine. Next, there were light yellow-green leaves, still curled up, as if reluctant to wake up for the summer ahead. The leaves opened up wider and grew greener and darker as I was rode south. Now in Georgia, the trees wore their full summer wardrobe in thick layers of dark greens. The flowers of spring had faded, and the start of their transformation into fall fruit was in full swing.

While I had ridden to the very beginning of spring, even to the end of winter; while approaching home through the summer South I was thinking about the spring of human life. I thought of the doe and the fawn I had seen back on the Blue Ridge Parkway, the fawn so new to life and with so much ahead of it. I was singing as many songs from my youth as I could remember in my helmet, doing some of my best, and my worst, singing I have ever done and remembering that special time in my life.

My mind wandered as the Georgia miles rolled past, filled with thoughts of first loves and awakening of desire, of the spring of youth and how special it is. I could see my old girlfriends, feel their young skin, and taste their lips and tongues. I was an aging man but realized that those feelings and thoughts had been a part of me, remained a part of me, and made my youth a wonderful time of urges, hopes, dreams, and even failures and broken hearts. The transitions I had been witnessing from winter to spring to summer brought all that alive in my thoughts and reminded me that I wanted to encourage my children to enjoy and appreciate the spring bloom of life while they could.

Life was about change, and I realized it should be embraced. There were walnuts in the trees in the North and here in Georgia were pecans. Shorelines had changed to mountains, and mountains had changed to foothills, then rolling hillsides, until finally I was whizzing through the flat Georgia pine lands. I had nearly frozen in Quebec and now was sweltering in the Southern sunshine and humidity. If it hadn't been for the contrast, there wouldn't have been the same experience, just as without broken hearts, there wouldn't have been love.

My reveries were interrupted by an orange low fuel light as I approached Hazlehurst. I pulled into a gas station and fueled up again and enjoyed a few minutes on my feet and off the bike.

Back on the road as I sped south on those empty and hot back Georgia roads, I laid down on my tank with my head behind the windscreen to escape the ever-present and raucous wind noise. I'd lie there in an envelope of relative quiet, with only the soothing low frequency and steady sound of the twin spinning below me until my neck could take the craning no more that it had to endure to enable me to see the road ahead while in that contorted pose. Head once again above the screen, the screaming wind would return while I alternately tried other postures to ease the pain I felt where the saddle met my butt—feet on highway pegs mounted to the crash bar out front, feet on the pillion pegs, feet below and back straight and head up, on my toes on the pegs then on my arches.

Douglas was coming up soon, which was where I had to decide the route to take into Valdosta. When I arrived I chose, in my disdain for cities, to opt for a country route so headed southwest on a minor Georgia back road. In twenty-six miles I turned right, just past Willachoochee. The small towns of Nashville and Adel were the only obstructions before my crossing I-75 as I rolled west-southwest into the countryside.

West of the crossing, the highway made a veer to the south-southwest and ran through quiet and beautiful rolling farm land. Everything was beginning to look familiar. On a previous trip to see Julie we had ridden this area two-up on the Bonnie toward Reed Bingham State Park, where we had opted for feet as our mode of transportation, walking along the trails in the park, discovering quiet waters and copperheads.

That day we had stopped at a fruit farm for fresh home-made ice cream full of chunks of locally grown fruit on the way back to her place. At Morven, I spotted the same farm on the northeastern corner of the intersection with GA 133. This time I skipped the ice cream and turned left on 133, doubling back toward I-75 on the last road before Julie's neighborhood, just fourteen miles away.

As I rode closer, I started watching for the diminutive road sign for Julie's street. The last time I had visited the large sign on the highway with the name of the subdivision in front of her neighborhood had been missing, and it was this time, too. I zipped past a likely candidate but was going to fast to make out the name on the tiny green street sign, the only guide now. I felt sure enough, however, to quickly turn around and approach from the east, this time slowing enough to confirm it was the right street. I turned left, and before the street circled around and back to the main highway, I turned into Julie's pine-straw covered driveway.

It was early enough in the afternoon to have some time to go inside and chat with Julie and her dad, Jack, before thinking about dinner. It was good to see Jack getting around, although with the help of a walker. When not in bed, he was pretty much confined to his easy chair in front of the television, where he loved to watch classic movies or read. He could still occasionally get out to the table in the backyard, which looked over into a pine forest across the yard, filled with birds and squirrels that he loved to watch, especially in the cool of the mornings.

Jack had continued his small abstract paintings. He showed me one with a pair of swirling red and white circles side by side on a blue field with a line connecting them from left to right in a sideways V pointing right and creating movement, with a pair of smaller circles in the middle and a blurred purple shading behind it all. It said "movement." Jack said it reminded him of me and my motorcycle.

When we were in high school, Julie, a handful of other friends, and I were all artists in one form or another. Later some of us applied our art experience towards careers in graphic design, as I had. But Julie had stuck to fine art and had never stopped creating from her heart, and I always have admired her for that.

Julie went to art school and painted wherever she was, almost always on the spot, doing pleine-aire work. She was often kayaking the streams and swamps of southern Georgia and northern Florida, gear on board and working from her boat. When time allowed it or a show in another area required her attendance, she took her tools with her and worked in new locations. With her bright expressionistic colors she painted the Appalachians, the US Southwest, and everywhere in between. Her rich colors and deep impasto reflects her love of the Impressionists and Expressionists. Parallels between her work and that of Gaugin, Van Gogh, and Monet are obvious.

On my next visit, Jack presented me with his painting, Julie also offered me one of hers. I had told her I wanted to buy one someday and wanted to pay her the normal price that she sells them for in a gallery. I think artists are often looked upon as people who should just give their work away. I feel different. Artists pay the same bills, more or less, as everyone else. Art is their job, and they need to receive pay just like everyone else, especially considering all the years of studying and painting before becoming good enough to leave the world a bit of extra beauty. Being something of an artist myself, I know how often one gets asked for "little favors" once others know you can paint or draw. On that visit, though, Julie insisted on me taking a small work "until you can afford a large piece." That little canvas of swirling paint, thick brush strokes, and rich deep burnt siennas, purples, pinks, ultramarine blues, and greens of all values and tints depicting a Southern pond edge with pines and palm tree now hangs in my office on the same wall with Jack's "motorcycle in motion" painting. It's good to look up and remember both of my dear friends with a single simple glance.

As evening was drawing near, Julie offered to take me out for pizza. We climbed in her truck and drove into Valdosta, finally settling in at a Mellow Mushroom. Anchovies was one of the choices of toppings, which Julie liked. I was feeling adventurous, so we ordered them along with all the other goodies on the entire pie. Of course, good beer washed it all down as we talked and passed each other news from each of our own little worlds.

Back at the house, dinner was followed up with more beer, and the conversation continued about old times and what we were doing now; about art, about politics, about everything, until we were all getting sleepy. Jack retired before us, but Julie and I soon followed. I wandered down the hall to what had become my bedroom when I visited. I checked in with Andrea—still good—set the alarm and fell asleep.

Chapter Seventeen

Day Fifteen

Heading Home

I took my time getting myself together the next morning. The ride home would be less than three hundred miles; no need to rush. I walked out to the kitchen, where I started the coffee. Soon hot black coffee was ready, and I poured myself a big cup. Soon, I was joined by Julie and Jack. We took our coffee outside to the little round table, sat down, and watched the world waking up as we sipped and chatted. Before long, Julie returned to the kitchen and rustled up some breakfast. Jack offered me one of his granola bars, which I washed down with more coffee.

I made one more call home, letting them know I would soon be on my way, then went back to the bedroom to gather up my stuff. In the garage the Bonnie was waiting for me, where I carefully strapped down all the gear for the last ride of the trip. Once everything was refilled and remounted, I walked back in to share goodbyes with Jack and Julie, who gave me a final hug for the road. I rolled the bike outside and started down the driveway while Julie took a photo of the departure. With a final wave, I turned onto the street and rolled through the quiet neighborhood among the pines to the stop sign at the main highway. I turned right and built up speed, heading toward Valdosta.

With the sun rising ahead of me, I crossed through the city along with the rest of the Saturday morning traffic, which was light once I had cleared the exits at Interstate 75. Skirting the southwestern edge of Valdosta, I accidentally ended up on Saint Augustine Road South that soon joined Old Clyattville Road. I had missed my turn onto US 221, which would have connected with US 41 South, the route I had planned to take out of Georgia. Old Clyattville Road would soon swing away from US 41, cross I-75, and go southwest to, where else, Clyattville, not the direction I wanted to go. I realized my mistake quickly and looked for my first opportunity to get back on track. An industrial road cut across and I hopped onto it, jogging back to my intended route.

I turned right and continued south out of Georgia toward the Florida border. I passed through the tiny villages of Dasher and then Lake Park. Within ten miles of exiting Lake Park I was once again in Florida and gassing up at Jennings and taking my first break of the day. I was in the quiet lonely countryside of north Florida and only sporadically passed through little towns on my way south.

I rolled through White Springs, passing Stephen Foster Folk Culture Center State Park as I rounded the bend in what could loosely be called "downtown" White Springs. I recalled camping there on one of my other rides back from the Blue Ridge Mountains. I had gone up to this small town another time with the entire family and met Julie there for the Florida Folk Festival, where we spent the day walking and watching demonstrations of traditional folk arts, with the kids taking part in some of the hands-on activities, and listening to folk music on several stands around the park. My family had gone back to our nearby campground early, and Julie and I stayed near the beer tent and the main stage, listening to different music acts while refreshing ourselves with some cold brews. Julie brought me back to camp later, then headed back home.

The weather had not been as cooperative as on this trip, and rain poured down during the rest of that afternoon and into the night, leaving us floating in three inches of water on our inflatable mattresses. It was all part of the experience of camping. Drying out in the campground's meeting building, no one was complaining, and all had a great time interacting with the other campers also seeking refuge inside. But on this ride, while passing that memorable spot, the sun was shining and there was no threat of rain as I rode past the park, across the Suwannee River, and through Big Shoals State Park.

I had one more sizeable town to pass through before I would be almost in isolation again, riding south on Florida's country roads. Lake City laid ahead, swollen in size due to its close vicinity to Interstate 75, one of the two main north-south corridors through peninsular Florida. I managed to avoid all the traffic pulling out or turning in along the stretch of highway approaching the Interstate, then popped out on the west side into rural, quiet Florida. Although I would pass through a few more small towns as I rolled south, none were very big or choked with traffic, but simply made for a pleasant contrast to the pine woods as I passed through the quaint little villages. I would have quiet and almost empty highways until at least Dunellon, when the buildup would begin as the route approached the Tampa Bay area.

Not long after crossing the I-75, at High Springs, US 27 joined 41 for the run south through Newberry, Archer, and finally Williston, where it peeled off on its own to the southeast to another crossing of I-75, then on to Ocala, The Villages, Lady Lake, and Leesburg. I let 27 run away on its own to that stoplight and traffic torture chamber it became east of I-75 and chose to stick to US 41 through the quiet pasture land toward Dunellon, where I knew the Tampa Bay bound traffic would start to pile up. Luckily for me, from Dunellon to Floral City, where I would turn onto back roads for much of the rest of the way home, was only twenty-five miles or so.

That balsam smell I loved was back in the air as I passed through woods of southern yellow pine. I followed, then passed, huge lumber trucks filled to the top of the side posts with the scaly trunks of those trees.

The highway ran through the quiet western Florida countryside, south of the Big Bend, where the panhandle pointed west to New Orleans like a wrinkled finger, and parallel to Interstate 75, but far enough west of it to be out of the traffic mayhem that Interstates tend to produce along their corridors. Pine and live oak draped with Spanish moss lined my way as I passed through small towns with few stop lights and light traffic.

I got lucky in Dunellon, where I found that traffic was still not very heavy. I continued south through Hernando and Inverness before the sea of vehicles became thick. At Floral City, at the only stoplight in town, I turned left and rode east downhill through the shady tunnel of trees and moss on Orange Avenue. I sped past dark hammocks of oak, fields with cattle grazing in the hot sun, and was kept entertained by the wide sweepers that appeared every so often on the way to crossing under I-75 and entering Bushnell just beyond.

I was in home territory, being within a wide circle with its center at Lake Wales that could contain most of my weekend riding. I had been through the area a lot, as it is my traffic avoidance route as I try to get out of the state on the way north or northeast.

In Bushnell, I made a right then a quick left onto Noble Avenue running east out of the little town. Crossing FL 471, my path became a narrow driveway-like road that cut through farmland with a few hard corners thrown in for fun as I passed under the big oaks planted on both sides separating the road from the fields. It delivered me to a T where I turned east. I was quickly in the tiny village of Center Hill and just as quickly out the other side. The road made a wide turn to the south and dumped me out on FL 50, the main and boring route from Brooksville in the west to Clermont in the east, where it crossed US 27. I turned left knowing I would not be on this busy route for long. I passed through the little joined-at-the-hip towns of Mascotte and Groveland, so close together you can't tell where one ended and the other began.

Beyond Groveland, my next road appeared on my right and I peeled south for the Green Swamp. The highway ran straight and flat for almost thirty miles to Polk City and Interstate 4, the state's hectic northeast-southwest main thoroughfare. I didn't follow it that far but, instead, turned off again twenty miles along onto a little gem of a back road called Deen Still Road that I've traveled a lot. It cut east across the swamp and out to US 27, well south of the mayhem of that highway farther north and did so with little traffic to slow my progress. Only a mile or so after I got on Deen Still, I turned south onto an even quieter Old Grade Road and headed for a crossing of Interstate 4. I was almost alone on the way to the Interstate and after passing over it, the only traffic to be had was at the lone gas station adjacent to the exit.

I took a left at the next road and swept southeast on a minor local road toward Haines City, which eventually took me through increasingly populated quiet neighborhoods as it approached US 27.

There, my choices of staying on small roads came to a halt. Ahead on my preferred route, FL 17, the way south from

Haines City was under construction. I preferred a little traffic to bumps and rattles and slow progress between safety cones, so I turned south on US 27. While 27 was a busy road, there it was not the corridor of stoplights it was between Leesburg and Ocala, and although the traffic was heavy, it flowed easily enough.

Once I was far enough south to clear the construction zone on FL 17, I turned east and found my over way to it, then turned south. That road ran within blocks of my house in Lake Wales, only twelve miles ahead. I could have ridden that section in my sleep, I had ridden it so many times before.

With Dundee behind me and Lake Wales ahead, I soon caught sight of Bok Tower, a pink marble tower set in the midst of a garden of native plants on the peak of Iron Mountain, the highest point in peninsular Florida and just up the street and around the corner from home.

I pulled into The Good Spot, formerly Fuzzy's, killed the bike, and climbed off. I shed my helmet and jacket and walked inside for my usual single celebratory beer I always have on the way back from extended rides. As I entered, the usual "Ozzy!" greeted me as I headed to a table to sit with a couple of my G Spot friends and ordered a draft. I hadn't shaved in over two weeks, but no one seemed to notice. It could be they had already had enough beers to not notice much, as most were not the light drinkers that I was. I didn't plan to stay very long, I just wanted a cold one and some time in the air conditioning before riding the couple more miles home to greet the family.

I rolled out, happy things had gone so well on my long ride. It was still early in the afternoon when I approached the house. As I rounded the last corner, I saw my sister-in-law stopped in front of the house and Andrea was bent to her window chatting, while the kids were gathered behind her in the yard. I turned in and did my usual U-turn in the grass in the front yard and lined my bike up on the narrow concrete tire path that constituted our driveway. I got a small wave from Andrea as I rode in—guess I wasn't missed as much as I thought—and Jacob walked slowly over to me as I was parking up.

I lined up the Bonnie on the one and a half foot wide strip, came to a stop, and flicked down the kickstand. I let the bike fall to the left, but the stand missed the edge of the concrete and fell into the void between the two cement paths. I could feel the heavily loaded bike going over. I told my son it was falling and I could not stop it. He stepped up to help, but it was too late. The bike fell onto its side, and with the mountains of gear like a huge camel hump on top giving it momentum, it rolled past horizontal and ended on it side with its wheels off the ground.

I had at least been able to slow the fall, and when I finally managed to get it upright, no damage was found, but it was quite an ignominious way to end an otherwise epic trip.

I'd been on the road for over five thousand miles, in two countries, eleven states, and two provinces; through traffic, cold weather, on twisting mountain roads and off-road; and after all that, my only mishap was in front of my own house.

I rolled the Bonnie backwards into the garage, relieved it of all the luggage, flicked off the light, and walked inside the house, lugging my gear and looking forward to a shower and my first shave in over two weeks.

It hadn't been the glorious, triumphant return I had envisioned, but I was happy to be home.

Chapter Eighteen

At Home

Slowly, as the trip had drawn out longer and longer, day by day the pressures and anxiety that had set the ride in motion had faded. Arriving back in central Florida, I felt rejuvenated. The weight of the stress and depression that had wrapped around me and was pulling me under had lifted . I could look ahead with some optimism, and much of my faith in humanity had been restored by so many interactions with people who, almost without exception, were kind and generous and ready to lend a hand. Real life had met social media and the evening news head on, and won.

My long ride, however, didn't fundamentally change the stresses that were a part of my everyday life; they were going to continue. But the experience gave me coping skills to deal with them and a different perspective that kept me from wandering too close to the deep end of my mind. In a way, the journey had perhaps saved my life. The change of environment the trip had forced was abrupt and extreme, and I woke up somewhere outside the hole I had fallen into.

Stress was perhaps going to be unavoidable along my path of self-employment, with deadline challenges of the magazine business and my own psychological shortcomings, but I could now approach each new problem from a different point of view, while reminding myself of the goodness of the world. I could cope, if I just did not only focus on the problems.

An old girlfriend of mine from Guatemala had explained to me many years ago that in her culture they called life "la lucha," or "the struggle." I could see the truth of that moniker. Whenever an obstacle was overcome, another popped up ahead in a never-ending cycle of struggles, then hopefully, triumphs, but always followed by more struggles.

Over another year, after I had returned to Florida, "la lucha" slowly caught up with me again. I could float but was still treading water. Even with a more positive attitude, as time went on the struggle would wear me down and sap my strength. I needed to do something to address the problem again before depression set in once more.

I wouldn't let that happen again. Part of my new skill-set was recognizing the early signs of fatigue and anxiety. I had found a way to restore myself, and it was time to do it again. But this time I would leave before it became a crisis.

NORTHWEST

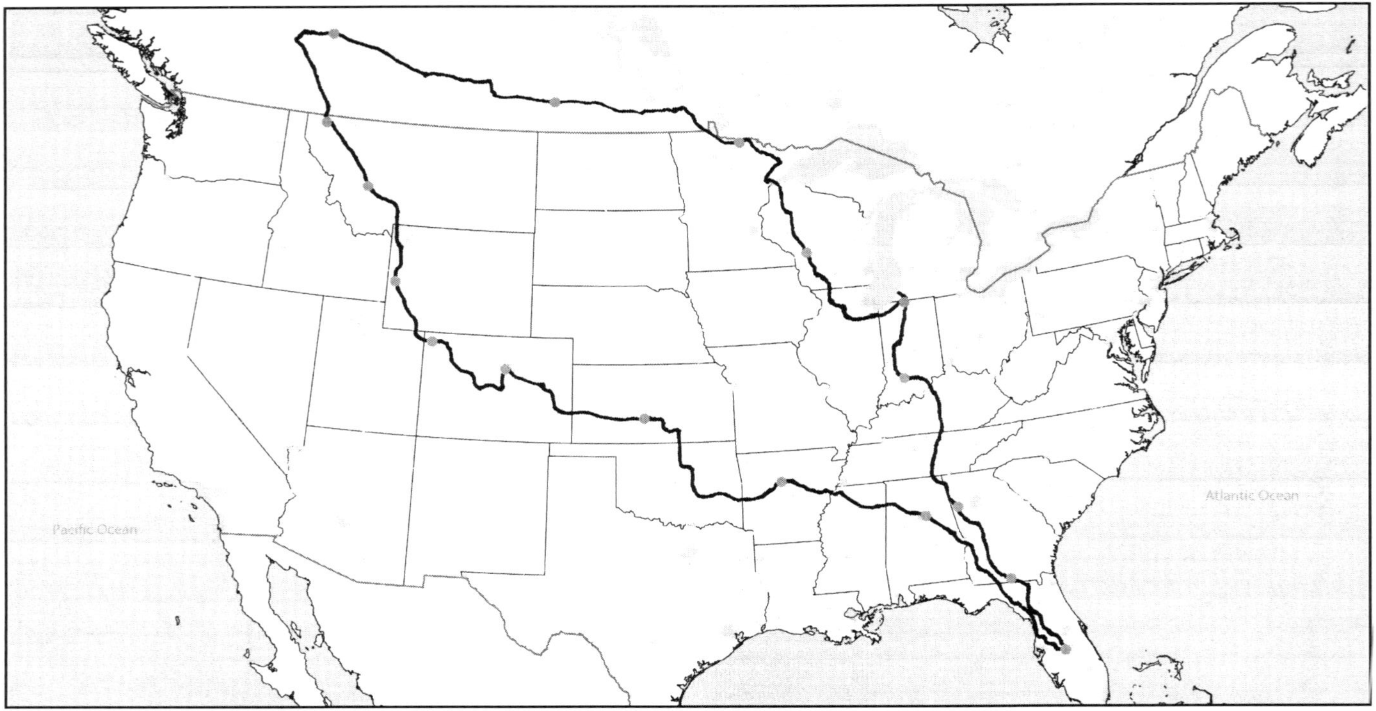
Pacific Ocean
Atlantic Ocean

Chapter One

Prompting, Planning, and Preparation

After that last bout with a particularly virulent episode of stress-induced depression, I did the only thing I could—I rode. That ride essentially became a mental reset for me, helping me out of the darkness I had almost been lost in. That trip I've come to call a "mental health ride."

As much as last year's ride staved off darkness and got me back on the right track mentally, the stress was rebuilding.

In the spring I discovered I had developed high blood pressure. Not being overweight, fairly active, and generally a healthy eater, stress had been the trigger. I tried to combat it with daily walks, usually three miles or so. Still, the high blood pressure remained, until one night I had chest pains with some radiating down my left arm. I had a borrowed blood pressure monitor that I used to keep track of my BP to see if the walks were helping, so I put it on and discovered my pressure was 178 over 127, a reading that indicates a trip to the emergency room was warranted. Still with no health insurance, that was not an option, so I spent an anxious night hoping for the best. The next day I went to a clinic, saw a doctor, and got a prescription, and a payment plan to go along with it. So then, not only my mental health was at stake, but a medical component was added to the formula. I had to do something to reduce my stress. By May, I decided another mental health ride was in order.

Planning was everything. I would have to ride on the cheap and after May 15, when I would put another issue of the magazine in the hands of the printer. A VJMC event was scheduled for June 22 through 25, which I would have to be at, so the logical choice was to hit the road and ride, catching the event on the way home.

I looked over maps, trying to pinpoint places I had not been, which looked interesting and different from the type of places I'd been before. The West looked promising. But like before, the Southwest didn't appeal to me because of all the accounts I had read by others, so that the idea of going there was like the negative end of a magnet pushing a negative me away. But I loved the mountains and had never been in the northern Rockies, even by car. Those massive cold peaks became the positive pole drawing me to the area. A plan was formulated that would take me to the Colorado Rockies, a place I had been many years ago with my parents and brothers, and then from there, I could work west and north into territory unexplored by me before.

Long before I was making preparations to leave, I had contemplated the possibility of this trip and had sent an email to my old college roommate, Dean, who lived in Wichita, Kansas, about possibly stopping there for the night on my way west if a trip materialized.

My first impressions of Dean was upon arrival at my dorm room as a new freshman at Anderson College in Indiana. When I opened the door to the room, it was immediately obvious that my roommate had already arrived. The room was strewn with cowboy hats and boots and all manner of "Western wear." I was a bit of a hippy, with long hair and a propensity to revere all things liberal, so as I had looked upon all the symbols of conservatism, I wondered how I would be received by this "cowboy" and how we would get along. When I met Dean, however, it was an immediate, if unlikely, friendship and we had gone through our first two years of college doing everything together. Dean was dating another classmate, Judy, and together we all got along great for the rest of our time together. When I had decided to quit school after my first two years, I followed Dean out to Kansas for the summer, where we worked side by side at his father's construction company. Judy also lived out in Kansas, in Liberal, so I was also able to continue to see her through the summer. Dean had gone on to marry Judy, and they had both been living in Wichita for years.

When I had called Dean, sometime back in February, he had invited me to stay with them and told me how excited Judy was for us all to get together again after so many years.

Now that the time had come to put my plan into action, and prepare for departure, I thought a quick call out to Dean to confirm my staying was in order soon. A week before I was to leave, but before I had called, I had been looking at Facebook, and to my shock, I learned that Judy had died suddenly. Only a couple months before she had been fine. Cancer had come and taken her quickly.

I called Dean a few days before my departure, sharing my shock and sadness over the loss of our friend. Seeing Dean was out of the question in my mind, imagining the grief he must be going through and the crowd of relatives that must still be gloomily sharing it. But Dean surprised me and said he still wanted to meet up. I decided I wouldn't ask if I could stay with him, so I made a plan to meet with him and leave it up to him whether he offered a place or not. I had found an ADV inmate near Wichita, who offered space for a tent, so I contacted him, explaining the situation and telling him that if my friend offered his place I would go there instead, but I may need a spot. I'd play it by ear when that day came.

Meanwhile, business was making sure I had plenty to do before launch. A warehouse I used in Colorado to store books until needed by my distributor had announced they were no longer going to warehouse for me and gave me until August 31 to get all 30,000 books out. The change would entail moving about half of the books to my place in Florida, where I would rearrange my woodshop temporarily to accommodate the books. They would be stacked to the ceiling and the shop made virtually unusable, but once the books were there, I made plans to build a shed dedicated to storing them. About half of the books would have to be destroyed because to store and move them all would be too costly. The books had been printed traditionally, but had already been set up to be produced on-demand by my distributor when they ran out, so destroying the old books saved the cost of moving and storing them, while not impacting my ability to continue to sell them via the print-on-demand process, albeit at a higher unit cost to me. Finally, a few of my best-selling hardcover books that were stored in Colorado would be shipped out to my distributor.

I had been working hard trying to get this done well before my departure and had it set up by the end of May—plenty of time, I thought, before I was going to be on the road. It turned out, however, that the warehouse would not be ready until June 10. I was set to leave by the 8th.

I contracted a trucking company to haul the books on the tenth, but if anything went awry, I would have to deal with it by phone and from the road, something I had hoped to avoid, so I was careful to have all contingencies covered so that the move would be automated. I lined up a few men to be available in Lake Wales to unload the truck when it arrived and left money with Andrea to pay them when they finished, and cleared the needed space for the number of books I expected.

I would be leaving only a couple days before school let out for the summer. The kids were old enough by then to stay by themselves, but I sat them down and had a talk with them about their behavior while I would be gone, emphasizing the need for them to help and support their mother.

On June 6th, Tropical Storm Colin was preparing to make landfall in North Florida. Luckily, the forecast was for it to be clear of the state by the 8th, and the most I should have to worry about is localized flooding in the low areas of Florida I would be passing through in the northern sections of the state.

Normally I would have begun to put together the August/September issue of the magazine on the 15th of June, but that time I started prepping the issue the week before I left, trying to get as much done before leaving as I could. The event in southern Indiana would be featured in the issue, so as soon as I returned to Florida, I would have to put together that story in a hurry. I tried to make sure everything else possible was done before I left, so I could concentrate on that last task when I returned.

During the last couple weeks, I was checking the ADVRider Tent Space thread and making contact with the inmates that would be on my route, setting up stops on the road. By the time I was finished, I had procured ADV spots for the first night in Alabama, a night in the Ozarks, Wyoming, and Montana. Other nights I would be at friends' places or be winging it.

On 7 June, I was back and forth from the computer, wrapping up work, to the Bonneville, stuffing every thing I could conceivably need into the already bulging luggage. By the evening, as much as I could do for the next magazine issue was done, as well as the planning for the book move in my absence. When I hit the sack, all I had left out for morning was my riding clothes, having packed away everything else on the bike.

Chapter Two

Day One

North to the Appalachians

The next morning—barely, it was 2 AM—I got dressed quietly, planted a kiss on the forehead of my sleeping wife, and walked out to the bike waiting for me in the garage. I rolled the Triumph out, gave it one more check over, then broke the silence by thumbing the starter. Pulling my helmet on, I threw my leg over and rolled into the darkness of the central Florida night.

My stomach was in knots, worrying about the family and if the kids would be okay. It was worse than usual, probably largely because so many details were not quite complete with the trucking arrangements and so many other things having been done at the very last minute. I hadn't had a chance to catch my breath after the flurry of hurried final activity.

The first order of business was to get out of Florida, hopefully by daylight and before the roads were filled with traffic. Rather than taking US 27 north then cutting across to the west through the Green Swamp, I headed west toward Bartow, our county seat, knowing the highway would be devoid of vehicles and I would only have to pass through one sizeable city, Lakeland, before plunging back into the countryside. In Bartow, I turned north in the direction of Lakeland and rolled out the other side into the quiet, empty night. I passed some of the best riding roads in Florida, stretching from Dade City up to Brooksville, but they would remain unvisited this time.

I rolled through the dark and patchy fog of a cool and humid Southern night with the fecund smell of dampness in the air. A gray shape dashed across in front of the speeding bike. A small deer had taken the chance to cross just as I approached, but was in the darkness of the opposite ditch by the time I had passed it's path.

As I rode in the quiet stillness, my nerves slowly unwound, and the road and all its sensations started to take the place of my last minute worries and anxiety.

It was a long haul on 98, running over two hundred miles from where I joined it in Bartow only fifteen miles from home, to Perry, Florida, in the area known as the Big Bend. I had turned west there many times before, continuing on 98 to trace the shoreline of the Gulf of Mexico as the road mirrored the beaches, which for many miles were only a stone's throw away. But that night I was going northwest, so I turned north at Perry toward Tallahassee. At Capps the road split, with the road I was on going west into the state capitol and the other heading north and crossing Interstate 10. When I took the right north at 8 AM, the sun was rising. I was in the land of the pecan tree, passing grove after grove between fields of young cotton plants as I rode north into Georgia, while the sun was struggling with the cool pine shadows for mastery of the day. By Camilla the sun had carried the day, and I could feel a hot day in the offing.

A Break at a Muddy Southern River

As I headed northwest, the elevation inched every upward as the Gulf of Mexico, now in my wake, grew more distant and the cordillera of the Appalachians grew closer.

I was only transiting a small part of southwestern Georgia as I worked my way north and west toward Albany and then Columbus, where I crossed the Chattahoochee River into Alabama, the third state of the trip.

North and west would be my mantra for most of the outbound trip, and I continued in that direction on US 280. This was a familiar route I had taken many times before enroute to the Barber Vintage Festival in Leeds, Alabama. There was a another bonus of taking this route, and that was AL 25, just a few miles to the north of the highway before 280 plunged into the metropolis. A short hop right there would get me to 25 which would take me toward the Barber Motorsports Park, on the east side of the big city, without getting entangled in the always snarled traffic in nearby Birmingham, which was an avoid-at-all-costs kind of town as far as traffic was concerned. The state road turned and twisted, climbed, and dropped across the mountains east of the city and landed me in Leeds—a nice, if short, bit of spirited riding to end a long night and day of mostly straight highways.

Just after noon, I arrived in Birmingham and met up with a fellow ADV inmate, Ken, who had a place just across the little creek bordering Barber Motorsports Park, where a nice shaded area for my tent was waiting for me below his house at the top of the hill. It was a relief to stop after close to six hundred miles in the saddle.

My Camp at Ken's in Birmingham

Ken offered cold beer and friendly conversation. I had bought a sub for dinner, so while Ken ran up to the house for more beers, I ate my dinner. Ken returned with a couple more, which were despatched quickly as we discussed bikes and riding and made plans for another visit during the upcoming Barber Vintage Festival. The ADVRider forum and its inmates were, of course, part of the discussion, and I let Ken know about a campout coming up the next February just a few miles south of Lake Wales, hosted by a fellow inmate, which he thought he might like to come down for.

The beer went down as quickly as the long day's ride had caught up with me. Ken brought out the rye, and as a last nod to the evening, we toasted the night and our friendship.

I made a quick phone call home, after which I made sure the phone was plugged in to charge, and headed back to the tent to escape the no-see-ums that had come out and to get some sleep, with the aim for an early rising to help me get through Birmingham before traffic was stirring. I drifted off to sleep to the sound of water gliding over rocks in the stream below the hill, while the night was lit by the sporadic flashes of fireflies in the cool night air.

Chapter Three

Day Two

Ozark Bound

The temperature had dropped overnight, so I put my wool shirt on underneath my jacket for my early morning departure knowing that at speed the air would be quite chilly in contrast to my afternoon arrival the day before. My destination was the TAT-Shak, a rustic cabin maintained by another ADV inmate for fellow forum members and riders of the mostly off-road Trans-America Trail, which was yards away in the Ozark woods, running from Tellico Plains, Tennessee, in the east to the southwestern Oregon coast in the west.

I had reluctantly planned on jumping on the Interstate for a little while just to get past the sprawl and downtown of Birmingham, but I missed the turn Ken had told me about. Instead, I shot through early morning downtown Birmingham, where a few wrong turns slowed me down. But I got through before the city had awakened and sailed out the northwestern edge, headed for the flat delta areas of Mississippi and Arkansas, and leaving the slowly diminishing southwestern Appalachian foothills behind me as the ribbon of highway rose and fell in decreasingly and almost imperceptible increments.

The Foothills Dissipate as I Leave the Appalachians Behind

Eventually, I found my way onto the Interstate for a short distance northwest, then turned off onto a smaller US highway, which ran more westerly into Mississippi. That route allowed me to miss the city of Tupelo and offered expansive views of cotton fields on all sides.

Before Clarksdale, I opted for a little squiggly gray line, MS 316, to connect with my next route north. Pear Orchard Road, as 316 was also known as, would pass through the tiny settlement of Jonestown, a throwback to the days of sharecroppers and Jim Crow nestled in the midst of the cotton fields in which the residents worked.

Although I was flying across the flat, rich bottomlands of the Mississippi Delta, covered in the muds left behind by millenniums of the great river's floods, the road swept left and right in surprisingly tight curves. Along with the deposits of soil, the river had left swirling narrow channels and creeks and skinny oxbows among the flats, and the narrow road snaked its way around these obstacles providing an exercise in riding curves not often found out of the mountains, albeit with no corresponding rise or fall in altitude, pegged at a steady 170 feet above sea level. The short diversion ended at US 49, where I turned north toward the bridge that would carry me across the Mississippi River and into Arkansas and the West, my second only bike excursion beyond that wide and muddy divider.

It was a short ride on a wide four lane divided highway to where 61 continued north and 49 went northwest, aiming for the big river. I veered northwest and soon was over the levee and approaching the bridge, guarded on the northeast side by the looming Isle of Capri Casino.

I approached the steel girder bridge up a long ascending ramp and was quickly above the river. At the top of the ascent and very middle of the girder span, high above the wide river, was a traffic light allowing only one lane of traffic to pass over at a time. I got the red and sat above the river with the delta spread out to the horizon in every direction below me. I could feel the bridge tremble and bounce as vehicles zipped past me bound for Mississippi. I looked south and north at the cream-in-coffee colored river far below, while tugs and their tows worked their way up against the slow but incessant and powerful current.

On the western side of the Mississippi, I left the balsam smell of the pine forests of the Southeast and rolled across farmland that could have been transplanted there from northern Indiana. The west side of the river had a decidedly deciduous flavor.

The highway continued west around the south end of an isolated island of bumpy hills stretched from the north-northwest, a scrap of the Ozarks flung away from the main group in the west, pointing like a finger toward the bridge with Helena, Arkansas, planted on its southeastern tip. Once past this Delta anomaly, the road turned north, and I followed it to a small state road that trended more westerly on its way predominantly northward, while 49 drifted on but trending toward the east. In a few more miles I jumped on a minor east-west route for the run west almost to Interstate-like US 167, which poured itself into Little Rock—another metropolis avoided. I hopped north again to US 64, which took me most of the rest of the way west for the day.

At Conway, the road mirrored the Interstate to the north and the Arkansas River to the south until I arrived at Atkins. I headed north, crossing I-40 again, away from the valley, while the altimeter started to rise again as I approached the Ozark Mountains. I turned onto the famous scenic AR 7 and toward the TAT-Shak. Closing in, I turned left onto Old Highway 7, the road the shack's address was on, which suddenly became gravel.

I figured I must be getting close and kept one eye on the road, my hand away from the front brake lever, and the other eye on the GPS until it said I had "arrived." All I saw was shadowy forest lining each side of the track. On my left was a closed and locked gate with a tractor parked beside it. "Could that be the drive to the Shak? Well, if it was, there was no getting myself and the bike past that gate."

I rode farther, still seeing no signs of any structure of any kind or even another dirt track running into the woods. I looked at my list of ADV contacts I had quickly created before I left, and of course, my TAT-Shack host was the only one that was not jotted down. Besides, I had no signal at all on my cell phone, and it was getting late in the afternoon. Deer would become a concern if I did not find the Shak very soon.

I abandoned the GPS and tried to remember the Google Map image with the red marker showing the location that I had studied so many times before on my computer at home. I rode back to Highway 7, turned south, then turned west where another small, but paved, road headed toward Hagerville, while keeping my eyes peeled for signs of the Shak in the area that I thought I recalled from my mental picture. I could have sworn it should have been there, somewhere past the curve that met up with the Ozark National Forest, but I saw nothing. I cursed myself for not having the forethought to mark it down on my road map.

The sun was dipping low toward the horizon, and the forest was already in twilight beneath the trees' dark branches. I headed back south again on 7, hoping to pick up a cell signal so I could get on Google Maps for another look for the location of the Shak. Racing the fading light, it wasn't until I got back to I-40 that a signal appeared. I pulled into a Best Western motel parking lot to take a look.

I had been so close, having ridden the gravel at the wrong end of Old Highway 7 and having passed the other end on the side road a couple times, just east of Big Piney Creek. By the time I stopped to check, however, darkness was almost upon me. I knew I'd be dodging deer by the time I got even close to the Shak if I tried to find it again, although by then I knew where it was. I admitted defeat for that day and booked a room at the motel.

It was nice to have a clean bed and air-conditioning, even if it did break the bank, but having to haul all the gear from the bike into the room was an ordeal that I would not have had to endure if I had found the Shak or camped out. At least the bike was just outside the window, so I could easily check on it if need be. A half hour after I had begun, the bike stood nude on its center stand, devoid of any scrap of luggage that might be a temptation to any passing thieves.

In the morning I could take advantage of a free breakfast, which was added justification for my stay, after I had lived on only handfuls of peanuts and breakfast bars since my sub the night before at Ken's.

I touched base with home and related the story of my day and my disappointment at having to spend so much money on a motel room on only my second night out. I also called

Dean, in anticipation of seeing him the following day in Wichita, and making sure he was still intent on meeting.

Earlier in the day I had called my shipper about the books to be moved from Colorado and was relieved to find out that they had talked to the warehouse guy in Fort Collins and had worked out all the details, and all was set for the move on Friday. I could sleep easier knowing that was organized and would be one less thing to stress about on this ride west meant to distance myself from worry.

Chapter Four

Day Three

A Bittersweet Reunion

I got up at 5 AM the next morning and had a solid meal and coffee at the breakfast bar. In spite of my early rising, it was 7 by the time I'd finished breakfast and all the bags I had removed the night before were resituated on the bike. A few years ago I had wandered around in the Ozarks in Arkansas and southern Missouri, so this morning I decided to go a bit out of my way and head west through the Ouachitas, instead.

The Ouachitas ranged from Little Rock along the south side of the Arkansas River and westward into Oklahoma, where the range dissolved into the interminable grasslands of the Midwestern prairies. I would leave the Ozarks behind, lying on the north side of the river and running west toward

Fort Smith, and cross the wide green valley of the Arkansas River, which divided the companion ranges.

Soon after crossing the river, I headed south on AR 7, which I had thought ran together with AR 28. I saw a sign for AR 28, pointing right and so turned that way. My map had 7 and 28 marked as one road heading down to Rover, where I wanted to pick up AR 27, another designated scenic highway, but because of scale I had missed that the roads split with 28 going southwest, before rejoining 7 miles south of where it had left after running well out of the way. I knew something was wrong as I rode in seemingly the wrong direction, but when the road intersected another state road, I saw a sign to Rover. Turning right got me back on track. Being lost for a while was actually pleasant and finally being on track I could enjoy the ride as the road passed through gently rolling terrain tucked between ranges of low mountains to the north and south.

The Blue Ridge-Like Ouchitas

At Rover I turned south and rode up and over Blue Ouachita Mountain and caught AR 88 west at Washita, following the blue map squiggle of the Ouachita River to Mena and past Queen Wilhelmena State Park where it was named Talimena Trail. The route continued west into Oklahoma, on through

Stair Mountain National Recreation Area. I had never thought of Oklahoma as being mountainous, let alone hilly, but the area surprised me. Although the peaks were not much over 2,600 feet, they fell off sharply to the valleys as I rode the ridge on a Cherohala-like parkway, and the views were very reminiscent of the Blue Ridge I had traveled so many times before, but with wider sweeping curves. The curves were signed for a suggested 45 mph but suitable for a spirited 65 mph, in defiance of the posted 55 mpg maximum speed limit.

Exiting the mountains, I continued west in continually flatter terrain, joining a bigger US highway at Hartshorne, and continuing west to Calvin. There the route split off to run southwest while I stayed on the main road running northwest, to Seminole, then turning northward again as straight as an arrow, shooting between Oklahoma City and Tulsa.

The terrain had completely flattened out by the time I was west of Tulsa, and oil wells appeared everywhere. The wells would accompany me all the way to the foothills of the Rockies as would the endless fields of wheat.

It had been warm all day, but the heat had increased dramatically since leaving Talimena, and a strong wind began to blow from the southwest as I approached Kansas. It was sweltering, and the wind did nothing to relieve the heat.

Once past I-44 the highway changed names but continued as a straight line heading north. When it jumped east a few miles, T-ing at a cross road, I turned left, instead. I resumed my northbound transit of the state just a few miles west of where I had turned. That route would take me all the way into Winfield, Kansas. Entering Kansas, huge electricity generating windmills joined the oil pumps among the prairie grasses.

The day was bittersweet for me. I was approaching a rendezvous with Dean, my old college roommate and now heart-broken friend. Dean's house was full of grieving family, so we had decided to meet up outside Wichita and have dinner together at least. As I reached Winfield, Kansas, I stopped for some ice tea to replace some of the moisture pulled from my body by the unrelenting heat and called him, making plans to meet up at a Pizza Hut in Goddard. While stopped, I also returned a missed call from my shipping company. The books had been picked up, and it was time for payment. I dug out my business debit card and gave the company the information they needed. That was progress at least, and while I had to cough up a one-time payment of thousands of dollars, I no longer would have to worry about paying the several hundred dollars a month just to store the books in Colorado. Hanging up the phone, another weight was lifted from my shoulders.

I wound my way around Wichita heading west, then north, and finally via a small unnamed gray map line that continued from Viola up to US 54.

It was nice to see Dean after twenty-four years, in spite of the circumstances, and I am sure it did him good to have a break away from his house that was surely filled with gloom. We shared a meal and caught up with each other. I asked about Dean's sister, Chris, who I had been in love with back when I lived in Kansas, in spite of the unfortunate and insurmountable obstacle of her being married to someone else at the time. Dean suggested calling her while we were together, but as the conversation twisted one way and another and in and out of different topics the idea was forgotten. It was just as well; one bittersweet moment at a time was enough. Dinner over, Dean insisted on picking up the tab. As we were heading outside to go, we promised to stay in better touch and not let another twenty-four years pass without seeing each other again. I climbed on the Bonnie and fired it up and waved goodbye as Dean left for home and his house full of mourners.

Dean had mentioned that if his place was not completely filled up with guests he would have offered me a place to stay, but there was not a square foot of space left. I considered the ADV inmates's offer, but it was in the opposite direction from where I was headed and not very close to Goddard.

Although it was late afternoon, I still had a couple hours of light left, so I thought I would make the best of it and try to make some westing before night fell completely. I'd take my chances on a camping spot. I thought, if nothing else, I could find a windbreak somewhere like I used to hunt in, duck into some place my tent and bike would not be seen, and hunker down for the night. I had a spot in the back of my mind that I had thought I might stop at for the night, if I got that far. I had seen it on Google Maps before I left home, near Dodge City, a little boat ramp area on a lake that offered free camping, but by the time I left Dean I could see I was not going to get that far without at least an hour or two riding in the dark across the prairie that was overpopulated by deer. However, Dean had mentioned during dinner that he thought that there was a small park on the side of the road in Pratt, the same town where we had lived and worked together back in 1978, and he thought he also remembered another roadside park on the highway even before there at Kingman.

Soon, I realized my time estimate on sunset was way off. Within thirty minutes, I entered Kingman as the sun was settling on the horizon, well before Pratt. Just as I entered the small farming town, I spotted a sign for Champlin Park on the right and pulled in. It was a tiny wayside park and picnic area. A sign said, "Traveling Campers Allowed, Must Have Permit." By then it was almost dark, and I wondered how in the world I could get a permit this late in the day. I rode a mile or so to the next gas station to ask about it, where I saw a state trooper just about to leave. I waved him down and asked him about the park and the possibility of camping there. He called his local counterpart and obtained permission for me, agreeing that my decision to stop before nightfall was wise because "We have way too many deer in Kansas."

I returned to the park and pitched the tent next to a recently cut field of wheat under the outstretched arms of a tree. The heat had not relented with sunset, and in my tent I sweltered in the warm night air as I listened to trucks rumble loudly by on the highway, just a hundred yards away, and tried to fall asleep.

Chapter Five

Day Four

The Great Plains to the Edge of the Rockies

The next morning, I got packed early and back on the road by 6 AM. I headed west on the unbending highway, soon passing though the little town of Pratt, where I had worked with Dean in the Kansas summer heat after my second year at Anderson College, becoming part of his family and forging our friendship forever. I stopped for gas next to the Sonic drive-in we used to cruise through on Saturday nights in my hopped-up little 1967 Datsun Roadster, doing our best to impress the local girls. The highway ran straight between endless fields of wheat. As I headed west, oil wells accompanied me, bobbing their heads here and there across the plains, busy feeding on the black oil among the wheat and prairie grasses.

At Mullinville, 54 took a turn to the southwest. I turned off, veering west then northwest toward Dodge City, leaving 54 traveling on without me, and headed on toward the famous Old West town.

The Bobbing Wells are Bigger than They Seem from the Highway

As I turned off, I immediately passed through the little village of Mullinville. As I rode out the far side I could not help but notice the huge field of hundreds of metal sculptures on the north side of the highway, just as the village gave way to the plains.

Feet from the road were rustic and rusty metal sculptures, many of which had obvious political meanings. The sculptures were mounted on rusting poles up to twenty feet high, creating a forest of metal and moving shapes. One had the name *Hillary* painted across it and a swastika with a woman's profile above; another labelled *Bailiff* depicted a man holding a beer mug with a hammer and sickle protruding from his head. The sculptor didn't play political party favorites, and ridiculous caricatures of Al Gore and Laura Bush stood side by side above the grass. Later, I learned the menagerie was the creation of folk artist M. T. Liggett (the M. T. stood for "Moon Tosser"), who lived in Mullinville, and whose works could be seen not only along

Route 400, but in at least one museum, the Folk Art Museum in Lucas, Kansas. He'd been quoted as saying, "If you like it, that's fine. If you don't, I don't care."

"Moon Tosser's" Field of Metal Political Statements

I stopped for a break, coffee, and a breakfast burrito in Dodge, spending less than two dollars and staying true to my low cost traveling plan.

By western Kansas, the Arkansas River, which had been a mighty river cutting Arkansas into a northern and southern half as it rolled toward the Mississippi, had become a small stream, only hinted at by the green of trees drawing moisture from it along its path. At the Colorado border it was a thin ribbon winding its way beside the highway.

I followed the Arkansas into the high plains of Colorado, the stream an emerald vein stitched into the gold carpeting of Colorado. As I travelled farther west into Colorado, the gold of wheat was replaced by the gold of prairie grasses.

US 400, which I had been following for 175 miles up the endless inclined plane of the Great Plains, was renamed US 50 at Granada, but didn't vary from the track west began by its predecessor. I stopped for fuel near Lamar, where across the highway was a huge field covered with wind generator blades, dwarfing the passing long-haul trucks. Hundreds of blades lay prone, waiting to be assembled onto their hubs, fitted to turbines, and hauled aloft onto towers in order to catch the prairie winds and produce electricity. Their size was truly amazing seen up close instead of miles away when they had been put to work on a wind farm. A truck and trailer measuring some seventy-five feet might span less than half of one blade's length.

Windmill Blades Waiting for Installation

Leaving Lamar, I soon turned north, leaving the diminutive Arkansas River to wander on toward the west, while I headed toward Kit Carson, sitting in an ocean of grasses in the perpetually blowing prairie wind.

The Kit Carson Museum on the High Plains Approach to Denver

I made a short stop at the Kit Carson Museum to learn a little about prairie life in the 1800s and to talk to the museum attendant about a book I had previously republished, *The Life of Kit Carson* by Edward Ellis, that was originally published in the late 1800s. We discussed the book and I made plans to send a review copy to her when I returned home.

At Kit Carson the highway made a northwestward bend toward Denver, and I followed it as far as Limon. I had not brought an extra quart of engine oil with me, so I stopped there at an auto parts store to pick one up, just in case. The young man behind the counter had noticed my ADV sticker on the Bonneville. He was an "inmate," too and as I left said it was cool that I was "rockin' the ADV."

From Limon, I headed west in an effort to avoid Denver, if at all possible. Among the wide grasslands I could imagine Wyeth's Christina laying in the fields with the rustic farm house and barn on the hilltop. Although in reality the scene was of a place far away in the Northeast in Maine, the rolling grasses and the treeless horizon vibrated sympathetically with the land of the high plains. I tried to imagine the area centuries before without the ribbons of highways crossing it and being covered horizon to horizon with bison.

Soon, I got my first view of the Rockies jutting abruptly above the horizon, with Pikes Peak to the southwest, still blanketed by snow at its peak.

At Kiowa I stopped for fuel. The Bonnie had never run so many miles without sputtering out of fuel—over 162 miles. The altitude combined with my fuel injection was working its magic and giving me much higher mpgs than usual. At lower elevations my low fuel warning light had been blinking on after 110 miles, but now it stayed unlit until 130.

I struck up a conversation with a fellow traveler at the station, during which my mind was eased by learning that I could bypass the thick of Denver traffic and skirt most of the metropolitan area on my way into Littleton.

Crossing I-25, the highway I was on connected with US 85 which ran all the way into Littleton, on the southwest side of the big city, more or less where I was aiming to stay for the night. Approaching Littleton just as the traffic snarl was getting crazy, I stopped to check the final directions. My stand-alone GPS had packed it in the day before, so I hooked my smart phone up to the bike's USB port and used the CoPilot app to find my destination off an exit west on CO 470, the southern loop bypass around Denver. I hopped onto the bypass and took it west just two exits, turned south, then right onto Deer Creek Canyon Road, heading southwest and away from the city. The route passed between red rock formations standing like sentinels guarding the canyon entrance, up a narrow road filled with bicyclists. Within a few miles, I found the side road I was looking for and turned off toward the campground where I was going to be staying.

After a mile or two of gravel, the gates of Mountain Air Ranch appeared. I've never been too body-ashamed, and Mountain Air was a nudist resort, just at the right place for my stop that day, that offered tent camping space. "Why not?" I thought. I missed out on experiencing such a place the year before in Canada, but now could check it out. There would be showers and a pool to enjoy for the rest of the hot afternoon; a kitchen set aside for the campers' use, making cooking an easy affair instead of having to pull out my stove and gas bottles; and getting dressed in the morning would be much easier being able to just step outside, rather than pulling everything back on in the cramped seven-by-seven foot tent that only had an interior height about as high as my waist.

We all being born naked, I never could see the logic in why society teaches us to be ashamed of our bodies, or that it is sinful for anyone to see them. How could being seen as we really are somehow be wrong? I was putting into practice what I believed but couldn't normally do because of the general unacceptance of society.

After pitching the tent, I decided to follow the maxim "When in Rome do as the Romans" and divested myself of my heavy riding clothes. The relief from the heat was instant. I shyly made friends with my neighboring tent campers when I saw them struggling with tent poles and flapping fabric. It had been a while since they had pitched it, and the correct method had been forgotten. Together we got the tent up, and I was rewarded with a cold beer that went down easily after a day in the saddle in what must have been 100 degrees almost the entire day. As I went back to my tent, my neighbor called out, "Help yourself; there are more in the cooler!"

My Camp at Mountain Air Ranch

I decided to go all in and explore the place. I headed up to the outside showers on the edge of camp and washed miles of road grime from my naked body. Then I walked up to the pool area, where I bought three bottles of water, downing them almost instantly. I picked a lounge chair near the pool and had just sat down when a distractingly beautiful

Asian-American woman came over to introduce herself and welcome me to the resort. She stood clothed in only the warm afternoon sunshine while she introduced herself then sat down on the foot of the lounger to chat. I found it a bit nerve-wracking at first but also liberating talking together this way, as if it was the most natural thing in the world, which actually it was.

In a while the nudist woman returned to her friends gathered nearby. I went back to the camping area as the afternoon waned, feeling a bit more comfortable in my skin.

Gathering my dinner stuff, I walked over to the kitchen, where I plugged in the phone, GoPro, and GoPro remote. I had the building to myself. I threw some spam on the communal stove for dinner then sat down at a table to eat while my electronics charged.

Back at camp, I enjoyed the rest of the day clothes-free as the sun settled behind the mountains, and the canyon I was in was clothed in increasing darkness. The air cooled quickly, with my camp site at over 6,000 feet in altitude, promising a comfortable night, a welcome relief after the sweat and noise of the night before.

I had lost my cell signal the moment I had entered the canyon, but before I went to sleep I sent a text message home, thinking if I did not get a signal here, then as soon as I emerged from the canyon in the morning it would be sent out. It was the best I could do.

Chapter Six

Day Five

Over the Continental Divide

I woke up to a chilly morning and mule deer walking across the campground fifty feet from my tent. The canyon was still in shadow, and my naked body was covered in chill bumps as I went up to the kitchen to make coffee and oatmeal, while checking to make sure I hadn't left anything plugged in that I had charged in there the day before. By the time I had finished breakfast, my tent was mostly free of dew, so I rolled it up and climbed back into my gear—a strange sensation after going without any clothes all the previous afternoon.

As I left, I clicked on my helmet-mounted GoPro in hopes of capturing some of the beauty surrounding Deer Creek Canyon Road, which I had viewed on the way in the day before. Unfortunately, going downhill out of the canyon the views were not as spectacular as they had been coming the other way.

I was going to wing it, hoping to find a place to camp along the way, having not found any suitable places in advance. I made vague plans to head south then west across Colorado, before making my way to the northwest corner of the state, stopping "somewhere." In the West there was an abundance of National Forests and Parks, and I hoped that finding a camping place would not be too difficult, and if need be I ought to be able to get far enough off the road to stealth camp.

I made my way back to US 85 south, leaving Littleton and Denver behind me. US 24 promised to move me west across the state and away from Colorado Springs, and shooting south out of the Denver area would get me to it, but that route would dump me onto it east of Colorado Springs. I would then have to negotiate that city to get back on the west side of Interstate 25, where I already was, and I had no desire to see Colorado from an Interstate highway. On my map, I spied another little wiggly gray line that connected to US 24 at Woodland Park from Sedalia and US 85. It looked just the thing to bypass Colorado Springs and put me on the desired highway, well into the Colorado countryside near Pike's Peak and away from any large cities.

15% Grade and Gravel on CO 67

I turned right onto my bypass and started a downward ride which quickly turned to gravel. The road dropped and dropped until a final plunge of a 15% grade plunged me into a valley on the back side of the most eastern range of the Rockies. Some twenty-two miles later the gravel ended. The rest of the way into Woodland Park was on pavement. I had been hoping to ride some dirt out West, and I accidentally had my first taste of it. The new Continentals TKC 70s did well, with no squirmy feeling at all on the gravel. I was impressed.

Arriving at the junction with US 24, I pulled over to send the kids text messages, which I tried to do fairly regularly so they would know they were on my mind and to include them a little in my journey. Somewhere along the way that morning my text from the night before had been sent.

I called Andrea to let her know I would most likely not have a signal most of the time, so if she did not hear from me that night she should not assume there was trouble.

A Spectacular View of Pike's Peak

Before rolling away, I took the time to take a photo of Pike's Peak towering overhead, south of the highway and sent it along with the text messages to the kids.

In spite of my breakfast bar and coffee that morning at the camp, I was getting hungry. Just before arriving in Johnson City, I caught sight of a little coffee and pie shop, Costello Street Coffee Shop, and pulled in. The place was a little high-end compared to my tea bag coffee, with varieties of gourmet blends available. The blueberry pie looked too good to resist, so I ordered a slice and a cup of coffee, then stepped out onto the shady patio to enjoy my splurge. The coffee and pie was delicious and from my relaxing spot I could check the phone's GPS and consider routes for the day.

Out of Woodland Park, I had started looking for opportunities to made some miles to the northwest. At Johnson Village, the highway I was on swooped north toward I-70, but I wanted to avoid the Interstate. As I gazed at the map, I spied a road cutting northwest toward Aspen that would intersect I-70 far west of where the other route would. It would not merge with I-70 as 24 did, but would cross it and join another small highway heading west at Glenwood Springs. That route would connect to another small road heading north at Rifle, and another at Meeker. From there the road headed into the northwestern corner of the state.

On the High Plains Heading to Independence Pass

It had been quite cold in the night, so I had put my wool shirt on beneath my riding jacket that morning. The day still had not warmed much, but when I turned onto my next road rain was threatening, so I added my rain and thermal liners to my jacket. As the road climbed toward Aspen, the heated grips became lifesavers and would stay on until I left the Rockies days later. The cold was quite a contrast to the day before.

I didn't know then that I was taking Independence Pass across the mountains, the highest paved pass that crossed the Continental Divide. The road wound ever higher as I approached the 12,093 foot pass to the west of Colorado's highest peak, Mount Elbert, another 2,347 feet above me. Rain, sleet, and then snow streaked my visor. Stopping at the top, I climbed off to walk a bit in the snow, still covering the mountains at that altitude. If I had headed that way too much earlier in the year I would have been turned back. The pass had not opened until May 26, and it was only June 12.

The Snow Field on Top of Independence Pass

I continued toward Aspen, accompanied all the way by a cold rain. In Aspen, when the sun finally appeared, deer wandered around the sidewalks mixed in with early tourists.

Leaving Aspen, the rain began fitfully again. It continued as I crossed I-70, where I followed a small highway on the its north side until Rifle, where the off-and-on rain stopped and the sun reappeared.

I turned north toward Meeker. From there, my route trended west along the valley of the White River, clinging first to one sage brush-covered valley wall, then the other, as open range whizzed by.

Approaching Rangely, the river and highway made an abrupt turn to the south. It was already late afternoon. I was looking for a place to camp when I passed a reservoir on my right, with a park nestled against its shores. There was a swimming hole, boat ramp, and picnic areas, but no obvious sign of camping spots. I decided to camp there anyway, if something did not turn up by Rangely, a few miles ahead.

I continued west into town, where I found a gas station and refueled. I usually kept a little cash on me and the rest stowed away safely on the bike, but I had run out of the on-hand cash. I reached into my tank bag, where I had stashed my main wad of cash only to find it missing. I started to panic, my mind racing to think of any possible places I could have dropped it or where someone would have had the opportunity to take it. I came up with nothing. I considered what I was going to do, then I patted my left jacket pocket and felt the money clip and lump of bills. What a relief. I must have needed cash back at the pie shop and stuck it in my pocket then.

I calmed myself down and walked in to ask the attendant if she knew of a place I could camp in the area. The only place she knew of was back at Kenney Reservoir, which confirmed my suspicions, so I turned around to head back.

Before leaving town, I stopped in at a tavern. It appeared to be the only place open beside the gas station. I had a nice cold craft beer, at a steep price, as an end-of-the-day reward. My thirst quenched and ready to return to the quiet of the countryside, I retraced my route back to the campground.

The Campground at Kenney Reservoir

Back at the reservoir, adjacent to the roped-off swimming area, I found an honor system drop box. The cost was just five dollars; my "senior" status giving me a discount. There was a slot in the box, so I reached into my pocket for a five. I didn't have one. The next denomination I had was a ten, and I didn't want to part with it unnecessarily. The best I could do was three ones. I thought, "How would they ever know it was me who shorted them." Guiltily, I dropped in my three dollar bills. About the time they left my hand, I realized they were not supposed go in the slot alone, but belonged in an envelope provided there, with places for my name, address, and tag number. If I didn't fill in the envelope and place the little tear-off tag on the pole by my site and someone checked, I would be busted, and if they opened my envelope and found no money in it I would be busted. It served me right, trying to be cheap in the first place. I filled out an envelope and inserted my ten, tore off the tab, and dropped in the envelope. It cost me thirteen dollars, instead of five, but it was still a bargain, and I felt better having paid the full amount.

I had arrived about eight o'clock, while the sun was just kissing the top of the ridge across the lake and about to leave me in shadow. I set up as its disk hid behind the far mountain and watched the world around me darken with the coming night, while the shadows climbed the hills on the eastern side of the lake.

As night progressed I ate my evening meal consisting of peanuts, a breakfast bar, and a bottle of water.

There were only two other campers there with plenty of spaces between, so no one felt crowded. I talked a little to my closest neighbor, a German-American in a Land Rover. He had been roaming Colorado trying to travel only on gravel roads as much as possible. The other camper was a couple in a pop-up Volkswagen Van. I left them to their solitude.

There would be no calls home tonight because, as predicted, I had no signal. I was glad I had warned Andrea that might happen.

I climbed into the tent as the wind came up and darkness fell. The tent whipped violently as the wind poured down from the hillsides, but once the valley was clothed in complete darkness the wind fell off and I went to sleep.

Chapter Seven

Day Six

Flaming Gorge and a Wild Ride into Jackson

Morning Sunlight Illuminating the Hills across Kenney Reservoir

I awoke to sunshine creeping down the face of the hills on the far side of the reservoir and a dry tent, there not having been any dew the night before. It would be nice to put it away dry for once, but as I started to take it down, a little stray cloud passed overhead and rain sprinkled down, while I frantically tried to get the tent rolled up and put away before it was soaked. Semi-dry would have to do.

Entering a New State

I reversed my track from the past afternoon, past the tavern and gas station and toward Dinosaur and the Utah border, just thirty miles away. The smell of sage permeated the morning air as I crossed the White River west of Rangely, where the route veered northwest into Dinosaur, just east of the Colorado/Utah line. East of there, a skinny, squiggly green line on the map ran into the extreme northwestern corner of the state to Dinosaur National Monument in the Uinta Mountains—shaped like a westward flying goose, or perhaps more aptly a pterodactyl, with wings in the Green and Yampa River Canyons and a long outstretched neck and head poking into neighboring Utah, where the two rivers joined and ran west toward Jensen, Utah. During the Jurassic period, unlucky dinosaurs were swept down river and were deposited at the confluence, where they were buried in sediment, until millions of years later erosion uncovered them, and much later, man found them. Other wonders there are petroglyphs made by the people of the prehistoric Fremont Culture a thousand years ago.

I debated making a quick stop, but the weather looked fickle, and I was to meet Brent and Julie in Jackson that afternoon and thought the limited time I could devote to this park would not do it justice. So, instead, I turned west into Utah, leaving Dinosaur until next time.

Flaming Gorge

In less than an hour I was in Vernal, Utah, a place a friend of mine had sung the praises of to me recently. Passing through town, I wondered what he was so charmed with, but as I made my way north, climbing toward Wyoming, a landscape emerged that was breathtaking, filled with red rock cliffs and a curving road winding its way past Red Canyon and the lake formed by damming the Green River at Flaming Gorge Dam. I turned before the dam and followed the canyon's contours west and then north toward Manila, then made another turn northwest for the run the rest of the way out of the state. The scenery was spectacular as I entered the southwest corner of Wyoming and headed north.

Thunderstorms had been threatening all day. As I kept rolling toward Jackson, I ran in and out of them. Lightning was shooting down from the darkening cloud bottoms overhead and rain and pea-sized hail took turns pelting me off and on.

Crossing yet another Interstate, I caught a shortcut over to US 189, which I would be following the rest of the way into Jackson, my stop for the night. I was running in a wide valley of rolling hills and converging with the Wind River Range, which was growing by the minute on my right, with its snow-capped peaks above the valley. On my left the Tetons were angling toward me as the valley narrowed and the two ranges met up at Gros Ventre Wilderness.

Approaching the head of the valley, heavy black clouds hung over the road ahead, discharging rain and innumerable lightning strikes to the world below, along with hail. As the darkness grew, the temperatures dropped. I stopped at a gas station and diner at Daniel to fill the bike and have some hot coffee and an appetizer of some sort, before tackling what lay ahead, hoping I might get a break and a chance to shoot though unscathed if I gave it some time and watched for my chance.

Bacon-Wrapped Stuffed Jalapeños at Daniel Junction

In Daniel's Junction Food Mart, I sipped my coffee as my hands slowly warmed, and I nibbled on some fantastic stuffed jalapeños wrapped with bacon and grilled. As I relaxed, all of a sudden the place was filled with a clattering noise. The clouds had let loose their load of hail on the roof, followed by wet snow. A minute later, there was another loud swoosh and a scraping sound from the roof as the load of hail and snow let go and cascaded down off the eaves and past the restaurant windows, burying everything in their way. As quickly as it had come, it was over. I walked out to see snow piled up in banks under the eaves and my bike's saddle covered in snow, with BBs of hail peppered throughout it.

Snow and Hail Left Behind by the Storm

I brushed off my saddle and climbed back on board, backing away from the restaurant, nicking it into first, and rolling back onto the northbound road toward the dark clouds and lightning strikes. Rain was on and off all the way, but I managed to miss the very worst of the lightning as I crossed over the ridges, where the two ranges had crashed into each other, and shot into "the hole," carved between the towering peaks by the Snake River.

Rain Ahead on the Wind River Range

The plan in Jackson was to meet up with Brent "Capt. Crash" Allen, who had written the first two books under my Road Dog imprint, and his wife, Julie. From there we planned to ride north together for a couple days. I found them at a Motel 6 as I entered Jackson.

We all decided we had enough saddle time that day. With the skies more or less cleared, we set off on foot for Bubba's, a barbecue joint that had been recommended to Brent by a friend. Julie did the navigating with her phone GPS, while Brent and I followed her lead through town. Returning to the motel after having the first full dinner in many days, I left them back at their room after having made plans to meet up in the morning, and headed off to Ed's place, another ADV inmate, not far away and inside town. After setting up my tent on his front lawn, Ed and I chatted bikes and travel while I enjoyed a beer he graciously offered as he showed me where I could plug in and recharge and where I could clean up and shower if I wished to.

There was another bike parked out front, a Buell. Ed told me it belonged to a couple also staying there that night. They were a young Dutch guy and an Italian-American girl, who had left one bike behind that day to ride two-up to

Yellowstone. It was getting late, but they had planned to be back that evening.

With no sign of the couple at nightfall, I hit the hay but later woke up to the sound of people talking in quiet tones outside. I had to pee, so I donned some clothes quickly, climbed out of the tent, and found them in the area outside the bathroom. We introduced ourselves and chatted a little about our plans. They had ridden up the Pacific Coast Highway from California to the Pacific Northwest, then crossed east toward Jackson. They had planned to head to Alaska but realized they were too late in the season to make it there and back, so had ended up in Jackson and were going to go to Utah. Having gotten to know my neighbors a little, I ambled back to my tent and slept the rest of the night undisturbed.

Chapter Eight

Day Seven

The Grand Tetons and North to Butte

Before eight, I had met up with Brent and Julie, and we were heading north out of Jackson. The drive out was spectacular as the first rays of the morning sun were peeping over the Wind River Range and lighting the tops of the Tetons on our left. The Tetons leaped almost surrealistically up, directly from the flat bottom of the "hole" with virtually no transition.

I wanted to get a still shot of the Tetons with my bike in the foreground, but Brent and Julie, with their photographer free to shoot "from the hip" on the pillion as they rode, kept riding. I saw a line of cars stopped ahead. Figuring it was my last chance for the photo and a handy place to stop, I pulled over, thinking surely I would soon be missed by the pair disappearing into the distance.

The Grand Tetons on My Left…

As I dismounted, I found out why all the cars had stopped as I glanced to the east and saw a small herd of bison grazing in the flat valley below the Wind River peaks. I spun around and got my photo of the Tetons and then a bonus shot of the bison with my telephoto lens before heading north again in hopes of catching my riding partners soon. I rode for a while then stopped to call them. They had stopped just past the toll gate at the entrance of Teton Park Road.

…and Bison and the Wind River Range on My Right

At the gate, I was astonished at the cost of admission—fifty dollars. I asked if they had a pass for all the National Parks and what that would cost, as I knew I would be passing through at least two more US National Parks. That turned out to be $80, a better deal, so I reluctantly pried the money from my pocket, and handed it to the attendant, but not until I had asked if there was a "senior discount" (not until age 67!).

I found Brent and Julie at the lay-by and explained why I had stopped. We agreed on signals in case I wanted to do some more photography.

We rode through the park, with the towering peaks always overhead on our left, and exited at the north end, almost instantly entering Yellowstone National Park.

Old Faithful with the Crowd of Tourists Carefully Cropped Out

We took the west loop and stopped at the visitor center at Old Faithful, where I successfully managed to get all my souvenir buying for my wife and kids out of the way. The geysers were impressive, but so many people crowded in the park and the shopping mall feel of the two huge shops ruined it for me and diminished the views. I think if one stopped in Yellowstone and camped for a few days, with some hikes out away from the throngs of tourists, it might fare much better as a scenic place. We did manage to see many more geysers with fewer people surrounding them and even some more bison, so the ride was pleasant, if not spectacular.

We worked our way around the west side of the park among the tourist cars and RVs and headed out the northwest corner into Montana, bound, eventually, for Glacier National Park on the Canadian border.

Rain clouds had threatened all day, and we had rain from time to time until we reached the state line, when the sun finally reappeared.

The mountains kept coming as we rode, with snow-frosted peaks in sight almost all day. As we continued, the hills on each side of the Madison River Valley, through which we were riding, were shorter and covered in grasses all the way to their tops, looking like a rolling prairie brought to a hilly extreme.

Pronghorn antelope were grazing on the side of the hills, while a wicked wind was blowing from the west, making our bikes heel over as if we were in a turn, as we made our way north. The wind was amazingly strong, and the gusts made it hard to stay on the road. We were running at about eighty mph, and the combination of speed and wind made for a very tiring day. It had remained cold all day, and I was dressed in everything I had, with the heated grips going all day.

We had decided Butte was a logical stopping place for the night. With the cold expected to be close to freezing after the day's wind and resulting exhaustion, I almost gave up on the idea of tent camping, but the Butte KOA was only $33, and I decided to save the money I might have spent on a motel room and use the tent after all.

Brent and Julie were staying in a motel, but before settling in for the night we all went to a Mexican restaurant that was nearby, recommended by the girl at the desk of the KOA. Other than a handful of peanuts, a breakfast bar, and coffee, it was all I had eaten all day, and Brent and Julie had also not eaten anything, so sitting down to a substantial hot meal was welcome by all.

After dinner, we went our separate ways, me riding back to the KOA to set up camp and my companions to their motel. After pitching the tent, I took a shower but didn't wash my hair so I would not have to spend the night in the cold with a wet head.

I pulled my dirty clothes over my clean body, with everything on except my Frog Tog rain pants and my riding jacket. I climbed into my bag in the tent and moved video from the GoPro to my laptop. I sent a quick note to Devon, a bartender back home who had grown up in Montana. I let her know I was in her home state and would be at Glacier the next afternoon.

I called Ken, the ADV inmate in Kila, Montana, where I was planning to stay the next night but got no answer. I texted him, letting him know where I was and that I would try to call again the following day.

Before going to sleep, a call to home was not encouraging. The air conditioning had gone out, and it might cost four hundred dollars to get fixed, with an additional one hundred or so to have the coils cleaned. Beside that, our son, Jacob, had given Andrea some kind of trouble that day. It was obvious from her tone that she was frazzled, but she didn't say what had happened.

It was not good stuff to go to sleep on, but I pulled the bag up around my neck, closed my eyes, and gave it a shot. Eventually the fatigue of the long cold day fighting the wind caught up with me, and I fell asleep.

Chapter Nine

Day Eight

Butte to Huckleberry Pie

I was up early, with plenty of time to enjoy a leisurely coffee or two and a morning snack at the KOA office, but to my dismay, as I walked up to the front door I found out it did not open until nine. Our plan was for Brent and Julie to meet me there at eight, which meant no breakfast for me for a while. At least the rain had finally gone, and the day turned out sunny and warmer.

My riding partners arrived right on time. Putting off coffee, we headed out on I-90, but only as far as Garrison, where we hopped off east to connect with MT 141 north, where we thought we'd find fuel.

Arriving at the junction, we explored the little settlement of Avon, but could find no gas. By then, fuel levels were getting critical on both bikes. We decided to head out of our way to the east, toward Helena, and return to our junction once we had fueled up. We figured there had to be something soon as the highway approached the fairly large city, just thirty miles away.

We found fuel at Elliston, where I had to make due with something for breakfast in the miniscule store there. I managed to find a decent muffin and hot coffee.

Full of fuel again, we headed back to 141, running north to MT 200, which arched west in a large semi-circle to connect with MT 83 at its apex.

We followed 83 north with the beautiful snow-capped mountains of the Continental Divide and the Lewis and Clarke National Forest shadowing us in the east. We passed Seeley Lake then Swan Lake, where Devon had told me her parents had a cabin. The lake flew by on our left, and once past it, after the road took a turn to the west, we turned north on a shortcut connecting to US 2, just east of Kalispell.

Approaching Glacier National Park

Just past Hungry Horse, at the very gates to the park, the road would take us to the turn-off to the Apgar Visitor Center and to Going to the Sun Highway. That route crosses to Saint

Mary over the towering mountains at Logan Pass. Once on the east side of the park, US 89 heads south along the eastern edge, then connects back to US 2 continuing around the southern edge of the national park and back north to West Glacier, just inside the park from Hungry Horse.

Going to the Sun Highway

We entered the park in hopes of following that loop all the way around the eastern and southern edges of the park before returning to Kalispell for the night. Stopping at the visitor center at West Glacier, however, we were informed that a large segment of Going to the Sun Highway was still closed by winter snows, and that we could only ride sixteen miles up. There we would have to turn around and return the way we came in.

We rode as far as was possible on the magnificent highway. Because of the closure, the route had little traffic, which was at least a little compensation for our being denied a crossing. On the way in and up we passed turquoise Lake McDonald and traced the flow of the McDonald Creek upriver, which was just starting its long circuitous journey to the Columbia River, and ultimately, the Pacific Ocean.

Falls South of Avalanche Creek

On the way back down we took a moment to stop for photos at falls south of the confluence of Avalanche Creek into McDonald Creek, where the afternoon sunlight was sparkling among the cascading water playing between translucent pools.

Exiting Glacier National Park, we stopped at the Huckleberry Patch for a taste of the local delicacy. Apparently, huckleberries here are highly valued, as I recall spring morell mushrooms were where I grew up in Michigan, with people having their secret patches that they reveal to no one, jealously guarding their find. The store and restaurant looked very much like a tourist trap out front, but inside was quite nice, with tasteful and tasty souvenirs and anything that could possibly be made with huckleberries for sale. I bought Devon a small jar of huckleberry preserves. She had told me before I left, "Whatever you do, make sure you try huckleberry pie when you are out there." After paying for the preserves, I made sure to do as she said, sitting down to lunch in the diner with Brent and Julie. I had an elk burger, washed down with coffee flavored with huckleberries and ordered a big slice of huckleberry pie to finish off the meal. Brent and Julie ordered their pie a la mode, with huckleberry ice cream atop their slices.

I Became a Fan of Huckleberries

Interrupting what would be our last meal together was a text message from home. There was trouble with the book delivery in Florida, and it had to be dealt with right then. The next day I would be in Canada and have no phone access. Mid-meal I had to step outside to get a clear signal and called Andrea.

The truck driver delivering the books had stopped in Lake Wales and asked a police officer how to get to our address. The officer had told the truck driver that he could not drive his truck through town to our place because the overhanging oak branches were too low.

That was ridiculous. I had lumber delivered by semi-truck many times before to the shop where I was going to store the books. Besides that, when I had set up the shipment I had made it very clear that while on the west end at pick up there would be a loading dock and fork lift, on the east end at delivery it would be residential, street-side, and hand unloading—all agreed to by the shipping agent and already paid for. The company was supposed to have notified Andrea at least a day in advance of delivery, as well, so she could arrange for the unloaders I had hired to be there, but the driver had called after he had arrived in Lake Wales.

I could feel my blood pressure surge as I tapped out the phone number of the shipping agent while my food got cold inside.

Thankfully, the shipping agent wasn't defensive and admitted it was not my fault but was theirs and assured me he would take care of it, even if that meant reloading the shipment into two smaller trucks for delivery.

Relieved, I returned to my pie while my agitation slowly dissipated with each bite of pie and sip of coffee. The wonderful flavor of the huckleberries won me over, turning me into a big fan, and quickened my recovery from the troublesome phone calls.

Leaving the Huckleberry Patch, we headed west toward Kalispell. Brent loves nostalgic, old-time roadside motels that still have that back-in-the-day aura about them, and so they stopped at a rustic motel, Kalispell Hilltop Inn, ten miles outside of town. Brent and Julie were heading back from there to Nampa, Idaho, in the morning, so we said out goodbyes outside the office of the motel.

I rolled on in search of Chris and his wife Kimberly's place, who had offered me a room for the night near Kila, just ten miles west of Kalispell.

I plugged in the address on Coon Hollow Road into my phone's GPS app. It sent me south of Kalispell and west of the southern route into town, instead of southwest on US 2, as the paper map indicated. Considering how addresses are sometimes oddly assigned, I thought it was not too far-fetched that Chris's place could be in that direction and still have a Kila address. I followed the phone directions, up twisting and branching gravel roads for miles, always climbing, until I saw a sign that told me I was on Coon Hollow Road. Now confident I was on track, I kept following the phone's instructions until the road came to a dead stop, with a locked gate across it and a wildly diminished and brushy path leading away from it on the other side, where the GPS indicated I was to go.

The long dusk of the mountains was upon me, and darkness was not far off. I had already seen deer beside the road on my way up, and of course, I had no cell signal, so I couldn't call Chris. I turned around, figuring I would return to US 2 the way I had come and head out to Kila on it. If I had a signal there, I would give Chris a call and tell him where I was, so I could get exact directions from that known spot on my map.

On my way down, I waved down a fellow rider who had passed me as I went up. He only got a hundred feet or so past me before he turned around and rode up to me. He was the epitome of a "biker," with braided beard, sitting on his chopped Harley rat bike, with an old helmet poised atop his headlight bucket instead of his head.

We chatted about bikes and Triumphs before he informed me that I had indeed been on Coon Hollow Road but that it crossed the mountain past the gate and went on to Kila. He told me that from the gate it was only passable on a small dirt bike and if you knew the way. He said he bet I should have gone on to Kila and gotten on the other end of Coon Hollow Road from there, and then gave me directions from US 2 at Kila.

He told me, in true generous biker fashion, that if I was unable to find my friend, I could return to his place and camp out there. I thanked him, we shook hands from bike to bike, then I rolled back down off the mountain and toward Kila as he roared up the gravel in the opposite direction.

At Kila, at the little pub my biker friend had told me about, I turned left and was soon back on the other gravelly end of Coon Hollow Road. The GPS gave me new directions to my stopover, and I finally rolled up into Chris's driveway with little light left.

The first order of business was a call home, but my phone showed no signal inside the house, but I was directed to a balcony upstairs where I might be able to get one. Standing on the balcony in the dwindling light, I watched two deer wandering around the yard while I talked to Andrea, catching her up on my day's travels.

Chris and his wife loved having riding guests and even had a guest book in the guest room set aside for visitors, in which Kimberly asked me to write my name, where I was from, and something about the trip I was on.

I was shown where the washer and drier was, and I took advantage of the first chance I'd had to wash clothes on the entire trip. I threw in my dirty clothes, which by that time were all of them.

While the clothes were whirling and tumbling, we all sat in the kitchen area and chatted about hunting and motorcycles, the two subjects that would get Chris engaged in talking. Otherwise he was a quiet man. Having been a hunting guide and having spent weeks at a time by himself in the mountains, he was used to solitude. Kimberly was more talkative and filled in the lulls in the conversation when it turned to other things. She mentioned they had an elk steak thawing in the fridge, in case I was interested in it then or for breakfast. I was still full after my elk burger and pie and opted for breakfast instead. We talked until ten, when I started feeling the need for sleep, said good night to my hosts, and headed off to my room.

Before lying down, I took a quick shower in the bathroom next to my room. It was nice not worrying about having a wet head in a chilly tent all night. I made sure all my electronics were plugged in and charging, climbed into a real bed, wrote down the day's details in my journal, and fell fast asleep under the thick, warm blankets.

Chapter Ten

Day Nine

O Canada!

After only a couple taps on the snooze button on my phone at 6:30, I got out of bed fully rested and made my way upstairs in hopes of some coffee. Chris and Kimberly were not coffee drinkers, so I got out some of my tea bag coffee while some water was heated up.

I gathered up my things and packed up my bags then sat at the kitchen island chatting with Chris about hunting and motorcycles until Chris had to leave for work and we said our goodbyes. Kimberly appeared about seven o'clock.

We talked for a bit about essential oils, which was a cottage industry for her, then she asked me what I would like for breakfast. I reminded her of the elk steak in the fridge. I had mentioned that on the road my breakfast is usually only a breakfast bar or some instant oatmeal with dates and walnuts, and Kimberly set to making some homemade steel-cut oatmeal while the elk sizzled in the pan in a pool of butter and garlic. While Kimberly cooked, I loaded my bags back on the Bonnie, then headed inside for a gourmet breakfast, with the elk melting in my mouth, despite Kimberly's claim that it was much tougher than usual.

By the time I finished loading, Kimberly had packed me a lunch of salad, a peanut butter and jelly sandwich, string cheese, and grapes for the road. We chatted about life in Montana and her life with Chris. When they got married, Chris had turned to carpentry and started making a living at that, while he worked on finishing up the house we were in, having started years before. I took a last sip of coffee, said goodbye and thanks, and headed out to the bike.

The deep gravel drive gave me a bit of trouble as I tried to back up and turn around to leave, with the bike sinking in an inch deeper with every foot I rolled it. Eventually, however, through pure determination and some brute force, the bike was turned around facing the road. I fired up the bike and nicked it into first, rolling onto Coon Hollow Road and back to the highway at Kila.

The Last of the Rain as I Head toward Canada

I fueled up in Kalispell then headed north toward the Canadian border and Roosville. The precipitation that had finally disappeared the day before had returned, and the day started rainy and misty and looking even darker ahead. By the time Canada hove into sight, however, the skies had cleared of rain again. Entering Canada was easy at the typically friendly Canadian border post.

The Kootenay River and the Southern Rocky Mountain Trench

Almost instantly as I entered Canada the landscape grew dramatic, with tall snow-capped peaks close by on my right, with more fading off into the distance behind the front line. The highway ran north through a wide valley that held the Kootenay River and its glacial snow-melt waters between two massive ridges on the west and east. The spectacle continued all the way to my turnoff into Banff National Park at Radium Hot Springs. I later found out I was riding the Southern Rocky Mountain Trench, with the Rockies above me on my right and the Purcell and Selkirk Ranges on my left.

In spite of the increasingly stunning scenery, my eyelids were drooping, and at Radium Hot Springs I found a Tim Horton's, where I stopped for a doughnut and a large coffee. A happy group of men were nearby my table talking. Most of them, apparently, were riders themselves. They asked me about my ride and whether their fellow Canadians were treating me alright. I replied that they had so far today and on my travels last year in their country, and that I loved Canadians and their country.

Near Fort Steele, another provincial highway had joined BC 93 for the trek north. At Radium Hot Springs the roads split again, and I turned toward the mountains on my right, on BC 93, while its former traveling companion climbed on to even higher latitudes and toward Jasper.

I reached up to the GoPro perched on my helmet and turned it on. Immediately, I was plunging through encroaching, towering walls of rock crowding the very edges of the highway as I passed through Sinclair Canyon, making a dramatic entrance into Banff National Park.

After a couple miles, I stopped at an unoccupied toll house with a sign that said tickets could be bought at a couple different visitors' centers. I rolled on and up into the mountains, but never found any of the centers that the sign had mentioned. I operated under the assumption that passage on the highway was free, but if I stopped to enjoy the trails and roadside attractions within the park I might need to pay a fee.

I clicked on the GoPro again and left it on until it ran out of power as I steadily climbed into the towering mountain range to ride the highway among the barren and snow-capped peaks.

Although the ride north in the States in the mountainous West so far had been spectacular, the views that opened around every bend in Banff blew me away. Around every curve another breathtaking view was exposed, and I felt tears involuntarily welling up in my eyes, brought on by the overwhelming beauty of the place. Not only were my surroundings awe-inspiring, but the spectacular views went on for a hundred miles, with each new turn revealing a new and magnificent landscape.

To think, I was only crossing a narrow waist of that range of the Rocky Mountains, a range that continued north for another couple thousand miles into the Yukon, eventually spilling into the slopes of the Alaskan ranges.

On CA 93 Crossing the Canadian Rockies

I wound past more peaks, clear blue-green river rapids, deep forests, glaciers high on the mountaintops, and falls dropping in threads of hundreds of feet from the glaciers feeding them. To perfect the scene, at the crest of the pass a very light snow was falling.

West of Banff on Canada 1 Looking at Mount Morquay

The ride across this range was overwhelming, perhaps not only because of the spectacle of nature all around and above me, but it was also the culmination of my journey. I was over 3,500 miles from home, and from there my route would slowly take me back toward Florida.

I pulled over onto the gravel beside an alpine river and got off the bike to take it all in without the motor thrumming in my ears. Months from then I knew I would long to be back with the quiet sounds of the water and the wind of the mountains. It was my last chance to breathe in the fresh high altitude air and relish in the rocky Mountain environment.

The drop down out of the Rockies was abrupt, with the range towering above the high plains, out of which they grew with almost no transition between plain and mountain.

The winds were very high coming down out of the mountains, so I decided to ride a bit farther before camping for the night, instead of stopping in Banff as I had planned, in hopes of avoiding the high winds by being farther out on the plains and away from the mountains.

Approaching Calgary on Canada 1, I spotted blue camping signs, but when I turned off to look for a campground all I found was row after row of new houses that must have sprung up so quickly they hadn't had time to remove the outdated signs. Finding my way back to the highway after a couple failed attempts, I got back on the "Trans-Canada" and took the by-pass around Calgary, hoping to find something on the eastern side.

Exiting the city I spotted a "campground," only to find out it only catered to RVs. I could have stayed there but would have been charged the same high rate as if I had been in one of those large, electricity sucking, behemoths. It was suggested I try Strathmore, a city a little farther along, but I saw nothing promising as I passed through it.

Once to the east of town, however, I spotted a campground sign and turned left into a gravel drive, where the old and obviously unoccupied and dilapidated buildings did not bode well. But I did see some small camper trailers parked behind the buildings fronting the highway, so I asked the half-toothless man who walked out to greet me if there was camping there. I was told there was and that I should ride around back and enter the house.

I rolled around to the house, parked the bike, and found my way to the entrance, when a woman suddenly appeared, apparently startled by someone actually stopping there. The fee was ten dollars, only about eight US dollars—cash, no receipt, no registration, just a finger pointed to where I could set up my tent.

The place was filled with about a dozen travel trailers and a collection of structures that looked like they had been assembled with used building materials, sporting unpainted plywood doors laid against openings. Other than a young man doing chores, the place was apparently deserted.

All I wanted was a place to lay my head for the night, and the price was right, so I moved to my site and set up the tent as the sun kissed the mountains to the west outlined above the open prairie.

After setting up camp, I strolled over to the bath house. While taking care of other necessities, I decided to skip a shower after seeing the dirt on the battered concrete floor and the multi-colored painted walls—dark blue which had once covered all the walls showing through a light blue that had been slapped on top where a previous toilet paper holder had hung and now was removed. It was really too cold, anyway, I told myself. I went back to my spot unwashed and watched the setting sun as the air grew chilly.

As the sun's disk fell behind the mountains, the air temperature dropped quickly. I slept fully clothed that night in my bag, insurance against the cold of the coming night. I was exhausted and turned in well before darkness fell.

I would have liked to have found accommodations farther west and earlier, but stopping where I did meant I would have a shorter ride the next day and could get farther east before stopping, and I wouldn't have to be in a big rush to make some real easting.

Earlier in the day, a lady who had stopped up in the mountains where I had stopped to take some photos of the river and absorb the beauty surrounding me had offered to take a photo of me with the mountains in the background. While we had chatted, she had said that the next few days were suppose to warm up. Now that I was going to be at lower elevations, it should be considerably warmer each day. I lay in my bag looking forward to a break from the cold, falling asleep while it was still light outside, in spite of it being almost ten o'clock—a result of my high latitude and it being only a few days from the summer solstice.

Chapter Eleven

Day Ten

Prairie and Wind

I woke up to daylight, no thanks to my phone's alarm clock, which had run dead in the night. Still, it was early, and I estimated it to be about half past seven. By eight, I was gone and heading more or less east again on the Trans-Canada Highway. The wind was wickedly strong, blowing out of the west-southwest.

The route made an abrupt jog south for several miles as I fought the gusts, then turned east again. After the turn, past Gleichen, I left my view of the mountains behind me, by then just a low pale-blue outline in my mirrors. I would not see any more mountains until I crossed my old friends, the Appalachians, after leaving the rally in southern Indiana and on my way home.

The road turned southeast around Bassano, heading for the town of Medicine Hat, on the eastern edge of Alberta. Over my right shoulder the wind was shrieking and blowing the bike hard. That stretch lasted maybe a hundred miles, but when I eventually turned due east, the world went silent, with only the engine sound in my ears and no perception of wind for most of the rest of the day, with the exceptions of when the road would veer slightly southeastward for short periods.

Before I was about to turn south off Canada 1 to get on some smaller back roads, I looked in vain for gas stations as my mileage added up and the reserve light glowed yellow.

Finally, the bike began to stutter. I knew what was coming, so I flipped the kill switch to keep from damaging the fuel pump by running it dry.

I could see a station just a mile up the hill from where I had stalled, of course. I took one of the liter MSR bottles from my pillion foot peg strut and poured its contents into the Bonnie's tank then rode to the top of the hill to fill the tank.

On the run between Strathmore and Medicine Hat, numerous oil wells appeared, pumping noticeably slower than their counterparts in Kansas. I wondered if the slow speed was due to them pumping from the Canadian oil sands, instead of pulling it up from pockets of liquid oil. By the Saskatchewan line the wells disappeared.

From Medicine Hat into Saskatchewan, until my turn south at Gull Lake south to catch the smaller eastern route SA 13, I rode through an area full of low, green buttes. Off to the south was the distant outline of a low line of mountains. The map put Cypress Hills Interprovincial Park in that area, and I saw a sign that indicated that in that direction lay the "Canadian Badlands."

The oil wells reappeared somewhere below Gull Lake and accompanied me for the rest of the day.

Montana is a huge state. Across Alberta and even into Saskatchewan I had been following the Montana line, just south of me. It was not until twenty or thirty miles before I stopped to camp that evening in eastern Saskatchewan that the state to the south changed to North Dakota.

I rode the provincial highway most of the way across the province through ground swells of grasses in every direction, except when broken by the line of a tree break. Among the rolling hills the green was peppered with busy oil wells perpetually bowing to the earth, then raising their heads.

It was so deserted on the plains and far between villages, which often had no gas, that my tank went dry again. It looked like I was not too far from Weyburn, so I just poured in the other liter from the other MSR bottle and kept going. Twelve miles passed, and I was still not at Weyburn. I stopped at the side of the road again, unloaded the tailbag, and got out my one gallon Rotopax that was tucked neatly under the tailbag. I knew that would get me the rest of the way. Although at first the gas mileage had dropped with the descent to lower elevations, the forty mile per hour tailwind had started to improve it again.

Weyburn showed up in just a few miles, along with a gas station. I took the time to refill not only the tank but the MSRs and Rotopax. I knew that in a day or two I would be in the wilderness of the Minnesota North Woods and would breathe easier having the backup supply back on board.

The day had warmed considerably, and by the time I had run out of gas the third time, I was sweltering in all my layers of clothing. The sky was cloudless all day except for a narrow strip of high clouds, at first off to the south, but which eventually moved overhead and then to the north and out of sight as the day had progressed, leaving the prairie skies solid blue and the sun free to heat the earth.

I was ready to stop for the night. I calculated I had ridden over 500 miles and had already gone farther than I had planned, giving me a good start for the next day. I decided to turn in at the first camping sign I saw. I had noticed earlier that Canadian highways have convenient blue signs for services and accommodations at intersections on even their minor routes.

I saw a blue camping sign at Stoughton. After turning left, I saw another sign, also pointing left, so I turned again onto a gravel road. Soon, that became dual track, so I turned around, thinking the sign must have meant the next paved road.

A girl was walking her dog on the road where it met the paved highway, so I stopped to ask her about the camping. She said I could follow the gravel road to get there, but if I took the next paved road and turned left I would go right to it. It was next to a huge building that apparently was for fairs and events, and I could see it from where we were when she pointed it out. I thanked her and rode on to the campground.

All Prairie Towns Have At Least One of These

There were three or four trailers parked there with accompanying vehicles, but no one was stirring about. I picked site number seven, two away from the nearest neighbor, and set up the tent.

Within minutes, a lady drove up in a pickup, registered me, and told me it would be ten Canadian dollars. I only had US currency, so I gave her a twenty and said ten dollars Canadian would be fine for change, as she had no US bills. They could use the extra money for the park in whatever way they chose. In effect, I had paid just over $13 US, which was still very cheap.

Apparently, it was very common in the little towns on the prairie to have a city park with sports fields and other facilities that also offered camping space for travelers. It would have been good to know the night before and for anyone traveling across Canada on the cheap like me. Just look for a grain elevator and you will find a town and, usually, one of those campgrounds. Ten Canadian dollars is cheap camping. The one I was at had a bathroom and shower, and I was able to pitch my tent in the shade on soft grass next to my own picnic table, too.

After a while, the dog walker I had encountered earlier passed through the park. I waved at her and said, "Thanks!"

The sun was setting, and a little chill set in, but not enough to warrant sleeping fully clothed again.

That night I fired up the stove for the first time, which I was starting to think would have been better left at home. I made a couple packets of instant oatmeal and a cup of coffee. Earlier that day, I had stopped for a cheap egg-on-muffin and coffee for breakfast at a Tim Horton's before I had left the Trans-Canadian. Other than the leftover grapes Kimberly had packed for me a couple days ago, which I had eaten on the side of the road midday when I had stopped to pour my reserve fuel into the bike's tank, that was all I had eaten all day.

I felt a sore throat coming on and hoped it would not escalate into something more serious, but the hot coffee soothed it temporarily. While waiting for evening to fall, I checked my phone, just in case I had a signal. I thought even if it was expensive I would try to call Andrea. The No Signal icon on the phone was on, however, so a call would have to wait until I was back in the States.

I have some nerve damage on my right foot's toes that I incurred a few years ago while repairing a floor at my brother's house. I had crouched all day and my two right toes began to burn. That pain returned from time to time, with no apparent reason, but when it did it was excruciating and felt like someone was holding a match to my toes. Usually this condition would last all day and then disappear until the next time it returned to torment me, in a week or in a couple months. Because of that, my wife had given me some of her strong pain pills, both controlled substances, just in case I would have a flare-up on the trip. Before I had left, I thoughtlessly dumped the pills into one of her old prescription bottles and threw the bottle in my bag.

I had not had the need to use them at all so far, but I would be returning to the US the next day, and now the idea of crossing back across the US border with two drugs not prescribed to me and mixed in one bottle seemed likely to cause trouble, possibly a lot of trouble if a border guard decided to do a thorough search. The thought of being delayed or worse, thrown in a holding cell, convinced me it was not worth trying to carry them with me anymore, so I flushed them and hoped my toes would not flare up again on the rest of the trip. I hit the sack, relieved I would not have anything to worry about when I reentered the US.

Chapter Twelve

Day Eleven

Leaving the Great Plains

The next morning I was up and out of Stoughton by 8 AM. I thought I had heard rain on the tent during the night, but that morning everything was dry. For once, the tent was put away completely dry. What I heard must have been the leaves of the trees rustling overhead.

Canada is huge and the prairie considerably wider than it is at the latitude of Colorado. It was taking me forever to cross it.

By the time I got well into Manitoba, the empty prairie was replaced by something similar to the terrain of northern Indiana at times and of southern Michigan at others. There were still large fields, but instead of being covered in prairie grasses they were planted with crops. There were more substantial woods among the fields, instead of the thin line of prairie wind breaks. Windmills and oil wells still were common most of the way. As I moved farther east, along with woods and planted fields, ponds and lakes appeared. Deer and moose crossing signs were often planted at the side of the road as I rode into and across Manitoba.

Wind Generators Dot the Prairies

I jogged south to catch another provincial highway across the bottom of the province, in order to avoid Winnipeg. It was a long time between gas stations again. Sometimes there were deserted farm co-op fueling stations I wasn't sure I could use. I had tried using one the day before, and my debit card had not worked. Luckily, that one had an attendant, and I had sought his assistance to get the pump to work. The ones I was passing in Manitoba were almost all self-service.

I was expecting The Bonnie to sputter to a stop at any moment when I spotted a lone pump and saw that someone was there. Relieved I didn't have to break out the extra fuel again, I pulled in, fueled up, then rolled back onto the highway and headed east once more.

I passed through Ninette, where town folk were lining both sides of the little town's main streets, and rode through the village with spectators watching me all the way through the three-block town. As I left town, I passed groups of young people, all dressed in costume and on horseback. Apparently they were the real parade, and the people downtown had not come out of mere curiosity to see a motorcycle roll through their town.

At Baldur, I stopped for a much needed coffee long after I should have. While taking to the waitress I mentioned the parade I had ridden through and asked her if there was a holiday that day in Canada. I was told it was a Solstice Celebration, although technically that would be on the Monday following the current weekend. There were plans in Baldur for the holiday, too. The people in the little diner were friendly, and we all chatted table to table as I drank several cups of coffee and had a grilled ham and cheese sandwich.

Leaving Baldur, I continued east for about ninety miles until the road ended at Morris, where I turned northeast toward Winnipeg. Before I got that far, however, I jumped east again on what would be equivalent to a county road in the US, to another provincial highway heading south. I hopped a few miles again only to turn east again to connect to my final highway out of Canada, MB 12.

By the time I reached the US border between Middlebro, Manitoba, and Warroad, Minnesota, it was getting late, or so it seemed due to the high clouds and heavy overcast skies that set in just as I was crossing into the States. But sunset was very late at that latitude, especially that close to the solstice, and by the time I found a place to camp hours later, I would feel the sun on my back again.

Leaving Canada was a breeze; there were no border guards there at all, and I simply rode through. Just past the booth was a souvenir store, where I stopped to look for a Canadian flag sticker for my windscreen.

The last time I had left Canada for my home country was in northern Maine. There was only one other family and me, and we all were searched thoroughly. When I had returned to my bike, all my luggage was scattered across the pavement surrounding the Bonnie. It seemed that one of the qualifications for being a US border agent is to be a dick.

I don't think they will even look at your resume for a border agent unless you can prove to them that your have disdain for the American citizens first. This crossing was no better than the last.

When I pulled up to the border, there was a sign that said "Proceed when lane is clear" and then a big red and green light shining a solid green, even though a car was ahead at the window a hundred feet ahead. A green light is almost universally understood to mean move ahead, so I did. When I did, the guard's hand was thrust out at me, brusquely signalling me to stop, and the agent's scowl looked like he thought I was public enemy number one.

When the car ahead of me had left and I had moved ahead again to his station with his permission, he asked me where I had been and where I was heading next. After answering him, I said, "Sorry, I didn't mean to move up too early, but the light was green." I got another disgusted scowl and an angry and short "The light is for an open lane, and the sign says to wait until clear!" I understood by then, but it was rather confusing having two conflicting messages, especially when a green light almost universally means "Go." It had been a simple error that could have been overlooked, but I would have wasted my breath saying any more and probably would have only incurred his wrath and caused myself more grief. I was glad I had dumped the pain pills. If I still had them and had offended him too much, he might have decided to search me and the bike, and things might have gone sideways from there.

It didn't seem right that the most anxiety-causing border crossings should be into my own country, and it was a shame that it is caused by agents who apparently don't know or care that they actually work for us. The only response to every situation does not have to be a hand on a gun and an angry display of authority.

Finally back in the US, by the time I reached Baudette, Minnesota, I was ready to stop and thought I would surely find a campground, as they seemingly had everything else, including a bar. I was hoping to have a cold beer after setting up camp. Unfortunately, downtown Baudette was closed due to construction, and I was routed around the small town.

At a gas stop, I asked a man about a place to camp and was told to look for one "just after the bridge." I crossed one on the other side of town where the detour reconnected with the main highway but saw no campground and kept going. I crossed another bridge and still saw no place to stop for the night.

I continued southeast until I saw a sign for a boat ramp and pulled in, hoping I might be able to set up there, but a sign said specifically, "No Camping." I saw a couple of teenage girls at the ramp messing around in the water of the Rainy River and asked them if they knew of any camping spots nearby. They answered no, but said I could camp there; no one would care as they were the only ones who ever went there. I was hesitant, thinking if I did camp there, I would surely be the one who got caught. It didn't appear to be as late as I had thought, now that the clouds were easing and the sky was lightening back up, even though I had spied deer moving around already. It was only half past six, so I asked the girls how far it was to International Falls. I thought there would surely be a campground there, being the largest town along my route. One of the girls said a half-hour, and the other said an hour. I decided to try to make it there, but if something showed up before I would stop at the first opportunity.

Within a few more miles, I saw a brown sign with a tent icon on it, along with another one depicting a boat ramp that pointed to the left. I followed it and soon found myself at the Rainy River, with Ontario facing me from the other bank. Looking at my map, I decided I must have been across from Emo, a town on the Canadian side of the river. And sure enough, there was free camping.

There were a handful of camping trailers parked up there already, but there were still plenty of open spaces. I picked out an empty one right on the shore of the river under a tree. The campers were apparently occupied by locals hanging out by the water for the weekend. I chatted with a couple of them, and they all seemed friendly.

My Camping Spot with a View of Ontario across the River

I broke out the stove, because the only food not requiring cooking I still had was a handful of peanuts. But I did have instant oatmeal. I connected the MSR bottle to the stove, let a little gas into the burner, turned it off, then flicked my lighter at it. It flared up, and after it had burned down enough to heat the burner, I reopened the gas valve. A cooking flame roared to life. I boiled water for oatmeal and a couple cups of coffee.

With coffee in hand, I walked over to one of the camps and asked if anyone had a forecast for the night and the next day. They replied that thunderstorms were predicted for that night, as was typical for that time of the year, but then it should be nice for the next couple days.

As the sun set, the last of the clouds drifted off to the east, and I hoped the rain would not arrive and that I would have nice weather ahead of me tomorrow for riding, or at least until I was in Wisconsin.

I had been out of touch with home for three days while in Canada, and I was hoping that, now in the US, I would have a phone signal and be able to touch base with Andrea. Apparently, at some point during my ride that day I had a signal, because I could see missed calls from Andrea and my parents and a text from my daughter now on the phone. But where I was camping, there was no service. I texted back to Andrea, anyway, letting her know I was back in the US in northern Minnesota, hoping the message would send tomorrow as I passed though signal areas. Nothing else could be done about it that night.

Chapter Thirteen

Day Twelve

A Foggy Lake and an Aerostich Miss

I woke to rain the next morning, trying to snooze-button it away, but it ignored me. The Rainy River was living up to its name. I guessed I should just have been thankful it was not called the Snowy River. The tent came down in the rain and got packed away wet.

I wanted to at least put on a clean pair of undershorts, even though every stitch of the rest of my clothes was filthy. There was a small open but screened structure, apparently intended as a place to behead and gut fish as indicated by the counter and sink, the stench, and bits of entrails. It became my changing room, but at least it was out of the rain. I repacked the bike in the drizzle, fired up the Bonnie, and headed back up the ramp to the highway. I continued east in the rain to

Pelland and toward International Falls, following the river along the border with Canada.

Arriving in International Falls, I spotted an open diner downtown. Riding a little way farther into town, to see what other options I might have, I saw no other restaurants. I did a U-turn and parked up in front of Coffee Landing Cafe, got off the bike, shook off the water, and got in out of the rain.

On the menu cover the diner was described as a "small town cafe with big city espresso bar." The place had a wide selection of coffees, but I opted for the brew of the day, good old strong black coffee. After the cold rain I had ridden through, the hot coffee felt and tasted marvelous.

I treated myself to a real breakfast of an omelet with onions, green peppers, black olives, and feta cheese. It was very good and came with toast and unlimited coffee refills, all for less than nine dollars. There was a broad selection of other mouth-watering sounding omelets and other breakfast and lunch fare.

It was fantastic to have found great food in a warm, dry spot and to encounter a diner full of friendly locals and tourists. I was glad I had not found anything else down the road, missing out on that great place. If I lived in the area, I am sure I would be a regular at Coffee Landing Cafe.

While enjoying my breakfast, the rain let up, but one of the waitresses announced that to the west was a storm coming our way with tennis ball-sized hail. The pea-sized hail back in Wyoming had hurt enough, and riding through tennis ball-sized bullets was something I did not want to stick around to experience. I decided I'd better leave and try to stay ahead of the storm. I wolfed down the last of my coffee and paid my bill.

I could ride 60 miles per hour. I calculated that even a fast moving storm would probably only do 30-35. It turned out my decision was the right one, and I found myself riding southeast through Kabetogama State Forest and out of the rain, with the sun coming out as the temperature rose.

At Angora, I topped up my fuel, even though it took almost nothing, because I was turning off to the east, and eventually southeast, through the wilderness of the Minnesota North Woods, through a series of state forests—Superior, Burntside, Bear Island, and Finland—to arrive on the shores of Lake Superior just above Silver Beach—a distance of 115 miles. At State Highway 1, I peeled off toward the east and into the woods. As the day warmed and the sun beat down, all my layers of clothing were getting uncomfortably warm. I thought about removing a layer or two, but was afraid I would regret it when I got near the cold waters of Lake Superior.

The North Woods in Superior National Forest on MN 1

At Ely, the road took a southeastern turn toward the big lake. About twenty-six miles from the change in direction, MN 2 offered the opportunity for a shortcut directly south to Lake Superior at Two Harbors, but I opted to continue on the road I was on so I would have more of the lake's shoreline to ride when I back-tracked on the coastal highway to Duluth.

As I rode over the last couple ridges before arriving at the coast, I could feel the temperature plummet ten degrees as I topped the hills and felt Superior's influence, then the temperature climbed again as I dropped down on the back sides of the hills. The fluctuation continued with each hill surmounted and descended until the last drop down to the lake.

While the highway promised to be a beautiful ride along the north shore as it hugged the beaches, with occasionally inland forays before returning to Superior, as I arrived, the lake was hidden under a deep veil of fog. I turned right, with only a grey blank wall to my left and tourist destinations to the right as I rode southwest.

When the route would leave the coast for more than a mile or two the temperature would climb, and as the road returned to the lake it would drop again. Not being able to see the lake and left with only the tourist shops on the highway and the many tourists traveling on the increasingly crowded road, I realized I could have taken the shortcut on 2 and not missed much.

The fog lifted very slowly as I headed toward Duluth, with it occasionally backing out to sea a quarter mile then returning right up to the shore below the bluff I was riding on.

A tunnel appeared ahead with a parking area on my left just before it. I turned off into the Silver Creek Cliff Wayside Park where part of the Gitchee Gami State Trail wound along the lake shore.

I parked and got off the bike, hoping that a hike down the trail might provide a better vantage point with less fog for a photo or two and a chance to stretch my legs.

I walked along the path that trailed along the cliff, through which the highway tunnel bored, but the fog did not cooperate. Still, it felt good to get out of the saddle for a while and walk. After a half hour or so, I walked back and climbed aboard, pulled out onto the coastal road, negotiated the tunnel, and soon passed Two Harbors. The GoPro had been turned on in photo mode when I had first got on the coastal highway in hopes of passing through some fog-free areas as I rolled toward Duluth, when I could click the shutter occasionally if the scenery deserved recording.

The sore throat I had worried about a couple days ago had gone but was replaced by an incessant sneezing. I would feel one coming on, grab my chin bar, throw it open, left one fly, then close the helmet again. It was unnerving to be blind for that split second when my visor was up and I was sneezing.

By Duluth the fog was gone and the heat was up. I stopped at a McDonald's, removed all my inner layers, and got a cold drink and a bite to eat. I checked the Aerostich website. I had wanted to stop by while I was passing through and had been looking forward to it for a while, even though the most I could afford to buy were a couple of zipper pull repair parts. The website gave their hours and open days. That's when I realized it was Sunday and they were closed.

Disappointed that I wasn't going to be able to visit Aerostich, I got back on the road and made my way through Duluth, with a couple wrong turns and back-tracking thrown in, and into Wisconsin.

I headed south out of Superior and left the great cold lake behind me as the route cut through Wisconsin, becoming almost Interstate-like as it approached Eau Claire. I bailed off the big highway at Chippewa Falls, heading east around the city, then south again once well east of it.

I had heard good things about southwestern Wisconsin, and had come this way so I could see it for myself, if only a small part, while passing through. My other day's goal as I rode south was to get onto the lower half of the two-page map I was using before stopping for the night. From there, getting to my friend Joe's the next day would be a fairly short ride and more relaxing.

The landscape changed to beautiful, rolling wooded hills, very reminiscent of Kentucky. The roads became windy. I could understand the appeal this part of the country had to motorcycle riders and was glad I was taking the time to pass through it.

I got onto the bottom half of my map, but by then it was fast approaching sunset. I spotted two deer, one of which crossed the road close in front of me. I was ready to stop and worried about deer only getting thicker as night approached. I couldn't find campsites, which farther north that day I had seen fairly regularly.

The Surprisingly Rolling Southwestern Wisconsin Countryside

Finally, I stopped at a station to fill up and went inside to ask about camping. I was told there was one ahead at Leon. I found the campground less than a mile east of the main road called simply Leon Valley Campground. I rolled in, and not seeing anyone at the office, I picked a spot among the RVs parked on a hill across the road from a pool. Soon a golf cart rolled by and one of the owners got out to tell me that my spot was generally for RVs and that there was another area for tents, but because it was late and they probably would not need the spot for anyone else, I could stay put.

Hoping my tent, which had been put away wet that morning would dry before I went to sleep, to kill some time I headed back out to the corner on the main highway where I had seen a small local tavern. There was a Blatz sign out front, a beer I remembered from my days when I was young and living in Michigan. I assumed that brand was long gone and only the old sign remained. I went in and asked if they really had Blatz. They said they surely did, so I asked for one. It tasted just like I remembered. Beer up North seemed to taste better to me than what we got in the South, and my unscientific theory was that the water they use to brew it comes from cold deep springs in the North. I had another beer while talking to the local fellow next to me about riding and about southwestern Wisconsin.

It was dark when I left for camp, so I rode very slowly and carefully, expecting encounters with deer around every corner, but I got back unscathed and to a relatively dry tent. I tried to call home, but again, I had no signal in that little pocket among the hills where the campground lay.

I went to sleep looking forward to seeing my old friend and having a day off the bike the following day. Joe was taking a day off work, and we would have a entire day to catch up, relax, and maybe visit some of the old haunts of our youth.

Chapter Fourteen

Day Thirteen

To the Land of My Youth

Rain and thunderstorms had kept me awake for an hour or so the night before, starting at about 3 AM. I could hear the storm moving from the northwest to the southeast in the sky overhead. I wondered if the tumult outside was the same storm that I had been trying to escape ever since leaving camp on the Rainy River and now had caught up with me. I hoped any hail in it had been dumped long before it arrived at my campsite. I lay in my bag listening to the thunder cracking above, worrying that perhaps camping under the canopy of a tree may not have been the best idea. But the thunder sounded like it was cloud to cloud, rather than cloud to ground, or at least that's what I told myself. Slowly the tempest abated as it passed on to terrorize Illinois and Indiana, and I soon fell asleep again.

I woke up about 7:30. Everything was wet, including clothes in the pillion bag, where I had also thrown all the rain and cold weather gear. Everything in the new Ortlieb panniers and the Nelson-Rigg tail bag stayed dry as a bone, including my laptop. The new purchases were paying their rent, and I didn't regret the high price I had paid for them. I couldn't do anything about the tent's wet state, however, so it was folded, rolled up, and put away dripping.

On the way out, I rode up to the office to deposit my camping fee in a drop box, when a man drove up on an ATV and opened the office. We both went inside, and he offered to make us some fresh hot coffee.

It turned out that he and his sister ran the campground, having inherited it from their parents. I handed him a twenty and three ones but he would only take the twenty.

We sat down and talked for a while. He had played music at a local biker club bar Friday night. He must have had a few too many while playing, because it was Tuesday morning and he was still feeling rough. The coffee did us both good and saved me a stop. I thanked him after a couple cups and headed back onto the road at around 8:30.

Near Cashton, there was a detour that took me through the hills on small country roads, including a very twisting and wooded one running along the Kickapoo River valley. It had curve after curve of fast sweepers. It was one of the most peasant rides of the entire trip. Back on my original route I rode southeast until Lone Rock, where I crossed the Wisconsin River, downriver from the famous Dells, a five mile long gorge of sandstone rock formations and water-filled canyons that feed it. As soon as I got across the river, I turned southeast and at State Road 23 turned south for a few miles.

I missed my turn onto State Road 191, a convenient shortcut running southeast and connecting with my next road east. Instead, I turned east on US 18 until I saw tiny County Road K, which I had noticed on the map connected with my next highway as well. K was paved but rustic and ran through pretty back country. I was glad I had missed my turn. Connecting with my next highway, I turned east.

Eventually, I turned south at New Glarius and headed into Illinois below Monroe, leaving the rolling Wisconsin hills behind and entering the flat farm country of Illinois.

The game then was to dodge the Chicago area as I headed around its southern edges toward South Bend, Indiana. I rode south until Dixon, crossing the Rock River in big city-like traffic, even in this small Midwestern town.

I crossed I-88 then turned southeast. I crossed another Interstate highway, jogged south again, shooting for a latitude south of the huge sprawling cities of Chicago, Joliet, Hammond, and Gary. I kept working my way east and south until I could safely travel east, always with an eye to avoiding the Chicago metro area.

I had almost caught up with the thunderstorms from last night. I could see them looming in the southeast ahead. I got close enough to the edge of the storms to get a few drops on my face shield but was spared a drenching. I would soon turn northeast toward South Bend as they roared southeast, ensuring a dry finish to my day's ride.

Approaching Kankakee, the last sizeable town I would pass through before South Bend, to the west and north of the highway were massive wind fields populated by innumerable windmills churning out power for Chicago and the areas around it. I was surprised, but guess I shouldn't have been, being so close to the "Windy City." It turned out, Illinois was second only to Iowa in wind-driven electrical production in the United States. It was a trend I was glad to see happening on this ride, not only here but in many other places across the Great Plains, both in the US and Canada.

It was mid-afternoon as I entered Indiana, where I could safely begin to make my way back to the north and east.

I started calculating how far it was and when I would arrive in South Bend. It didn't look good for avoiding the numerous deer darting across from clumps of trees on each side of the road among the cornfields. I started getting nervous as it was getting quiet and shady under the trees, so I kept a careful eye on the edges of the road ahead and occasionally covered the brake as I made my way east and north toward Walkerton, now that the Chicago and Gary areas were left behind over my left shoulder.

I arrived in Walkerton, a little town filled with memories from when I had gone there with my dad and grandpa to attend horse auctions when I was a kid.

I took IN 23 from Walkerton, which ran straight, more or less, into South Bend. Halfway there, I hit a detour and was forced east. I went for miles and never saw another detour to get me back on 23, but realized I was on IN 4, which I knew would intersect on US 31/20, the new loop around the South Bend and Mishawaka that I wanted to get on.

I passed Potato Creek State Park and soon was on the eastern side of the loop. Ironwood Drive was just a couple miles from there, and it headed toward Joe's.

The sun was still peeking over the horizon when I found Joe's street, stopped, and messaged him to let him know I was just around the corner. After only one U-turn, I found his house and him standing in the drive.

I pulled up into the drive, killed the bike, and reached out a hand to greet Joe. We moved the bike into the garage, where I pulled off stuff I would need inside. Wet stuff was spread around the garage to dry, then I headed inside. A shower was my first priority, since the last time I had one had been in Kila, Montana, five days earlier.

The sopped and dirty clothes in the pillion bag and my riding pants that had been worn for thirteen days and a couple cold nights were due for a wash, but my hopes for that were dashed. The storm I had slept through in Wisconsin had passed through South Bend ahead of me and left most of the city without power.

I had my shower by candlelight as soon as I had downed the beer Joe had waiting for me, then chatted with Joe and his wife, Jan, messaged home, and uploaded videos to the laptop from the GoPro while I ate cold leftover pizza.

I hit the sack clean, dry, and satisfied and didn't bother to set the alarm.

Chapter Fifteen

Day Fourteen

A Day Off

It was so nice to finally not have to wake up to an alarm. What a luxury to get up at 8:30, without the need to get on the road and make miles.

Joe and his youngest daughter, Olivia, and I went to breakfast, because the power was still out at Joe's. Unless we wanted cold leftovers, going out was the only option. Apparently, the storm damage had been repaired sporadically across the city, and we were able to find a restaurant that was serving hot food. Halfway through breakfast, Olivia rushed off for an eye appointment and left Joe and I munching our breakfast, having coffee, and talking about old friends and the old days while we leisurely finished.

Back at the house and finally with a cell signal, I sat outside and called my parents; my Uncle Max, who lived in South

Bend, and Andrea and filled them in on how things were going and my time table for the rest of the trip.

Not long after I wrapped up my calls, Olivia returned, and we three drove toward Lake Michigan to Warren Dunes State Park, where we used to camp and play back when we were young. On the way, we stopped at Joe's sister Lisa's place in Niles, which had been built where their childhood home that had burned a few years ago had been. It was sad to see the old house gone, but good to see that Lisa was building on the same footprint. The view into the trees from the bluff above Brandywine Creek from the living room picture window was still there, lending a relaxing and peaceful ambiance to the new house, as it had to the old. Lisa decided to join us for the ride to the dunes.

Olivia Tackles Tower Hill ahead of Us Slowpokes

We all climbed the big dune, where I recalled hang gliders taking off in past years, although the gliders had long ago been banned. We walked down to the beach far below and relaxed for a bit. The water was surprisingly warm, even though at the entrance booth the sign said it was 73 degrees F. I remember only a very few days that the water was not numbingly frigid, so the warmth was a welcome surprise. I went swimming for a while, enjoying the refreshing, salt-free water, before returning to my spot on the sand to write the log entry for the day before.

Nothing had changed, and all the bikinied girls walking around on the beach and at the top of the dune reminded me of being up there in my youth and how entranced I was with those young, lithe bodies.

Lake Michigan from the Top of Tower Hill

Returning to Joe's that afternoon, I took time to carefully clean my windscreen and adhere the stickers for Utah, Yellowstone, and Glacier National Park I had picked up on the trip. It was getting to be a challenge finding a place on the crowded windscreen, but I managed to get them all on and still leave a bit of clear screen at the top.

The power was still out, so for dinner Joe cooked hot dogs and corn on the cob on the grill. We also had some salad and fruit that didn't require an electric stove to prepare. Joe and I opened some Pinot Noir that was actually quite good, in spite of it being contained in a box, and had a few glasses while we relaxed and talked.

We moved inside when the neighbor fired up his loud and jarring generator. Luckily, not long after that, the power came back on. I chucked my dirty clothes into the washing machine and got them started. Joe said his good nights early, with work waiting for him the next morning. Jan and I stayed up talking politics, while my clothes flopped around in the dryer and my riding jacket benefited from a wash too, before we both went off to bed.

It looked like only 275 miles or so for the next day to Spring Mill State Park. I fell asleep looking forward to an easy and short day of riding.

Chapter Sixteen

Day Fifteen

Flat Farmland to Rolling Hills above the Ohio

I had set the alarm for seven, as late as I could, but still be able to see Joe before he went off to work. There was no hurry to get on the road, with only a couple hundred miles or so between South Bend and Mitchell, Indiana, and Spring Mill State Park, where the VJMC was having their national rally. I would be getting into work mode there, making sure we had the needed photos of the event for the upcoming magazine issue.

By the time I walked into the dining room, there was a breakfast of scrambled eggs, bacon, and toast along with hot French-pressed coffee waiting for me. Joe soon left, and then between sips of coffee, I methodically reloaded the bike, stuffing the clean clothes I was not wearing that day in the panniers. I had checked the engine oil and Scottoiler reservoir the night before and had topped up the chain oil, so nothing else was left to do to ready the bike but load it back up with all the stuff I had spread around the garage to dry.

By ten, I was ready to go. I rolled the bike out of the garage, being careful not to let the now top-heavy bike tip too much on the sloped driveway. I gave Jan a hug, offered her and Joe a place to stay in Florida and encouraged them to visit us, and rolled back onto the road.

I wound my way back out of South Bend on vaguely familiar streets, which I hadn't been on in many years. I found my way to Old US 31, now called 931, avoiding the Interstate-like new 31, which wrapped itself around the city. Construction detoured me off the old highway and onto State Road 331 for the run south to Rochester in the flat, fertile northern Indiana farmland, carpeted with green thigh-high corn and low soybean plants.

At Rochester, I got off the divided highway and onto quiet back country roads again, first south-southwest to Logansport then turning south toward Boyleston. I turned right to avoid the sprawl of Indianapolis, passing to its west, then turned south again at Frankfort. The high school I passed there proudly announced to the world in large block letters across its front "THE HOME OF THE HOTDOGS." I wondered how the students felt about the moniker bequeathed them by their school board.

At Martinsville, I veered southwest for several miles until I could take a short connector road to my final road for the day, State Road 37. I had only one more large city to pass through, Bloomington, before being spat out into the countryside again into the rolling and forested area of southwestern Indiana, with Mitchell dead ahead. The stretch into Bloomington was an ordeal, being under construction from Martinsville to the home of Indiana University at Bloomington, a stretch of sixteen miles.

Clearing the construction, I made easy progress, arriving at Mitchell about 1:30 in the afternoon. By the time I had unloaded all the gear and had deposited it in my room at the Spring Mill Inn, it was after 2 PM.

I wandered downstairs to find my fellow club members. I found them in the banquet hall, getting ready to check early arrivals in for the rally. I passed a couple hours chatting and plugging stuff in to recharge when the plan was announced to meet up at the Dairy Master in Loogootee, a diminutive town to the west. Some would drive and others would ride, so I joined the riders.

As I had pulled in at the state park, I had noticed a strange sound coming from the Bonnie, but I didn't notice it any more after getting on the road with the group of a half dozen riders. Arriving at the diner after a slow speed ride of about thirty miles, the sound appeared again. I took a closer look in the parking lot. It was obvious that the chain was very loose, with two or three inches of slop, and as it went around it would bounce and scrape on the foot of the center stand. We all went in the diner to eat, and I made a mental note to adjust the chain as soon as we returned to the inn.

I opted for a lunch of fish and chips, although the specialty of the house was a pork tenderloin sandwich, which turned out to be fried like a large wienerschnitzel and by all accounts was worth the calories.

On the way back to the park, I babied the bike, being cautious of rolling on and off the throttle too aggressively and taking care crossing rough railroad tracks. I made plans to break out the tools the moment I got back and while it was still light enough to see to adjust it. Meanwhile, our group got slowed down by my friend, Jim, on an old Honda CB350 Four as it slowly lost charging capacity and fell to the back of the group. I watched in my mirrors as its headlight got dimmer and yellower, then went out altogether. Eventually, a trailer had to be sent back out from the inn to pick up Jim and the ailing bike.

I had made it back in fading light, but by the time I had gotten out of jacket and boots, retrieved my tools from the room, and gotten back to the bike, the sun had settled behind the trees. The flashlight, which I had the forethought to grab with the tools, came in very handy. Unfortunately, the small ratchet that came in my tool roll wasn't up to the task of turning the big 25 millimeter axle nut. Luckily, with all the bike guys around, it wasn't long before a large adjustable wrench was offered and the axle was freed enough for me to turn the adjusters and take the enormous slack out of the chain. The chain had developed a stretched section, so with it adjusted properly in one spot, upon spinning the wheel and moving the chain to a new position it yielded either slack or tight points.

The Gathering Place at the Inn after Dinner

The chain was shot and would have to go. I hoped it would be good enough to get me home, so I could do the replacement there. I thought it strange, though, that when I last checked the chain in Jackson, roughly halfway through the ride and after 3,000 miles, it was exactly the same as it had been back home before I had left. What had stretched it since then was a mystery. I did recall having hit a rough railroad crossing particularly hard (hard enough to have bottomed out the forks and rear shocks) on the way from South Bend to

Mitchell, so I had a suspicion that might have caused a sudden stretch in one spot.

At Spring Mill, I had no cell signal again, but did have access to Wi-Fi provided by the hotel, so I was able to Facebook message Andrea and let her know I was in for the day. I also got a couple Facebook posts in and received a message from my friend, Julie, who invited me to stop by her place for the night on my way home. That left me with only one night to wing it looking for a campsite.

As evening settled in and members sat around talking at the front of the inn, we watched the crippled CB350 Four roll in on a trailer. I called it a night and headed up to my room early, setting the alarm for 7:30, the time the restaurant at the inn opened for breakfast.

Chapter Seventeen

Days Sixteen, Seventeen, & Eighteen

A Gathering of Vintage Motorcycles

I had a restful sleep in the luxuriously air conditioned room and in the morning headed downstairs to have breakfast in the hotel dining room. I sat with Mary and Charles, good friends from the club who hailed from Louisiana. I had once held a commercial captains license and Charles had once operated a tugboat on the Mississippi, so we had boating stuff in common to talk about.

We had a nice conversation while I was downing a bowl of oatmeal with raisins, dried cranberries, walnuts, and honey gathered from the extensive breakfast bar. I limited myself to my usual oatmeal. I had lost seven pounds so far on the ride and didn't want to gain it all back, which would have been easy to do there with all the activities revolving around lunch stops and big buffet dinners each night during the rally. Plus, to avail myself of the entire breakfast buffet would cost ten dollars with coffee, while the oatmeal with coffee would only run me four dollars, keeping my budget on the frugal end of the scale. Besides, I could never eat my money's worth out of an all-you-can-eat breakfast bar and would be mostly wasting the money on it. That morning, however, Charles insisted on buying my meal, so it cost me nothing but some delightful conversation.

I went upstairs and changed into my riding clothes in anticipation of another group ride. Although I was worried about my chain, I had to get some photographic coverage of rides this weekend. I chose one to the Medora covered bridge, built in 1875 and one of the longest in the country, with a stop at an unusual round barn and lunch at a Dairy Queen. I took photos of the group at stops and the bridge and some video of the riders going through the covered bridge for the club website, ensuring my cache of representative photos of that part of the rally would be sufficient.

Medora Covered Bridge

Back at the hotel I went swimming in the pool, which became my afternoon refuge from the unusually hot weather. After the swim, there was just enough time to grab a shower and check Facebook before the evenings' banquets. Downstairs the banquet room's glass wall looked out upon the canopy of trees rooted far below at the base of a ridge upon which the hotel was perched. The scene cast a green radiance throughout the room, as I wandered here and there adding more event photos to my SD card.

After dinner each night, there was more socializing on the outside patio where I continued my photographic duties between beers.

Group Rides Came and Went All Weekend

The day had been filled with the comings and goings of multiple group rides, while many members were still showing up and getting their bikes ready for the big show the next day. The mortar that held all these things together was the camaraderie of the big group of vintage motorcycle enthusiasts, a huge family we were all part of. Of course, a grand buffet was laid out that evening again, followed by the ritual of a late night on the patio, where a raccoon walked around the perimeter on a low stone wall, insisting he really *had* been invited. The smell of sausages, brought out as hors d'oeuvres, I think had been his motivation.

It had not been long since the solstice, so it was still quite late before darkness fell completely. That night I didn't get back to my room and in bed until after eleven, probably the latest I had stayed up on the entire trip.

In the morning after another breakfast of oatmeal and coffee, I walked outside to take a look at the many bikes gathered in the circle in front of the inn as the bike show registration got underway. There was a wide variety of vintage Japanese motorcycles arrayed around the circular driveway, from daily runners to showroom-condition, pristine examples of rare models. People lined up at the registration tent or rolled their beauties into place among the other entrants, while I snapped photos for the magazine. Having booked the entire inn except for two rooms, gave us the run of the place, and soon the entire circle was filled with bike after bike facing into the center of the circle like so many metal and rubber flower petals.

The Inn's Circular Drive Hosted the Bike Show

As much fun as the group riding was in this rolling and forested corner of Indiana, I didn't join in that day, thinking the less miles I put on my ailing chain, the better my chances would be of making it home with it still in one piece.

After shooting enough to feel secure that I had enough photos and having voted my choices for the various classes, I sought the refuge of the pool once again, while the day heated up and the food was being prepared for the final evening's awards banquet.

Vintage Japanese Bikes Lined Up in Front of the Inn

By six, it was time for the massive buffet. I tried to restrain myself as I passed down the long group of tables covered with three entrees, salads, sides, and desserts. After I had finished my meal, I moved about the room taking more photos. Finally, I gave in and had a piece of pie and some more coffee, before the event moved on to awards for the day's bike show, followed by the awarding of the many raffle prizes.

The grand prize for the raffle was a Shoei NeoTec helmet, Shoei's pricey top-of-the-line modular. I had been riding in a helmet I hated, a Fulmer M2 modular that pulled my hair so badly when I took it off that, if I didn't wear a doo-rag, I could barely extricate myself from it. The seal at the top of the visor on one side was hanging down, refusing to do its job no matter how many times I "fixed" it. I was waiting anxiously for the grand prize winner, the last ticket, to be drawn. I kept my fingers crossed and hoped I would finally have something decent to wear. Numerous other prizes were drawn without mine being called, so I figured my chances were improving as time went on, but someone else won the coveted prize at the end of the night to my chagrin. Oh, well, it had been a long shot. The Fulmer would have to continue on top of my head for the rest of the trip, regardless of its raggedness.

On the patio again after dinner, I put away my camera to freely enjoy the last time with my friends and fellow members before we all departed in the morning.

While I did not plan to get all the way to Valdosta the next day, I wanted to get as far as possible so the ride the rest of the way there would be an easy one the following day. With that in mind, I made it an early night, went upstairs to repack, and went to bed, leaving the partiers to continue on without me on the patio below.

Chapter Eighteen

Day Nineteen

Across the Mason-Dixon, Bound for Georgia

I got up at 7 AM and started gathering all my bags, which I had repacked the night before, and brought them down to the bike. I had brought the Bonnie to the now mostly empty circle in front of the inn to make loading easier, but it also put the whole operation in front of an audience. Many passersby commented on the massive load, while I was re-securing all the RokStraps.

I was about to leave by about 8:30, when my hotel roommate, Rob, told me Peter, my friend and vice-president of the club, had sent him out to get me to come back in to have breakfast with him and some others before I left. I wasn't in a big rush, so I went back in to eat and had a couple more coffees, in addition to the two I had already outside while packing the bike. Peter grabbed the bill before I could and told me it was the least he could do for the help which I had provided and was about to provide again. He needed my help to load his Valkyrie onto a trailer. I went out to the parking garage and fired up Peter's bike and rode it up onto the trailer so Rob could secure it. That task done, I said goodbye to everyone and rolled out of the park and headed southeast.

Crossing the Ohio River

I planned to go east and cross over the Ohio River at Madison, far from the busy city of Louisville. I followed the highway southeast as far as Salem, where I switched to another running straighter east for the rest of the run to the river crossing. Once across and in the Blue Grass State, I headed to Frankfort, then followed US 127 all the rest of the way through the state, across the rolling Kentucky hills and into the Volunteer State.

In Tennessee, the highway continued its southern trend, crossing I-40 and the Cumberland Plateau, and rolled toward Chattanooga. There was talk of thunderstorms in the forecast, yet the first half of the day was dry, partly sunny, and hot, but I could see the gathering storm out ahead of me. I hoped it would move out before I caught up with it, but I ended up getting soaked as I approached Chattanooga from the northwest.

Before the route dove into the city, I turned southwest onto a connecting route to US 72 at I-24, where the rains finally dissipated, leaving me with a dry run into northeastern Alabama.

I sliced across the corner of the state, then turned southeast, crossing the Tennessee River and continuing into the northwestern corner of Georgia.

This path ran southwest of Cloudland Canyon State Park, a gem and little known beauty of a park hidden away not far from the big city of Chattanooga. I had thought about stopping there for the night, but there were finally dry skies and more daylight remaining. I decided to carry on southward at least as far as Rome, where I had stopped years ago on the first Motorcycle Kickstart Classic ride that had run from Maggie Valley to the Barber Vintage Festival that year, with a night's stop at Panhead City.

The highway joined US 27. I followed it into Rome and out the other side and started looking for a place to stop for the night.

I decided I would take the first campground that presented itself, thinking that along 27, being an old pre-Interstate main route between the North and Florida, it would have some mom-and-pop campgrounds still hanging on.

As I rode on with darkness approaching, I had my eyes peeled for deer and a place to camp. My luck finding a campground was fading like the light around me, when I spotted a gas station ahead. Although my reserve light had not come on yet, I thought I would fill up, which would give me a chance to ask inside if they knew of any place to camp nearby.

The clerk said he didn't know of one but told me to ask a couple who were in the store that lived in the area. They couldn't think of anything, except for what they called

"Seabreeze." They debated with each other whether camping was allowed there, but neither was sure. It was very close, just left at the next light and a short distance east, so I figured it was worth a shot.

I pulled back out and headed toward Seabreeze. What I found was VFW Post 7402 and a lake with a beautiful park and boat ramp. I pulled in, and a fellow walked out from a permanently parked camper near the office. In answer to my query, he told me camping was ten dollars. While we talked, he mentioned he rode, which spun into a conversation about bikes and Triumphs for a bit. He had traveled a lot by motorcycle too and was sympathetic to my situation. We shared some road stories, before I moved down to the lakeside area where he indicated I could set up. He let me set up first then walk back to pay him, so I would not have to pitch my tent in complete darkness.

The tent site was pleasant, on soft grass and near the lake. I also had a cell signal, so I called Andrea for the first time since I had left South Bend. I also let Julie know I would be at her place the next day, which would be a short ride of only three hundred miles from my camp site. As soon as I had camp set up and my calls made, I crawled into the tent, stripped down, and fell fast asleep.

Chapter Nineteen

Day Twenty

A Romp through West Georgia

I got up at seven and leisurely got the camp picked up and the bike loaded. I was on the road by 8:30 and found my way back to US 27. I thought about stopping early to get a coffee but didn't see anything other than gas stop/convenience stores. I was hoping to find a little country diner somewhere, where I could sit inside in comfort and enjoy some coffee and maybe a light bite, so I kept heading south with my eyes open for the first opportunity.

US 27 continued south and crossed I-20, the main east-west corridor out of Atlanta on its west side. Not long after the Interstate, I turned off 27 and tried to get on Alt US 27, which headed more southeasterly toward Newnan and from there south toward Greenville. Instead, at Newnan, I got confused and ended up taking a bypass the wrong way out of town on another state highway, which, if I had followed it, would have dumped me in the mess around Atlanta—the last thing I wanted. The road was divided, with a deep grassy median between the east and west lanes, but I chanced crossing it, got turned around, then jumped on I-85 to the first exit to get back to Alt US 27, to continue south the way I had planned. At Greenville I turned east on a small state highway, which would connect with my next route about halfway to Thomaston.

Just before Thomaston, in the tiny gathering of homes called Sunset Village, I spotted the Sunny Side Up Café on my right, two hours after I had left the campground. I pulled into the small gravel driveway, parked, and walked into the little café. It was a small local diner as I had hoped that was empty, except for a pretty, dark-haired young lady sitting in the first booth. I asked if I could sit anywhere. She laughed and told me she was waiting for food for take out and would not be my waitress.

The owner came out, gave the girl her order, then poured me some coffee, and kept pouring as I drained each cup until I left. I also ordered an egg and cheese sandwich, which was an entire two dollars before tax. As I ate and enjoyed my first coffee of the day, the owner and I chatted, while he tended to his business.

At Thomaston, I turned south onto the next half-page of the Georgia map that I had torn from the atlas and tucked under the clear cover of the tank bag. Before I had gotten onto that second half of the map, the mountains had faded away and had been left behind. I rode on through rolling farmland planted with peanuts and cotton.

My route took me all the way to Albany, passing just a few miles east of Jimmy Carter's hometown of Plains. In Albany, I caught my last highway of the day, GA 133, which ran southeast and right past Julie's neighborhood, just a few miles west of Valdosta and the I-75 corridor.

I arrived at Julie's early. The house had been left unlocked, so I let myself in and got a shower while she was still at work at the university.

I got finished with the shower and wandered out into the kitchen and dining room area, not bothering to get dressed, knowing it would be some time before Julie got home. I sat down at the table, opened my laptop, and checked Facebook in the buff. What I had not realized was that Lisa, one of Julie's friends, who had a trailer in the backyard and often came to stay with Julie, was there. Lisa walked into the kitchen and past me sitting naked at the table. I cleared my throat and let her know I was there and warned her I was naked, trying to make a joke out of it. All was okay, though, as both Julie and Lisa lived rather Bohemian lifestyles, and nakedness was not a shock to them. Lisa just went on doing whatever she had been doing in the kitchen, while we both talked about the trip and the new stuff in our lives.

Eventually, Lisa went outside, and I pulled on some shorts before Julie arrived. Julie made dinner while we chatted and had some beers.

It was oddly empty at Julie's, now that her dad, Jack, had passed away earlier in the year. Jack had been a fixture in his chair in front of the television, talking about good books he had read, philosophy, and the current political situation. He loved it when I showed up on a bike and always asked which one I was riding.

This had been the first time I had seen Julie since her dad had passed away, and we talked a little about that recent sadness. Lisa joined in, and all we caught up with each other and talked until we were all too tired to go on, when we all headed to our beds for some sleep.

Chapter Twenty

Day Twenty-One

Homeward Bound

I got up early and had coffee and more conversation with Julie, securing a promise that she'd come down sometime soon to visit us in Florida. I loaded the couple bags I had removed from the Bonnie the afternoon before and headed back onto the road.

I hated riding on Interstates and especially I-75, the big highway that cuts south through the Florida peninsula, so instead, I headed east into Valdosta and caught US 41, which ran through the countryside toward Jasper in the extreme northern part of Florida.

At Jasper, the route intersected US 129, the same road that eventually climbed its way up into the Smokies and would become the Tail of the Dragon as it twisted and turned its way into Tennessee, six hundred miles away from where the highway ends in Florida. In northern Florida, I followed the highway as it rolled south, crossed I-75, and transited the quiet countryside, where only tiny towns occasionally sat at crossroads and lumber trucks filled with the trunks of southern yellow pine were almost the only other traffic. I turned off US 129 in Trenton, before its terminus at Chiefland, and cut diagonally across toward Bronson and on to US 41 at Williston.

From Williston to Citrus Springs there was only one town of any size, Dunellon, and little traffic. I only had to deal with the traffic from Citrus Springs for a little way south, where I turned off at Floral City and headed back into the uncrowded Florida countryside on familiar back roads.

I was on home turf then, having ridden the area many times before on weekend rides or as I had transited the state on my way out on long distance trips as I had the previous spring coming back from Quebec. At Bushnell, I shot underneath I-75, then rode east, continuing on a little county road that was not much more than a tree-lined narrow path, with several tight turns along it as it twisted around farms. It deposited my Bonnie on a road just outside little Center Hill, where I picked up another county road to State Road 50. From there I ran east through the twin cities of Mascotte and Groveland at the northern edge of the Green Swamp.

Passing through Groveland, I turned south and ran through the heart of the swamp, just as I had done the year before, with the huge Green Swamp Wildlife Management Area stretching beside me to the west. Entering my home county of Polk, I turned east on Deen Still Road and within a few miles turned south onto Old Grade Road, crossing over the Interstate and turned southeast to ward Haines City and US 27, the north-south route that passes Lake Wales on its journey to its end in Miami, two hundred miles away.

I guess I was a creature of habit using the same route regularly, but avoiding US 27 or I-75 or I-95 while trying to go north from Lake Wales didn't leave many traffic-free options.

Turning south on 27, I only took it as far as Dundee Road where I turned left, passing through the small town and onto FL 17, also known as Scenic Highway.

The road wound south all the way into my neighborhood, where I turned left downhill and past Spook Hill Elementary School, where my kids had attended, then around the corner onto North Wales Drive. Negotiating a couple more curves past little dried up North Lake Wales, and I was in my driveway.

Before backing the bike into the garage I took the final mileage. I had ridden 7,635.8 miles altogether on this second "mental health" ride. My route had taken me through some of the most beautiful areas in North America and across seventeen states and four provinces, thirteen of which I had never before traveled through by motorcycle. I had visited three national parks in the US and one in Canada and passed through uncounted national forests in both countries. Best of all, and as I had experienced before, I got to meet some of the most interesting, friendly, gracious, and generous people I had ever known. Homes were opened wide to me and meals were offered numerous times. Most of all, my faith in people had been renewed and stress had disappeared. Even my blood pressure responded to the relief the ride had brought and was down to the normal range when I got home.

Epilogue

Restoration

When I started these stories, I wrote a lot about my depression and disappointment with life. I didn't mention all that to garner pity or to whine. I considered not mentioning it at all, knowing how it might be perceived, and just leaving the stories as rolling travelogues. When revealing oneself like that, you never know how much to say and who you might be hurt if you say too much, or if you may be perceived as weak or self-absorbed.

While my family has our own unique struggles, my kids did not cause my depression, my wife did not cause it, or even our financial fortunes; it was my reaction to many things, and I did it to myself. Someone else might have reacted completely different to the same circumstances. I should have reacted differently to life's troubles and taken a deep breath, sat back, and tried to gain a different perspective. I could have told myself that life is short, and in the end all that matters is how you live it—a life lived in worry is a wasted life. But I adopted a negative attitude; it grew and came to rule my life, eventually digging that hole that I couldn't crawl out of.

I mentioned the setting that prompted my leaving on these rides because I didn't want to pretend to be some happy go lucky wanderer, without a care in the world. There is a story behind every ride; maybe it's bright and cheery, but sometimes it is dark or dreary. No one does touring or adventure travel in a vacuum, or at least no one I know does, be it around the world or just across a few states, in a group or alone. Everyone has something to deal with, maybe it's financial, maybe psychological, maybe emotional, maybe they have a physical disability or limited time between other responsibilities in which to fit their wandering and are hard-pressed to get away at all.

As I started reading my notes I had taken on the road and was preparing to set this down, I noticed I had not written down much about my state of mind, except in the first few days, and only sporadically afterwards. And I think I know why that is—the act of operating a motorcycle demanded my full attention.

Riding put me in the midst of nature; I felt the wind, and smelled the passing forests, I heard the motor and wind whipping around my helmet. I felt the cold, the heat, and the rain. On a bike, all the sensations felt are added to the simultaneous need to always be in control of the machine. Steering, shifting, rolling on and off the throttle, listening for telltale sounds that might indicate a mechanical problem, and minding that my gear didn't come loose consumed most of my attention. Add to all that the need to constantly be aware of my surroundings, watching my mirror, scanning for hazards ahead, be they there already or soon to develop, and my being was saturated with the experience.

The riding experience didn't allow me time to dwell on much else but the activity I was in the midst of, and that is the very thing I needed when I was seemingly overwhelmed by problems. I had to let them go, set them aside, and concentrate on what I was doing. Even at the end of the day, stopped and at camp or in my tent, the exhaustion of the ride and the residual effects of the new experiences were too fresh to allow for many other thoughts to intrude.

On a long ride, the more days that pass, the easier it is for me to set aside worries and just live the experience. Given enough time, riding can act as a reset. Like a Zen clap, startling me out of my current state of consciousness, riding shook me into a different perspective.

Removed from the world of social media, I had a chance to interact with people face to face and see them as they really were, not as anonymous faces in a substitute, artificial world. And the biggest difference was being able to distinguish which world was real and which was not.

Now, as a result of these rides, when depression raises its head and wants to take over, I can look back and understand that, in spite of the darkness, life can be good and joyful, because it has been that way for me before. I know people are usually kind and hospitable, because they have been that way toward me before. Those thoughts help me keep hope alive during dark times. Those experiences also prompt me to try to be one of those kind and generous people myself, which elevates life and is a buffer against a return to disillusionment.

Can riding cure depression? I don't think so. The work of dealing with depression enough that blackness is replaced with light and doesn't return takes more than a long ride and time alone. Overcoming it is still ahead of me. For now, however, riding helps me to get to a place where I'm not overwhelmed by it.

Siddhartha, by Herman Hesse, a book I first read when I was a teenager and have reread many times since, has perhaps an apt passage. The main character, Siddhartha, who had searched his entire life for enlightenment and contentment, had finally given up. He approached a river, about to throw himself in and end it all.

> *And full he was, full of the feeling of being sick of it, full of misery, full of death, there was nothing left in this world which could have attracted him, given him joy, given him comfort.*

> *Passionately he wished to know nothing about himself any more, to have rest, to be dead...*

> *...In deep tiredness, he took his arm away from the trunk of the tree and turned a bit, in order to let himself fall straight down, in order to finally drown. With his eyes closed, he slipped toward death.*

> *Then...a sound stirred up. It was a word, a syllable, which he, without thinking, with a slurred voice, spoke to himself, the old word which is the beginning and the end of all prayers of the Brahmans, the holy Om... And in the moment when the sound of Om touched Siddhartha's ear, his dormant spirit suddenly woke up and realized the foolishness of his actions.*

> *...when the Om entered his consciousness: he became aware of himself in his misery and in his error.*

And later, the old ferryman, Vasudeva, who takes in Siddhartha, says...

> *It is as I thought. The river has spoken to you. It is your friend as well, it speaks to you as well. This is good, that is very good.*

The road had been my river, and my Om had emanated from it. The spinning wheel and the path passing underneath me had emitted the Om. What it had taught me was not that everything was good, not that there were no problems, no evil, no lies; it taught me acceptance.

Like a baptism, the road and my experiences on it had washed away years of anxiety, worry, and disillusionment, and when I came up from the water there was a new world waiting for me, not a world of sunshine and happiness only, but a world of good and bad, truth and falsehood—the world as it really is and not a dark world composed of only negatives.

I was reading another book recently in which the author was describing going through unlit and curving mountain tunnels in Eastern Europe. As he entered, everything was pitch black outside the dim beam of his headlight. He might as well have been in space. The darkness might continue for quite a distance. Eventually, however, the road would make another turn, and a little glimmer would appear on the outside of the curving tunnel walls. The glimmer would grow until the final turn was completed. Then a growing arch of light would materialize and grow until he passed through it and into the bright sunshine. That description seems a good analogy of the lessons learned on the road. As depression deepens and life seems dark, I know that, sooner or later, the last bend will appear and light will return, in spite of the darkness I am passing through at the moment.

The darkness does not have the hold on me as it might have if I hadn't stepped away and got on the road again on the back of a bike.

Now the pressures of my life have returned. I have good days and bad. As time passes, stress builds up like water above a rickety dam. But a chance to reset is just around the corner. In the meantime, I'll watch for that glimmer on the wall and expect to see daylight growing once again ahead of me.

Graham Field said in *In Search of Greener Grass*: "But a frame of mind can change around the corner from the seat of a motorbike," and for me, that was true. But while it was the road that had brought me back to my senses, I don't think that the road is the only way back from darkness toward light. What's important is to step out of ordinary life and be immersed in something that demands full attention for an extended period of time. It might be sailing, it might be hiking the Appalachian Trail, it might be volunteering in some foreign land that delivers that Zen slap and diverts a path heading toward darkness toward the light. There are as many ways toward restoration as there are depressed and stress-filled people.

The motivation for the rides in this story was not solely to deal with my depression, either. I had, and still have, a strong drive to see parts of the world I've never seen before, especially from the saddle of a motorcycle. One day I'd like to see places far away on other continents, but a lifetime can be filled just experiencing the magnificence of our North America. I have only scratched the surface, in spite of tens of thousands of miles of riding across it. There are many more mountains to climb, valleys to cross, and wild lonely places in which to pitch a tent, where the only companions are the wind and the weather.

After these journeys, I was able to get some relief for my depression in the form of an anti-depressant. The best explanation I have heard of how these drugs work was by the comic and writer Neal Brennan, who describes them as "raising the floor" of the depression, allowing one to cope more easily with it. The anti-depressant helps but does not remove all the symptoms, it just keeps the dips from getting too low. Time will bring more pressures and stress, I am sure, but more mental health rides to raise the floor a bit higher are only time and planning away.

So, the only question for me remains: Where to next?

Appendix I
Gear and Statistics

Northeast

The Bike

2011 Triumph Bonneville T100, with Pirelli Scorpion Trail dual-sport tires, home-made bash plate of aluminum "diamond plate," Scottoiler, rear brake caliper relocated to top of swing arm

Equipment

First Gear Onyx magnetic tank bag

Expandable Cortech Sport Saddlebags and top bag

First Gear Silverstone expandable tailbag

Large cheap dry bag holding sleeping bag and Thermarest sleeping pad (until they were lost somewhere southwest of the Catskills)

Cheap Walmart three person dome tent (really appropriately sized for one person), packs small

Small three-legged camp stool

One Rotopax one gallon fuel container carried on stock Bonneville tail rack underneath tail bag

Two MSR one liter fuel containers, one mounted on each pillion footrest strut in bicycle water bottle carriers on homemade mounts.

Sliders Kevlar-lined three-quarter mesh jacket with rain and thermal liners and ECE back, shoulder, and elbow armor

Sliders Kevlar-lined cargo pants with ECE knee armor

Generic leather winter gloves and Tourmaster perforated leather summer gloves

GoPro Hero 3 video camera

Canon Rebel DSLR

Magellan RoadMate automobile GPS

Trip Statistics

Fifteen Days

Temperatures, from 90°F to 32°F

Total mileage, 5,142 miles

Twelve states and two provinces

Fuel cost, $330

Motel and dinner in Quebec, $92

Cash spent, mainly food, $187

Total spent, not including souvenir gifts, $609

Northwest

The Bike

2011 Triumph Bonneville T100, with Continental TKC 70 dual-sport tires, home-made bash plate of aluminum "diamond plate," Scottoiler, rear brake caliper relocated to top of swing arm, Oxford heated grips (I learned my lesson in the NE)

Equipment

Same as NE, First Gear Onyx magnetic tank bag

Same as NE, expandable Cortech Sport top bag only

Nelson-Rigg waterproof tailbag

Ortlieb Moto QRL quick release waterproof panniers attached to home-made pannier racks

Fender bag on front holding spare inner tube

Large cheap dry bag holding sleeping bag and Thermarest sleeping pad

Same as NE, Walmart three person dome tent (really appropriately sized for one person), packs small

Same as NE, small three legged camp stool

Same as NE, Rotopax one gallon fuel container carried on stock Bonneville tail rack underneath tail bag

Same as NE, two MSR one liter fuel containers, one mounted on each pillion footrest strut in bicycle water bottle carriers on homemade mounts.

Same as NE, Sliders Kevlar-lined three-quarter mesh jacket with rain and thermal liners and ECE back, shoulder, and elbow armor

Same as NE, Sliders Kevlar-lined cargo pants with ECE knee armor

Forma Adventure waterproof boots (highly recommended)

Generic leather winter gloves and Tourmaster perforated leather summer gloves

Same as NE, GoPro Hero 3 video camera

Nikon D5300 DSLR and

Same as NE, Magellan RoadMate automobile GPS (quit working two days out)

Trip Statistics

Twenty-one days

Temperatures, from 100°F to 30°F

Total mileage, 7,636 miles

Seventeen states and four provinces

Fuel cost, $458

Cash spent, mainly food, $502

Accommodations, including one night in motel, $118

Total spent, not including souvenir gifts, $1080

Appendix II

Complete Route Turn by Turn

Northeast

Day One—543 Miles

FL 17 north to Dundee, FL—Dundee Road west—US 27 north to Ocala—North US 301 to Starke, FL—FL 16 to FL 121—FL 121 north to GA 23—GA 23 north to US 301—US 301 north to Statesboro, GA—US 25 north to Augusta, GA—I-520 west to I-20 to GA 28—GA 28 north to SC 28—SC 28 joins US 221 to McCormick, SC—US 221 north to east shore of Lake Greenwood

Day Two—376 Miles

SC 72 north to Whitmire, SC—US 176 north to Jonesville, SC—SC 18 north to SC 211—SC 211 east to Sharon, SC—SC 49 north to York, SC—US 321 north to Bus US 321—Bus US 321 through Lincolnton to NC 16—NC 16 north to Tazewell VA—US 19 to Camp Creek Road—Camp Creek Road north to Camp Creek State Forest, WV

Day Three—379 Miles

Camp Creek Road south to US 19—US 19 south to US 460—US 460 east to US 219—US 219 north to I-68—68 east to US 219—US 219 north to Berlin, PA—PA 160 to Reels Corner—US 30 east to PA 96—PA 96 to Weyant—Mowry's Mill Road to Sarah Furnace Road—Sarah Furnace Road to Bus US 220/I-99—Bus US 220/I-99 into Altoona

Day Four—27 Miles

Spent exploring the area around Altoona

Day Five—333 Miles

Bus 220 north to Bald Eagle—PA 350 north to Phillipsburg, PA—PA 53 north to Moshannon, PA—PA 144 north to Renovo, PA—PA 122 east to US 220 (alternately take Hyner's Run east to PA 44 before Hyner View State Park)—US 220 east to PA 44—PA 44 north to Tomb, PA—PA 973 east to Loyalsockville, PA—PA 87 east to Russell Hill, PA—US 6 east to PA 92—PA 92 northeast to Gelatt, PA—PA 2046 north to PA 171—PA 171 north almost to Ararat, PA—PA 370 northeast to NY 17—NY 17 east to NY 30—NY 30 to Shinhopple, NY, and River Road—River Road south to Peaceful Valley Campground

Day Six—293 Miles

River Road to NY 30—NY 30 northeast to Gilmantown, NY—NY 8 northeast to the NY 9N and Lake George—NY 9N north to Hap's Corner in Crown Point, NY—(side trek to vista point)—Creek Rd. west to White Church Road (NY 7) north to Lang Rd.—Lang Road east to Lang Cemetery—Park up and walk to the point over the boulder strewn path.

NY 9N north along Lake Champlain to NY 22—NY 22 north to Essex, NY—Essex Ferry east across Lake Champlain to Charlotte, VT—Ferry Road east to VT 116—(I was lost here. Following is the recommended route to VT 128. Once there it should be clear sailing to Fairfax.)—VT 116 north to VT 2A—VT 2A north to VT 15—VT 15 east to VT 128—VT 128 north to Fairfax, VT

Day Seven—395 Miles

VT 104 north to VT 105—VT 105 east to Richford—VT 139 to the Canadian Border—QC 139 north to Sutton, QC—(I was lost here. Following is the recommended route)—QC 215 north to QC 241—QC 241 to Roxton Falls, QC—QC 139 north to Acton Vale, QC—QC 116 northeast to Plessisville, QC—QC 165 southeast to QC 112—QC 112 northeast to Frampton, QC—QC 275 northwest to QC 216—QC 216 northeast to QC 204—QC 204 northwest to QC 132 and the Saint Lawrence River—QC 132 northeast to Rivière-du-Loup, QC

Day Eight—396 Miles

QC 132 to Rimouski, QC—QC 232 south to QC 289—QC 289 southeast to Lac Baker where it enter New Brunswick and becomes NB 120—NB 120 to Claire, NB, and the US border—ME 11 south from Fort Kent, ME, to Milo—ME 6 west to ME 23—ME 23 south to Sangerville, ME

Day Nine—242 Miles

ME 23 north to ME 6—ME 6 to ME 16—ME 16 west to New Hampshire where it becomes NH 16—NH 16 south to Mount Washington—(Side trek-Mt. Washington Auto Road to the top of the mountain at 6,288 feet and back to NH 16)—NH 16 south to North Conway, NH

Day Ten—491 Miles

NH 16 to NH 112 (Kancamagus Highway)—NH 112 to US 3—US 3 south to NH 104—NH 104 west to US 4—US 4 west into Vermont and to West Bridgewater, VT—VT 100 south to Wilmington, VT—VT 9 west into New York where it becomes NY 7—NY 7 south to Denison Road—(Lost again. Following is the recommended route.)—Denison Road becomes Vly Road and goes to NY 155—NY 155 south to Voorhesville, NY—NY 85A east to NY 85—NY 85 east to NY 140—NY 140 east to Elsmere, NY 335—NY 335 south to NY 32—NY 32 south to NY 23—NY 23 west to NY 296—NY 296 south to NY 23A—NY 23A to NY 214—NY 214 south to NY 28—NY 28 east to US 209—US 209 southwest to NY 17—NY 17 south to Goshen, NY

Day Eleven—271 Miles

Cheechunk Road which becomes Echo Lake Road west to McVeigh Road—McVeigh Road to Dolsontown Road—Dolsontown Road west to Mount Hope Road—Mount Hope Road (County Road 11) west to Otisville, NY—NY 211 west to US 209—US 209 (Federal Road) south then west into Pennsylvania—US 209 west to US 443—US 443 west to US 22 and the Susquehanna River—US 22 south to I-81—I-81 west across the river and to PA 34—PA 34 south to Bus US 15—Bus US 15 south to Bullfrog Road—Bullfrog Road northwest to Gordon Road—Cross Middle Creek (Don't go alone and be careful!) on Gordon to Middle Creek Road—Middle Creek Road North to Pumping Station Road

Day Twelve—387 Miles

Emmitsburg Road (Bus US 15) south to Fairplay, PA—US 15 south to US 340—US 340 southwest to US 522—US 522/US 340 south to Front Royal, VA—Skyline Drive south—Skyline Drive becomes Blue Ridge Parkway at Afton, VA—BRP to Smart View Recreation Area—(Side trek to campground, first few miles gravel and steep twisting downhill)—VA 793 (Runnet Bag Road) to VA 40 (Franklin Street)—VA 40 (Franklin Street becomes Charity Highway) southwest to Idlewood Lane—Idlewood Lane east to VA 622 (Deer Run Road)—VA 622 (Deer Run Road) to Deer Run Campground, Ferrum, VA

Day Thirteen—407 Miles

Idlewood Lane to VA 40 (Charity Highway) southwest to Woolwine, VA—VA 8 northwest to Blue Ridge Parkway—BRP southwest to NC 80—NC 80 south to US 70—US 70 west to NC 9—NC 9 south to Mill Springs, NC—NC 108 joins US 176—US 176 southeast to SC 14 southwest to SC 11 (Cherokee Scenic Highway)—SC 11 west to US 25—US 25 south to SC 247—SC 247 south to US 178—US 178 south to US 76—US 76 northeast to SC 252—SC 252 east to Ware Shoals, SC—US 25 north to SC 252—SC 252 east to Neely Ferry Road—Neely Ferry Road south becomes Todd Quarter Road—Todd Quarter Road to US 221—US 221 south to SC 72/US 221 at Lake Greenwood

Day Fourteen—315 Miles

US 221 south to Clark's Hill, SC—Into Georgia across Strom Thurmond Dam on US 221 south—US 221 south to Douglas, GA—GA 135 southwest to GA 76—GA 76 southwest to GA 133—GA 133 east to Valdosta, GA

Day Fifteen—287 Miles

GA 133 east to Saint Augustine Road—Saint Augustine Road south becomes Old Clyattville Road—Gill Harbin Industrial Boulevard to Bus US 41—Bus US 41 south to US 41—US 41 south to Floral City, FL—FL 48 east to US 301—US 301 south to Noble Avenue—Noble Avenue east becomes CR 567—CR 567 to FL 48—FL 48 east to CR 469—CR 469 to FL 50—FL 50 east to FL 33—FL 33 south through the Green Swamp to Deen Still Road—Deen Still Road east to Old Grade Road—Old Grade Road south to Old Polk City Road—Old Polk City Road east to Haines City—US 27 south to CR 546—CR 546 east to FL 17—FL 17 south into Lake Wales, FL

Northwest

Day One—578 Miles

FL 60 west to US 98—US 98 north to US 27/US 19—US 27/US 19 to Capps, FL—US 19 north to Americus, GA—US 280 northwest to AL 25/US 231—AL 25/US 231 north to AL 25—AL 25 north to Leeds, AL—US 78 west to Birmingham, AL

Day Two—572 Miles

US 78 west to I-22—I-22 to AL 44—AL 44 southwest to US 278—US 278 west to MS 316—MS 316 northwest to US 61/US 49—US 49 into Arkansas—US 49 west then north to AR 17—AR 17 north to AR 38—AR 38 west to AR 31—AR 31 north to US 64—AR 64 west to Atkins, AR—AR 105 north to AR 7—AR 7 north to Old Highway 7—(Here I was lost looking for the TAT Shak.)—Old Highway 7 west a few miles then turned around—AR 7 south to AR 164—AR 164 northwest to Hagerville, AR, then turned around—(Later I discovered that just east of the Big Piney Creek crossing on 164 was the western entrance to Old Highway 7 Road, the correct way to TAT Shak.)—AR 7 south to AR 27—AR 27 south to I-40

Day Three—566 Miles

AR 28 south to AR 154—AR 154 east to AR 7/AR 28—AR 7/AR 28 to Rover—AR 27 south to AR 88—AR 88 west to OK 1—OK 1 west to US 270—US 270 northwest to US 377—US 377 north to OK 99—OK 99 north to OK 33—OK 33 west to US 177—US 177 north to McCord, OK—US 77 north into Kansas to Winfield, KS—US 160 west to KS 49—KS 49 north to South 263rd Street West to US 54—US 54 to east to Goddard, KS—US 54 west to Kingman, KS

Day Four—482 Miles

US 54 west to US 400—US 400 west to Granada, CO—US 50 west to US 287—US 287 northwest to Limon, CO—

I-70 west to CO 86—CO 86 west to US 85—US 85 north to CO 470—CO 470 west to CO 121—CO 121 south to Deer Creek Canyon Road—Deer Creek Canyon Road to Mountain Air Ranch

Day Five—377 Miles

Deer Creek Canyon Road to CO 121—CO 121 north to CO 470—CO 470 east to US 85—US 85 south to Sedalia—CO 67 (Gravel and curves on a downhill grade until the North Platte River) to Woodland Park, CO—US 24 west to CO 82—CO 82 northwest to US 6—US 6 west to CO 13—CO 13 north to CO 64—CO 64 west to Rangely

Day Six—376 Miles

CO 64 northwest to US 40—US 40 west into Utah to Vernal, UT—US 191 north to UT 44—UT 44 west then north to WY 414—WY 414 northwest to Urie, WY—WY 412 northwest to US 189—US 189 north into Jackson, WY

Day Seven—310 Miles

US 26 north to Teton Park Road—Teton Park Road north to US 89/US 191/US 287—US 287 north to I-90—90 west to Butte, MT

Day Eight—365 Miles

I-90 to US 12—US 12 northeast to MT 141—MT 141 north to MT 200—MT 200 west to MT 83—MT 83 north to MT 35—MT 35 north to CR 206—CR 206 to US 2—US 2 into Glacier National Park—US 2 west to Kila, MT—(Side trek out of Kalispell to the wrong end of Coon Hollow Road. Miles of gravel and uphill winding riding.)—Airport Road south to NF-2991—NF-2991 becomes Emmons Creek Road—Emmons Creek Road to Truman Creek Road—Truman Creek Road north to Coon Hollow Road—(Now you have to turn around and retrace your steps out.)

Day Nine—454 Miles

US 2 east to US 93—US 93 north to Canada at Roosville—BC 93 north joins BC 95—BC 93/BC 95 north to Radium

Hot Springs, BC—BC 93 north and east across the Rockies to CA-1—1 east to Strathmore, AB

Day Ten—534 Miles

CA-1 east and south to SA 37—SA 37 south to SA 13—SA 13 east to Stoughton, SA

Day Eleven—492 Miles

SA 13 becomes MB 2—MB 2 east to MB 10—MB 10 south to MB 23—MB 23 east to MB 75—MB 75 northeast to 305—305 east to MB 59—MB 59 south to MB 52—MB 52 east to MB 12—MB 12 into the US at Warroad—MN 313 southeast to MN 11—MN 11 southeast to the Rainy River across from Emo, ON

Day Twelve—544 Miles

MN 11 to International Falls, MN—US 53 southeast to Angora, MN—MN 1 east then southeast to MN 61—MN 61 southwest to Duluth, MN—US 53 south to WI 29—WI 29 east to WI 27—WI 27 south to Leon, WI

Day Thirteen—479 Miles

WI 27 south to Cashton, WI—WI 33 east to WI 131—WI 131 to County Road P—County Road P west US 14—US 14 southeast to Lone Rock, WI—WI 133 south the WI 130—WI 130 south to join WI 23—WI 23 south to US 18—US 18 east to Country Road K—County Road K south to WI 191—WI 191 southeast to WI 39—WI 39 east to WI 69—WI 69 south to Illinois and IL 26—IL 26 south to US 52—US 52 southeast to IL 23—IL 23 south to IL 18—IL 18 east then south to IL 7—IL 7 east to Indiana and IN 2—IN 2 east then north to IN 8—IN 8 east to US 35—US 35 north to US 6—US 6 east to IN 23—IN 23 northeast to IN 4—IN 4 east to US 31—US 31 north to US 20—US 20 east to Ironwood Drive—Ironwood Drive north to Brookmede Drive—Brookmede Drive west to Woodmont Drive, South Bend, IN

Day Fourteen

(Side trek by car to Lake Michigan.)—IN 933 north into Michigan and MI 51—MI 51 north to US 12—US 12 west to Three Oaks, MI—North Elm Street becomes Three Oaks Road north to Red Arrow Highway—Red Arrow Highway north to Warren Dunes State Park

Day Fifteen—234 Miles

IN 931 south to IN 331 (Old Dixie Highway)—In 331 south to IN 25—In 25 south to IN 29—IN 29 south to IN 28—IN 28 west to IN 39—IN 39 south to IN 39/IN 67—IN 39/IN 67 southwest to IN 39—IN 39 southeast to IN 37—IN 37 south to Mitchell, IN—IN 60 east to Spring Mill State Park

Days Fifteen through Eighteen, 150 Miles

Day Nineteen—552 Miles

IN 60 east to IN 56—IN 56 east to US 421—US 421 south into Kentucky—US 421 southeast to US 127—US 127 south into Tennessee and to TN 28—TN 28 south to I-24—I-24 west to US 72—US 72 south into Alabama and to AL 117—AL 117 southeast into Georgia becoming GA 48 and to US 27—US 27 south to GA 120—GA 120 east to Seabreeze Park

Day Twenty—289 Miles

US 27 south to US 27 Alt-US 27 Alt south to GA 18—GA 18 southeast to GA 74—GA 74 southeast to US 19—US 19 south to GA 133—GA 133 southeast to Valdosta, GA

Day Twenty-One—282 Miles

GA 133 east to US 41—US 41 south to US 129—US 129 south to NE CR 339—NE CR 339 southeast to US 27 Alt—US 27 Alt south to US 41—US 41 south to CR 476—CR 476 east to CR 567—CR 567 east then south to FL 48—FL 48 east to CR 469—CR 469 south to FL 50—FL 50 east to FL 33—FL 33 south to Deen Still Road—Deen Still Road east to Old Grade Road—Old Grade Road southeast to US

27—US 27 south to Dundee Road—Dundee Road east to FL 17—FL 17 to Lake Wales, FL

Acknowledgements

A huge thanks goes out to ADVRider.com, the great Tent Space Sign Up thread, and all those willing to offer a place for those of us on the road. These trips would have been much harder and much more expensive, maybe impossible, were it not for their kindness and generosity.

Thanks to Randy Warren, for her willingness to help with and proofread not only my work but *Vintage Japanese Motorcycle Magazine* and other books from Road Dog Publications. And to all the Road Dog authors, who have inspired me not only in riding, but in writing, as well.

A final thanks to my family, especially my wife, Andrea, who accepts my wanderlust and allows me, without complaint, to fulfill that need.

Other Books from Road Dog Publications

Also by Michael Fitterling

Thoughts on the Road[1,2]

The founder of Road Dog Publications and Editor of *Vintage Japanese Motorcycle Magazine*, ponders his experience with motorcycles and riding, and how those two things intersect and influence his life.

Other Authors

Motorcycles, Life, and...[1,2] — *by Brent Allen*

Sit down and talk motorcycles, life and...(fill in the blank) with award winning riding instructor and creator of the popular "Howzit Done?" video series, Brent "Capt. Crash" Allen. Here are his thoughts about riding and life and how they combine told in a lighthearted tone.

The Elemental Motorcyclist[1,2] — *by Brent Allen*

Brent's second book offers more insights into life and riding and how they go together. This volume, while still told in the author's typical easy-going tone, gets down to more specifics about being a better rider.

A Tale of Two Dusters & Other Stories[1,2] — *by Kirk Swanick*

In this collection of tales, Kirk Swanick tells of growing up a gear head behind both the wheels of muscle cars and the handlebars of motorcycles and describes the joys and trials of riding

Bonneville Go or Bust[1,2] — *by Zoë Cano*

Zoë Cano dreamed of riding across the US, so she scrimped and saved, and poured over maps. Finally, she took a leap of faith, flew to the US, and began the adventure of a lifetime—riding solo from Boston to LA on a Triumph Bonneville.

Southern Escapades[1,2] — *by Zoë Cano*

Zoë takes in a corner of the US missed on her previous journey. Riding from Florida to Alabama and back through Georgia, she finds her way to Barber Vintage Festival, AIMExpo, and Daytona Bike Week.

Beads in the Headlight[1] — *by Isabel Dyson*

A British couple tackle riding from Alaska to Tierra del Fuego two-up on a 31 year-old BMW "airhead." Join them on this epic journey across two continents.

A great blend of travel, motorcycling, determination, and humor.—Dee (★★★★★ Amazon Review)

A Short Ride in the Jungle[1,2] — *by Antonia Bolingbroke-Kent*

A young woman tackles the famed Ho Chi Minh Trail alone on a diminutive pink Honda Cub armed only with her love of Southeast Asia and its people and her wits.

Asphalt & Dirt[1,2] — *by Aaron Heinrich*

A compilation of profiles of both famous and relatively unknown people who ride, dispelling the myth of the stereotypical "biker" image.

In Search of Greener Grass[1] — *by Graham Field*

With his game show winnings, Graham sets out solo on his KLR for Mongolia and beyond.

Eureka[1] — *by Graham Field*

Graham sets out on a journey to Kazahkstan only to realize his contrived goal is not making him happy. He has a "Eureka!" moment and turns around and begins to enjoy the ride as the ride itself becomes the destination.

Different Natures[1] — *by Graham Field*

The story of two early journeys Graham made while living in the US, one north to Alaska and the other south through Mexico. Follow along as Graham tells the stories in his own unique way.

Distributed by:

NBN national book network

Road Dog PUBLICATIONS

www.roaddogpub.com

Also available for [1] Kindle from amazon.com & [2] Nook from bn.com